Other books by the author:

Patchwork
Between Earth and Sky
The River Road
Centerville

The Music Book

Karen Osborn

Livingston Press

The University of West Alabama

Library of Congress Control Number 20200932306
Printed on acid-free paper
Printed in the United States of America by
Publishers Graphics

Hardcover binding by: HF Group
Typesetting and page layout: Sarah Coffey
Proofreading: Maddie Owen, Tricia Taylor, Jenna Frye

Cover Design: Joe Taylor

Cover Photograph: Beth Marie Read

This is a work of fiction. Any resemblance
to persons living or dead is coincidental.
Livingston Press is part of The University of West Alabama,
and thereby has non-profit status.
Donations are tax-deductible.

First edition

6 5 4 3 3 2 1

The Music Book

Karen Osborn

For my mother, sisters, and daughters

First Movement:
The Exposition

Chapter 1

1953, Providence, Rhode Island. The train stopped and her cello hit up against her side. "Here, Miss." A young man handed her suitcase down, and she went quickly out ahead across the crowded platform and through the small station. Outside, cars were bumper to bumper, windshields flashed in the sun. Businessmen hurried toward the station, and a woman dragged a suitcase and a child, one in each hand. The sunlight was hot on the concrete sidewalk. She held a hand above her eyes and spotted the DeSoto they'd told her to look for behind a large station wagon with wooden panels. Charles Breedlove sprang from the driver's seat.

"Irena, right? Irena Siesel?"

She was twenty-one and newly graduated from the conservatory. There was that blouse she'd worn with a scalloped neckline and a dark skirt, gathered at the waist. She was strong looking, large boned with wide shoulders and a square, determined jaw, soft gray eyes and long hair that fell forward when she played the cello, parting like a curtain to reveal a driven but dreamy expression, as if she saw phantom shadows.

She'd been hired to perform at the music festival last minute because the cellist with The Modern Strings, a new ensemble group in New York City, had broken his arm. Patrick Dempsey, the group's violist had phoned her. They'd had trouble finding someone, and John Pincer who taught her at the conservatory had given him her name. They were playing the final event in a four-day festival that would showcase classical music from the Baroques to the moderns and debut a new composition by Arthur Cohen, a rising young composer and their pianist. Was she available, could she do it? Had she studied or performed modern classical music? It was a difficult piece.

Yes, she'd answered readily to each question, though the conservatory hadn't taught the new modern composers. "I'll take the train down Monday morning."

He said they'd fit in rehearsals during the festival and he'd mail her the music. Charles Breedlove, the quartet's violinist, would pick her up at the station in Providence.

A few days earlier, she'd been offered a teaching job at the music academy in Boston where she'd once taken lessons, but if you were good enough, and at the conservatory they'd called her gifted, exceptional even, you performed, you didn't teach. Mildred Ridley had managed a career performing the cello, and so had Phyllis Kraeuter. Erica Morini, the only female solo violinist in recent years (there were no solo violists or cellists), claimed the problem with women performers was they lacked the single-minded devotion necessary to sacrifice everything to their instruments.

Charles drove through the crowded streets. Cars glistened in the sunlight, horns blared. At the far side of town, she smelled the stink of the fish canneries through the open windows. Then they reached the city's outskirts where they drove faster. A small track of recently built houses appeared then disappeared, and billboards flashed by too fast to read them. As they left the city, the road wound closer to the ocean where tall sea grasses grew by the roadside and the water appeared in patches.

"I love a road that winds along the coast, don't you?" Charles called out.

A damp wind blew through the car as they turned onto a two-lane road close to the water. When they crossed the bridge that spanned the inlet, her hair streamed out the window. Above her the sky felt huge.

Charles asked about her name, and she told him she'd been named after her grandmother and called Reenie when she was growing up.

"Reenie," he repeated. "That's brilliant. Reenie, you are."

Later she was introduced that way and her name differed only on the program.

Charles drove casually, ignoring speed limits and not slowing even when they crossed a high, narrow bridge with open grating above the inlet. One hand stayed on the steering wheel and the other waved about. "Have you heard Arthur Cohen's recent recording? We're featured on it. He and Patrick met at Yale, and last year when they both moved to New York City, they formed The Modern Strings. We've played to several good-sized audiences, but this performance will be the biggest." He glanced across the seat at her. "You have a copy of the score, don't you? Patrick said he'd sent it to you. John Pincer claims you're very talented. In fact, he says you're unprecedented. We were lucky to get you, since we only learned last week that Les Carmichael broke his arm." He glanced across the seat at her. "Water skiing," he added. "No doubt he had a girl on both sides."

They passed marshes and fields thick with brush. In the bright air, everything gleamed—beach front hotels, the small white houses with dark green trim, and the ocean behind them. The sun was a glowing white ball. Something was about to happen that would change whatever happened afterward.

"We're very forward looking," Charles called out over the rush of wind blowing past the windows. "It's implied, after all, in the name, so it's perfect that we'll be the one group at the festival with a female musician."

"Don't worry, I'll fit in," she laughed. "I'll wear trousers."

He said they'd be playing the final concert and the other concerts, featuring Bach, Beethoven, and Brahms, would lead up to theirs. The festival, held in a mansion in Newport, would attract a large, wealthy audience. There were great opportunities for musicians who performed the new and more difficult music. Did she know? Did she realize? He tossed out the names of modern artists—Mark Rothko and Willem De Kooning.

"David Tudor, John Cage, and the likes of them are equally transforming music," he said. "It's revolutionary."

"Yes," she answered, "of course," and in the distance, she made out a line of events, each opening toward the next in a vast spread of opportunity.

They had a ferry ride to the island where Charles bought them hot dogs, and Reenie stood on the deck watching the narrow island's coast spread into view. Mansions dangled at the top of the cliffs, like a strand of beads on a fancy necklace. They hung over the steep descent to the water. Charles pointed at one of the largest, named The Breakers, a sprawling white mansion he said the Jamesons had rented for the performances.

"I love this, don't you?" he asked. "Pretending for a few days that we're rich?"

When the ferry reached the island, they retrieved the car and drove away from the small town toward the island's point. She saw walls of white and blue hydrangeas, a field of blue delphiniums, boats in the harbors, and the ocean laced with waves. White stones shimmered in the heat through a screen of greenery. They passed a pasture with a yellow barn, then tall hedges growing close to the road, hiding vast grounds and long drives leading to the houses along the coast.

"That's where the performances will be held, behind that black iron-gate," Charles told her, pointing at a placard with "The Breakers" written on it. A mile or so farther up the coast, the Jameson's driveway cut a circle through boxwoods, and a rambling, three-story Tudor rose up out of the sand.

"They've put us all in the main house, except for Arthur who's staying in one of the cottages. Did you say you'd heard that recording of his? You must if you haven't. He's taken every piece of music written and synthesized them into his own style. Perform Arthur Cohen now, and you'll end up in Carnegie Hall or the Met. That's what it feels like. That's what I predict."

Men milled about the cars and taxis, unloading suitcases and instruments. Charles walked her to the doorway. "Oh look, there's Thomas Baxter and Louis Heath. They're performing Bach tomorrow evening."

They walked onto the front portico lined with potted ferns and stepped inside a large entryway with a chandelier the size of a dining room table. Her room, Charles told her, was upstairs, the fourth door on the right, just down from his. He set her suitcase and cello by the stairs.

"They can sleep up to thirty people here, and I think our numbers are close to that, with all the performing musicians, along with a few guests."

She followed him down a central hallway, past a parlor and dining room. "Patrick and Arthur are by the water. Come, I'll show you. I'll introduce you."

A comfortable looking living room in the back of the house opened to the outside through a pair of glass doors that led to a stone patio. White hydrangeas ringed the lawn, and near the terrace yellow roses bloomed. Beyond them, she saw the ocean, light glinting off the waves. Three men and a woman stood at the end of the lawn, looking out at the sea.

"The two on the right are Harmon Rothschild and George Shields," Charles said waving.

"Didn't Harmon Rothschild perform as a soloist with the Philadelphia Symphony this past winter?"

"Yes, I believe you're right. See that man on the left next to the woman? That's Patrick Dempsey, our violist who telephoned you."

"Who is the woman?"

"Adele Jameson, our patron. Patrick and Arthur met her last year. She's funding the entire festival."

Patrick bent toward Adele Jameson, and his head obscured hers. Beyond them the cliffs fell off sharply, and below that was a rocky beach. Close to the shore, the water was pale blue with white foam. The sunlight blinded where it touched the ocean, but when Reenie squinted, she could see far out where the blue sky darkened.

"Arthur is the one in the ocean. Do you see him?"

She held her hand above her eyes. Other musicians were walking out onto the lawn. She felt pulled toward something she couldn't see, something important.

"That's his dark head above the waves," Charles said. "Earlier this summer we performed at an event on Long Island. A group of us stayed up late drinking the night before. Arthur stayed the latest, but the next morning he was up before the rest of us, swimming laps. I watched him going back and forth along the shoreline and thought, how does he do it? Then of course, his performance was the most remarked upon." He paused, waiting for her to respond.

"Strange," she said.

"Impressive. Do you swim?"

"No," she answered.

"He'll get you in the water at some point. He has a way of convincing us all."

In the distance, the dark head skimmed above the waves. It looked like the swimmer was approaching the shore, but just before he reached it, he turned and swam back out into deeper water.

Later that evening, a group of them gathered outside on the lawn. The sun was about to drop into the water, all that fiery light being extinguished. Arthur stood next to her, smoking. He'd just told her a story about a whale that had washed up onto shore.

She didn't find him immediately attractive, not with his straight, dark hair worn a little too long, and she was on her guard. Violet Hammer at the conservatory had had that affair with her violin instructor that had ended so badly. No one was surprised when she didn't pass her solo performance.

"It's a true story," Arthur insisted about the whale. "I heard it from a fisherman near the island's point when I went for a walk. The whale washed up onto the shore, and the fisherman happened upon it. It was still living when he found it."

"Was the fisherman able to save it?"

Arthur shook his head. "He got help and they tried to pull it into the ocean, but the whale was too heavy and the waves kept bringing it back. They migrate at the end of the summer, and sometimes one comes too close to the island." He gestured toward the water. "They're swimming out there somewhere, just beyond the point." She peered far out into the ocean. "You received my music, didn't you?"

She told him she had. It was the hardest piece of music she'd ever played, but she told him it was interesting and impressive. He was older, had studied composing with Paul Hindemith at Yale and then with Walter Piston at Harvard. He'd already won those awards for his piano playing.

He talked about Schoenberg and the importance of serialism and atonal music, giving vague descriptions of what he called "new" music that broke with tradition. The new music sounded nothing like the old, and the world needed boldness, not composers like Leonard Bernstein who catered to popular taste. "The fundamentals of music are rapidly changing," he said, "and we won't know who the most influential composers are for many years. We have to constantly reconsider what makes music, music."

"I guess that's the work of a composer," she said, surprised at how he'd dismissed Bernstein.

"It's not just the work of a composer," he told her. "It's the work of any serious musician."

The sun had dropped into the water, pulling all the light out of the sky. The only piece left was a deep pink glow at the horizon. His voice had a ring of certainty. *I'll be such a musician*, she told herself.

She knew, didn't know. She was in the memory unit when the envelope with the music book arrived. It came by post, a thick brown envelope addressed to Irena Reynolds at the house on Hickory Street, then forwarded to her room #139 in the memory unit. The envelope contained a sonata composed by Arthur Cohen and left for her in his will. There was also a letter from Deborah Cohen, his niece and executor of his estate, along with a copy of his obituary and a music program from the Newport, Rhode Island Festival in 1953.

She forgot to dress, didn't seem to know or hear. Her mind was elsewhere. They worried about loss of balance and falling was a danger. She'd moved into the memory unit several months ago because of the strokes. Words didn't string together. She stuttered on sounds, didn't know how they fit, and she forgot what day it was, couldn't be counted on to know, couldn't count. She didn't follow or understand, but she heard everything—voices in the hallway, machines beeping, intercoms speaking. The memory unit contained endless floors and halls, each with countless rooms. She heard them all around her, a labyrinth.

Arrangements had been made. Her will and directives were signed. Did she want to review them? Her daughter Judith had many questions, a sudden interest in family history. Where was Irena's father buried, and when and how did he die? What part of Germany had Irena's grandmother immigrated from, and was she Jewish by any chance? Wasn't there a story about her speaking Yiddish the last years of her life when she moved in with Irena's mother? And who was this composer, Arthur Cohen? Do you remember playing with him at a festival in Newport, Rhode Island? He must have held you in high esteem. The letter says you were the only person outside the estate to receive his music. If you died before him, he wanted the composition destroyed.

Outside the window clouds circled, an eye peered through the glass panes. A giant ear noted everything. Nothing was solid. People sat in wheel chairs or drifted ghost-like in the hallways.

Come with me.

Wait here.

I'll be right back.

She heard pieces of what was said, couldn't follow, didn't reply. She heard Judith's voice, the words that were her questions. She heard footsteps in the hallway, heard other voices in other rooms and the sound of a great machine, a sound that never stopped. It rose up from the basement and poured through the rooms and hallways.

Judith showed her the program of the music festival from 1953. Do you remember playing in it? It would have been several years after the war, and it says here that Arthur Cohen was part of that post-war generation. The composition he left you in his will has never been performed, but his niece thinks it the best of his work, greater even than his piece that won the Pulitzer. He was briefly famous after an opera he composed about the Viet Nam War and then he won the Pulitzer a few years later, but after that his music was rarely performed. The obituary says his music always began with a vision of a gold or yellow rectangle. The piece that won the Pulitzer was called "Those Golden Fields." *The Times* says his music was lush with echoes of the composer Rachmaninoff. Do you remember? Do you agree? And didn't you play in that opera? I have a vague memory that you did.

Rachmaninoff? She didn't know, couldn't say. She'd once had a copy of the program like the one in the envelope, but she'd thrown it away, along with that newspaper article. The notes in the music book were hand written in dense, dark notation. When she touched the backs of the pages, she felt the circles of the notes with her fingertips. It was a sonata for the piano and cello, and his niece had found it while cataloging his music. Until then she hadn't been sure the piece actually existed. She'd eventually found many versions of it.

Judith said, I want you to hear it performed. I think it might help. The doctor said… He claimed… Music has certain effects on the listener. I've spoken with Deborah Cohen and we're arranging for a performance.

The woman who did the straightening came in and a toilet flushed. Shadows moved upon shadows. Rooms superimposed on one another. There were things Irena had never told anyone and now she wouldn't say them. It was impossible. Dates didn't matter. She forgot where she was, forgot that she had granddaughter in college and that a therapist came three days a week. She forgot the time when the therapist came and forgot the therapist. Time meant nothing. They said it was August and soon it wouldn't be so hot, but she was cold in the memory unit. She wore sweaters and the fleece jackets Judith bought her. They told her to come out in the hall and walk and they held her arm. They said just take small steps when she'd always been sturdy and strong, a good walker.

The hallway of the memory unit was brightly lit. Cords dangled from the walls in case of emergencies. She heard a phone ringing and someone said the man in 109 needed help. She heard him shouting but couldn't hear the words, couldn't make sense. Other things crowded in, loomed vividly. She heard music she'd performed. She heard what she'd said and what others had said. She saw what she'd done, saw what others had done, and felt it all over again, felt it more deeply. At night she had so many memories she couldn't sleep. She saw the house on Hickory Street and the academy where she'd taught cello lessons. She saw symphony hall. And now she saw those four days in Newport with Arthur Cohen and The Modern Strings. They rose up before her even though she didn't know when Judith was coming and couldn't follow what she said. The present was blurred but her memory was detailed and distinct. A door that had shut long ago was open, and a performance was happening. She'd gone to that festival a few months after turning down Benjamin's proposal and feeling so distraught. *You'll regret this the rest of your life*, he'd told her as she got up to leave the restaurant in tears. Then the offer had come to play in the festival, and she'd taken the train down and driven along the ocean to the island with Charles. There'd been that white blouse with the tiny buttons up the back and all those skirts she'd folded and packed in her suitcase. Trousers weren't an option. She'd joked about wearing them, but never would have. She'd worn exclusively skirts to practice and perform in, amid all those jokes about female cellists opening their legs to play their instruments.

*Oh sister, oh baby. Play me like that. Think of the sounds
we could make.*

Music had poured out of the bedrooms and the downstairs
parlor and living room of the Jameson's house at all hours. She
heard snatches of Bach, Schumann, Brahms and Mozart—all
blending together. She had never heard so much music at once,
including at the conservatory where practice rooms were sound
proof. The next morning when she woke, Charles stood on the
lawn playing Beethoven's "Ode to Joy" on his violin facing the
ocean. His suit jacket strained across his shoulders, and the violin looked like a toy in his large hand, but he drew the bow
back and forth with such grace. The sun had just come up and
the light was still pale and the music made her weep. She became someone else, listening, and stayed in her room practicing
Arthur's difficult piece. She was being steered toward it, her
future, which was nothing like a future in Boston. This other
future swept down and lifted her.

At the conservatory when they rehearsed, they broke
down difficult passages and talked about them before playing
a piece through. They put on the metronome and followed the
instructor's directions. But when The Modern Strings met the
first morning to rehearse, they just started playing. She thought
maybe they would play the entire piece through without direction, but when they reached the end of the first movement, they
paged back and started again, this time stopping repeatedly.

They critiqued phrasing and intonation, then spent twenty minutes or more tuning chords, arguing about who was flat.
Someone told her to play the notes on different strings and she
did. Was she flat still? She couldn't tell. Nothing made sense,
including the music's constantly changing time signatures and
the passages with hundreds of notes crammed into just a couple
of measures. She entered late, then too early. They said she still
had the wrong sound. At the end when the others started packing up and Patrick announced they'd finished with enough time

to walk down to the ocean before dinner, she went on playing, trying to find the right sound. She would have played until her fingers bled.

"Come on, Reenie," Charles said before he left the house. "You have to stop and come with us."

"In a minute," she told him. "Go on ahead. I'll catch up."

She lowered her cello into the case, feeling like she'd stepped off the planet. She had no idea what "you have the wrong sound" meant. She walked outside and crossed the lawn to the top of the wooden steps that looked out over the ocean. Something had slammed into her, or she had slammed into it. An abyss had opened. Beyond the threshold, she couldn't say, didn't know, but the moment when she could turn back was gone. She was already falling.

The sun was bright and the rocks gleamed with bits of mica. The tide was out and below her she saw a narrow sand beach. The men had already reached it. They took off their shoes and rolled up their pants legs, pushing one another and joking about the waves, which could knock you against the rocky shoreline if you weren't a strong enough swimmer. The jagged cliff jutted out over the water. Colors were so bright they hurt, and the sound of the ocean saturated everything. The performance was what mattered, she told herself, not a first rehearsal.

She turned and began to walk along the cliff edge, high above the water. Next to her, the shoreline fell off sharply. Far below, bits of sand beach spilled out from the rocks, and the waves flashed with white foam. What was the right sound? What made music, music? And how could she have made those wrong entrances? Behind her, she heard a voice and turned. It was Arthur, several feet back, shoeless and without his jacket and tie. His pants legs were still rolled.

"I liked your playing," he shouted. "We're perfectionists and modern music is difficult. Not every musician has a feel for it."

"You don't need to compliment me," she called back. He

was trying to make her feel better, worried she'd quit and they'd need to find a substitute for the substitute. "I can handle criticism."

"Patrick and Charles have had the music longer, and we've been playing together for a while now. We're used to each other."

Below them, an outcropping of smooth, rounded stones jutted out into the water. Years later Benjamin would show her the geodes that sometimes hid inside stones like those. On the outside they were gray granite, but if you cracked one open, you might find a cavity of crystal or a tiny, glittering cave. Arthur walked a few paces behind her. She moved as fast as she could, concentrating on the narrow trail.

"That duet between the piano and cello in the final movement isn't easy. I'm sorry for bringing you in at the last minute, especially to play something that's difficult."

"I can manage it," she said, shouting over the sound of the waves and the wind. "It's an exciting piece. I like a challenge."

"I think you probably can. You've got the facility to play it and I like your style."

What style, she wanted to shout back. She was surprised they hadn't sent her back to Boston.

"Even while we were working hard on that difficult passage, you just focused on playing the notes," he added. "You didn't try to show off your technique."

"But technique is everything," she said, thinking that if it weren't for technique she wouldn't have been able to play those difficult measures at all.

"The music itself is everything," he countered. "Technique is only what we use to make music."

"But it's not music until it's played."

"It is music," he argued. "Maybe it's the only real music."

She stopped and slipped off her shoes. The ground was hot but she hardly felt it, and she walked quickly ahead. Down below, the ocean was a mass of glittering points, as if the sun

21

touched every wave. She couldn't think straight, and behind her, Arthur kept talking.

"When we play a piece of music, we have to get out of its way. We should disappear. Technique should disappear. I can't stand musicians who talk about interpretation. It's presumptuous. Our duty is to lift the notes off the page, and it's a sacred duty. That means sensing what the composer meant and what the music itself means, not imposing your own meaning on it. That's true for any piece of music. People think that abstract music gives them more license for interpretation, but it doesn't."

They had to walk single-file, and she stayed ahead of him. She was all nerves and everything he said made it worse. "You're quibbling with semantics," she told him boldly. "Technique doesn't need to be a controlling system. If we feel the music, if we go through the process of not just playing the notes but becoming the notes, as you say, disappearing into them, then we make the music new every time we play it. That's true interpretation, and it has everything to do with connecting with one's own sense of the music, one's own sound. Interpretation and technique make that process possible. They're what make music come alive, whether it's new music like yours or a symphony written in the 1700's."

The path widened and Arthur came abreast of her, shaking his head. His longish hair swung back and forth. It gleamed under the sun.

"That is exactly what I'm against," he said. "Believing in one's technique and one's ability to interpret the music is simply ego, and I don't care if the person doing the interpreting is a conductor or a musician. The idea that one's individual ego can be greater than the music itself is dangerous presumption. It destroys good music. Listen to that recent recording of Stravinsky's *Suite Number One*, and you'll hear what I mean."

"But if you're a musician, you find the meaning of the music, that essence, or purity, or whatever you want to call it, that's beyond you or anything you could ever mean on your own, by going inside yourself and connecting with it. That experience is true interpretation, and it leads you out of the ego, not further into it. I don't know about the recording you referred to, but I know what I experience when I play."

"True music divorces itself from technique and expectations. That was Schoenberg's purpose in creating serial music, to do away with expectations. We're living in an unpredictable world, and music divorced from expectations and technique is the only relevant expression of it."

"And what are you left with if you do away with expectations and technique?" she asked. Nothing she told herself. Chaos.

"Sound," he said, answering her right away. He didn't even have to take a second to think. He already knew. "Not a performer's ego, but pure and powerful sound."

"Well, I know what I experience when I play," she said. She wasn't shouting, but she spoke fiercely. Something had snapped into place. It was herself. "You can't tell me that what I experience is ego—it's not."

"I'm not trying to tell you what you experience." He threw up his hands. The path curved close to the edge of the cliffs. Rocks and scrub brush fell away to one side, and on the other side she saw verdant lawns and flowering bushes.

"You can't know what happens inside a musician," she said. "You can hear the music that's produced, but you can't see inside the musician and know what he or she is experiencing."

"That's not what I'm saying. I'm just saying that the music is bigger than we are." He stopped walking but she kept going, so that he was forced to shout. She pictured him screaming at the ocean, the ridiculousness of that. He was claiming that ego was what kept musicians from playing well, yet he seemed subsumed by his own importance. His sonata was more difficult than any music she'd ever played. Some of the musical patterns made no sense, and there was no consistent melody. Maybe it was difficult simply because it was bad. She wondered how much knowledge he had of the cello.

"Any piece of music has its own life," Arthur shouted. "Our work is to experience that life. Performance isn't about making an audience happy or making them understand or appreciate anything. It isn't about the audience or about the musician. It's about the music itself. The medium is everything."

The sky was darkening, but the air was still bright, shimmering with heat. She could see far out into the ocean, all the way to the thick line of the horizon. They'd descended closer to the water and reached a break in the path where it was possible to scramble down to the ocean over the rocks. She held her shoes in one hand and didn't stop until she reached the bottom. She threw herself down on a narrow strip of sand and shells next to the water.

Moments later, breathing heavily, Arthur lowered himself beside her. If she wasn't so tired, she would have stood up and walked back at the fastest possible pace. His hair whipped in front of his face with the wind. He was breathless from shouting. She hated the sound of his voice, so passionate and certain, and yet she could have lived off that sound. It cut both ways, straight through her.

"Performing new music demands courage. You have to reinvent yourself to play it, but it's the only music worth playing." He looked at her, glaring with sudden intensity. "Patrick says you were offered a teaching position at a music academy in Boston."

"Yes," she told him.

He moved closer, inches away. She could see every line in his face, the way his cheekbones were too prominent and his forehead too high. "If you could even consider teaching at a music academy, you shouldn't be performing."

For a long second, she stared back. She had a terrible urge to spit at him. "What do you know about it?"

"You're talented, and I think you may have the ability to actually produce a pure or true sound with your instrument, as you've argued. But in order to do that you'll need to devote yourself. To be a true musician, you have to want to play music badly enough that you can't think of doing anything else. That's the one thing I do know."

For a moment, they continued to stare at each other. Then she grabbed two fistfuls of his hair. It slid between her fingers, the type of hair that would untangle easily if you took a brush to it. She yanked hard enough that she expected some of it to come out in her hands, but instead his face moved into hers. Everything about it looked distorted—the shelf of his nose, the indentations where his eyes rested. What happened next happened quickly, without her thinking about it.

The small stones and sand ground into her. He pulled at her skirt, fumbling with the slip, but he didn't let go of her mouth. She felt like her teeth were locked around him. For a second she worried someone in one of the houses above might see them, and then he moved his hips into hers and she felt a sudden sharp pain.

"Some people are greater than the music," she told him. "Some people are meant to be its medium."

She slid under his grasp and everything rippled, turned and thickened. She and Benjamin had kissed for hours, fumbling to find each other's body parts underneath their clothing, but stopping there as if it were an end-point. This was not like that—not tentative or based on the assumption that spending long moments with one's mouth open to another's could be endlessly enjoyable. It was more like wrestling on the lawn with her brothers, pushing and shoving. She had liked that endless kissing, but now it seemed pointless. Here she was someone else.

Next to them, the ocean crashed against the rocks. She saw the dark outline of his head and saw his shirt, white against the bright air. Her skirt bunched around her waist. He was grinding her into the sand. She heard his breath quicken, and for another few minutes, his weight bore down on her. Then he lifted himself and she pulled her skirt down. There was blood on her slip.

It had seeped through to the sand where it spread into a circle the size of a sand dollar.

"That was your first time," he said, watching her. "You should have said something."

She pulled off her underwear and slip and walked down to the water to rinse off the blood. After dipping them in the ocean, she wrung them out and shook them dry in the hot air, then splashed the cold seawater between her legs under her skirt. The sun had dropped close to the horizon, and a second sun, a mirror image, bled into the water's surface. She fixed her sight closer in, on the breaking waves. They were gleaming also. In the concentrated light, everything was splitting apart.

"Are you alright?" Arthur asked from behind her.

She couldn't explain why she'd done what she'd done. Benjamin had called her a damn mystery when she'd refused his proposal. She didn't know. She was a mystery to herself.

"I'm fine," she told him. "But the dinner must be starting soon. We need to hurry back."

It would be a long way to walk, past the Jameson's to The Breakers, and they wouldn't get there in time. She began climbing back toward the path. Just before reaching the top, she stopped and slid her damp underwear up under her skirt, unbuttoned her blouse and pulled the slip over her head.

"I'm not dressed properly for the dinner and concert," she said as she refastened the buttons on her blouse.

"You're completely presentable," he told her, coming up behind her. "A beautifully presentable performer."

"Less than thirty minutes ago, you were telling me there was no reason for me to play music."

She stepped away and they began to walk, linking hands for a moment before the path narrowed. She was herself walking with him, yet she wasn't.

"I was telling you there was every reason for you to play music," he said just before they dropped hands and quickened their pace, trying to get back before the dinner was over.

Chapter 2

You're so lovely they had told her and you play like an angel. You have the face of an angel. At the conservatory, they asked her out and critiqued her abilities. They tested her over and over, she was always being tested and they explained why or why not she would qualify for the orchestra. Then she'd auditioned her first semester and been accepted when usually students didn't make orchestra until their second year. They taught her bowing methods and how to make ponticello with no pressure and how to play legato. They taught her staccato and spicatto. They taught her how to play with tension and without tension and when to bow close to the bridge and when to bow further away. The quality of the sound came from the bowing. In the windowless, sound-proof practice rooms where the lessons were given, they put their arms around her demonstrating. They embraced her, all the while talking about posture and positioning. When their hands brushed her neck or touched the front of her blouse, she kept her eyes on the music as if nothing else was happening. They corrected her and inspired her and intimidated her. They asked did she want to meet them somewhere later. They assigned her grades and decided her future, and she had to be careful answering them, saying no without rejecting or insulting. She kept her head down and practiced eight hours a day. She wore gathered skirts that draped between her legs, avoided shoes with heels, and favored thick stockings over the finer nylon ones. She made herself unattractive, wearing little makeup and tying her hair straight back. At night in the female dorm rooms, they talked about romantic motion pictures, weddings and engagements. She knew almost nothing about sex. They said you couldn't get pregnant the first time. Katie Sharpe had thought she was pregnant but eventually got her period. Someone said there were barriers—this part was especially vague—that prevented it all together.

Let's have lunch today.

Let's sit you up.

Let's lie you down.

Here in this chair by the window.

She was in the memory unit, remembering. She'd gone off to that festival just a few months after graduating.

Holding her shoes in one hand, she hurried barefoot along the path. Arthur's black hair glistened, and everything looked deeply colored because the sun was setting, scattering light in tiny pieces. When they reached The Breakers mansion, they walked up separately to the lawn where dinner was being eaten but ended up sitting at different ends of the same table. She had put her shoes back on by then, and Arthur had picked up his jacket when they passed by the Jameson's house. She said she'd been out walking and gone farther than she'd meant. Arthur said he'd lost track of time while playing music in the cottage. One minute she convinced herself everyone believed them, the next she knew they didn't. She felt like she'd fallen off a cliff face.

"Sit here next to me," Adele Jameson told her, as a folding chair was quickly put in place.

Across the table, they were talking about Arthur's piece being premiered on the festival's final night. Patrick claimed Arthur's music was completely original. "It's without predecessors," he said.

"But any piece of music has predecessors," someone protested.

"Not Arthur's and not most of the music The Modern Strings performs. Am I right?" Charles asked, then went on without waiting for an answer. "The new music we play questions the relevance of the old. If we are now facing the end of civilization, what is the point of melody? Bombs exist, therefore Beethoven no longer matters."

"That's a pithy summary, Charles," Patrick told him.

"Pithy but true. I've heard you and Arthur more than once downgrading all three of the composers being featured here."

"I've spent many years revering Beethoven," Patrick objected.

"But not the last ten."

"Well, perhaps not the last five," Patrick conceded. "But I still very much admire his use of color."

Reenie watched Arthur—the shape of his hands when he picked up his wineglass and how his dark hair fell into his eyes as he argued with Henry Jameson. "Of course music is political," she heard him say. "All art's political. It has to be, by its very nature." His voice had the same insistence she'd heard down by the water. He *was* that insistence.

The lawn where they were eating stretched from the back of the mansion to the cliffs. Beyond the tables, she glimpsed wild rose bushes, and beyond them the sea grasses that grew in the sand near the ocean. She listened to the conversations, but barely followed, couldn't think straight, and had a thousand thoughts and impressions. Had fascism destroyed the arts? Did the fact that Strauss was a political opportunist mean his music was backward, as Arthur was insisting? And what made Stravinsky different? The German language was despised, but German music was revered—Beethoven, Brahms, even Wagner was great. The women around her wore dresses with gathered skirts. She should have changed her clothes, but that would have meant going up to the house, and there'd been no time. She'd walked as fast as she could with Arthur's argument sloshing in her head. What did it mean to play music? How much of the music's sound was determined by the notes and how much by the musician? What was a true sound? Was there even such a thing? And if she found it, if she learned to play it? Her mind raced.

The women seated near her asked about her training and what she'd studied. They said they'd never met a woman cellist before and wanted to know what she wore when she performed.

Adele Jameson said she loved the idea of a female cellist. "I can just picture you in Toscanini's orchestra, seated among those rows of tuxedos with your long flowing hair. You would upend things!"

Toscanini was the most well-known conductor in the country. His performances were broadcast live. "A woman will never play with Toscanini," Reenie said. "I can't imagine it."

Across the table, someone was saying how unfair it was that Aaron Copland was questioned by the government.

"If you're a patriot, there's no reason for concern," Henry Jameson told them.

"That sounds a lot like the Soviets. They're all about patriotic music," Charles said.

"Leave it alone, Charles," Patrick told him.

"Just like the Germans were," someone else said. "Nothing like an insistence on patriotic to ruin a piece of music."

"Do you know," Charles went on, "Someone recently told me the penalty in New York State for being a card-carrying communist is the loss of one's fishing license. Let's have a show of hands. Has anyone at the table even got a fishing license?"

Everyone glanced around the table, but no one raised a hand, except for a chagrined violist who after a moment or two of needling confessed that yes, he had one. He loved to fish and had recently stayed two weeks on a lake in the middle of nowhere alone, just so he could. "It was so quiet you could hear them moving through the water."

"Impossible," the others objected.

"Not impossible," Arthur said. "One small sound heard in isolation can be especially beautiful."

Dessert came, a summer cobbler piled high with whipcream. Charles finished his, and when he excused himself to get a seat for the concert, Reenie followed. She quickly caught up.

"Arthur's the only one who can speak out and argue with people at an event like this and not suffer for it," he told her. "Did you hear him? He challenges Henry Jameson who's funding the event and the debut of his piece, and he comes off sounding brilliant and impassioned while I look like a fool."

"Not a fool," she said.

"Well, everyone ignores my opinions."

They walked up to The Breakers. At the top of a long slope, light poured from the back of the mansion. They entered through a glass loggia that opened onto the Great Hall where the ceiling rose three stories above them and dozens of paintings hung on the walls. In the back, large windows displayed the setting sun. At the other end of the hall, a red carpet led up a wide, curving stairway, and high above them gilded frescos of garlands, shells, and cavorting figures lined the domed ceiling. At the ceiling's apex, someone had painted a pale turquoise sky with white cottony clouds.

"It's meant to make us feel we're outside," Charles said, pointing up at it, but being in the Great Hall felt nothing like being outside. Charles noted everything. "The pillars along the balcony are painted. Do you see that design done in blue? And look at the seashells along the ceiling, and below them, those figures I believe are meant to be sea-gods. Each one of those doors leads to a reception room. Can you imagine the wealth it took to build this? That portrait is of one of the Vanderbilts. Isn't she lovely? I heard all that gold paint on the trim is made from the actual metal. They had to melt it down. Can you imagine the difficult work of it?"

Around them, the seats in the hall filled with concert-goers—men in dress suits and women wearing pastel blues, greens, pinks, and golden yellows. At the front the five musicians in tuxedos tuned their instruments. Reenie said she couldn't imagine the high ceilings would produce good acoustics, but when the quintet struck the first notes of Bach's concerto, they were perfectly clear, and a well-ordered Baroque world rose up like the tall fluted columns that lined the room and the evenly spaced archways with gold trim around the ceiling. She didn't know this concerto, had not studied it or heard it performed before, but it felt familiar. Bach's music made sense. Her ear picked up the brightness of the flute against the lower register of the cello in the background. Five instruments were conversing, and the second movement arrived without surprises, like a well-planned garden planted on purpose for variations in color. She understood such musical phrasing built on repetition and variations. It was a balm. Every muscle let go, her heart rate slowed. Language slipped, but not the ear, not the heart. It went on listening. The first time she'd heard a cello, it had been playing Bach in a small concert hall. She'd tucked her feet under her on the seat to get up high enough to see. "What is that instrument?" she'd whispered, pulling on her father's jacket, falling in love with the cello's sound in an instant, like a stone falling through water.

The concerto ended and applause swelled, as row after row stood clapping until she stood also, filled with a surge. When the applause died down and everyone began to gather their programs, she walked back outside across the lawn, toward the ocean where a group of musicians waited for Charles and the others who had gone to find flashlights. Torches flared in the darkness. She heard laughter and the sound of the water. Around the front of the mansion, car engines were starting up, and she made out headlights in the distance.

Arthur stood apart from the others near the hedges, smoking. "It was a lovely concert," she told him.

"Yes. This is the perfect setting for Baroque music."

"I never heard Bach played like that before. The intricate patterns were so clear and precise." Her voice sounded dreamy. She saw the tops of the hedges as her eyes adjusted. Above them, the stars seemed close and fiercely bright. Her body was humming. Something had opened inside her, large and amorphous.

"Baroque music is dead," Arthur said. "It's popularity rests with the fact that it's well known, but it can't speak to us anymore."

"But it has a timeless quality," she said.

"All good music has a timeless quality, but that won't save it. The careful arrangements and those patterns you describe can't express anything meaningful anymore. It doesn't resonate."

"But it does resonate," she said. "It did."

His eyes gleamed in the darkness. She could make out the shape of his head and shoulders and the white shirt where his jacket opened. "Siesel—that's a German name, isn't it? But you don't have an accent."

"Yes, German," she said. "But I was born in the United States."

"I attended Darmstadt last year, for the composer's competition. It was strange to be in Germany." He smoked for a minute then added, "They had one of those camps there, in Liebigschule. I saw where it was. I can't even describe how terrible that was. The next day I listened to Schoenberg's lecture about the need to destroy the rage for order, on which western classical music is founded. He presented a good case that would wipe out our reverence for most of the greatest composers."

"A rage for order," she repeated. "What does that mean?"

"Those intricate patterns you described." He tossed down his cigarette butt and ground it into the grass. There was an awkward silence, the thrum of the ocean still there in the background. She would never have described the need for patterns as a rage.

"We could leave now and start back without the others," he said.

Across the lawn small globes of light bobbed in the darkness. Charles and his group were headed toward them. Nothing felt real—the sound of the ocean, the lit sky, the slope of his shoulders, the way she'd grabbed his hair earlier, or the ordered beauty of the concert. Then before she could answer, the flashlights came closer and Charles called out, "We've got light," as the group of men swarmed around them.

"We'll have to stay close together," Charles told them.

"Reenie, you should walk somewhere in the middle, and we should all hold onto one another. One wrong step and I can't imagine what a fall from the height of those cliffs would do."

She fell into line toward the middle, and Arthur was somewhere at the back. Thomas Baxter, the violinist who had performed, walked just behind her with one of the flashlights, and she had no trouble seeing the path back to the Jameson's. The small beam lit the way.

Chapter 3

She was in the memory unit. A sound rose from beneath the building, a loud thrum. It blew through the vents in the hallways and rooms. It absorbed all other sound. It *wa*s all other sound.

Confusion and sleeping off and on throughout the day were normal. Her mind was not functioning and they couldn't say when and where the strokes would strike. Scans and images didn't help. The strokes occurred like flashes of lightning, but instead of coming from outside, the brain was assaulting itself from within. Judith asked many questions. Why weren't the medications working? What about studies showing that lost abilities could be regained? Would more therapy sessions help? And why did her mother keep having more of the strokes? Irena had signed a paper to prevent fluids when she could no longer drink which was how they said it would likely go in the end. A month, perhaps several or even a year. She had a strong heart which might keep going. It was not the question. Thinking would eventually cease. The brain would shut down. The orchestra would release its instruments after the finale. But silence was not possible.

She sat in a chair, lay down on the bed, ate less and less food and drank fewer liquids. She climbed hills, lugged her instrument, lifted herself into automobiles, ran and walked and slipped on the flat wet surfaces. It was all up close and very vivid. She was split into many different people, many different ears, and she heard everything simultaneously. Underneath the performance hall there were hundreds of practice rooms, each one sound proof, without windows, its own tiny cell. They filled one hallway after another. She practiced ten hours a day in them. Then the conductor told the orchestra they would be there longer getting it right. That solo she'd performed, that piece of music that was so difficult she'd forgotten it as soon as the performance ended and hoped never to play it again.

"Hurry," they kept calling. She was down by the ocean. "Come out here with us."

The tide was high and she had to pull her skirt up to keep it from getting wet. Charles said there were jellyfish and that someone had been stung. Patrick and Arthur wanted her to get her suit on and come in. They stood in the waist-high water waving.

"They'll keep at you until you agree," Charles said.

She liked that they kept calling out to her, that they wanted her with them. "Is dunking in the ocean one of the requirements for playing with your quartet?"

"Yes," Charles said. "It's part of the hazing of musicians, and I regret all I've surrendered to it."

Patrick bobbed in the waves close to shore, but Arthur swam farther out and then in a line parallel to the coast, skimming along the surface as if the current had no hold. After a few minutes, she couldn't see him, just the sun glinting off the water.

She went up to the house and ate biscuits drenched in butter and drank too much coffee. After breakfast when the group met for another rehearsal, Arthur was in high spirits, teasing that he'd get her in the water eventually. They began by playing the first movement a few times before moving onto the second. In one section, her timing was too slow, and they went back and played the same passage again and again.

"That time you played it too fast," they told her. "Stop listening. Just count."

Arthur had them page back and start the passage from the beginning. "Just count," he repeated. The music was fast and the tempo kept changing. She counted the beats in each measure, not thinking about anything else, and finally she got the entrance right, but she couldn't tell any longer if she was playing the right notes. If she stopped counting for even one second, they seemed to know and told her, "Keep counting."

She nodded and went on counting. Her mind screamed numbers and she got the timing right, but it didn't feel like she was making music. Instead she felt like a counting machine, and she grew more and more furious about the counting and frustrated with herself that she had to do it. Yet gradually, as she kept counting, the notes took on life. It happened without her noticing at first, and it happened precisely because she was counting. She couldn't explain it. Unexpectedly, her instrument was singing. She was stuck inside time and she was not stuck. Counting, it turned out, was everything.

Nearby, Patrick's viola and Charles's violin skimmed the high notes, while she and Arthur wove lower notes beneath them. She forgot how hard the music was, forgot the other instruments, but heard them, heard the other world they were making. She played faster, racing against the violin, then against the piano. Her fingers moved with more agility than she'd thought possible, and her whole body swayed with the motion of her bowing arm. It was like looking into a vast window and seeing the window inside of that window and then the one that came next and next. There was no end to the sounds that existed between the four instruments.

At the end of the movement, the rhythm became more regular. The tempo slowed and the sound faded to nothing. For a few seconds, the room was silent and then the music roared back with a boom. The final notes exploded. They lit a place inside her she hadn't known existed, a place that pitched and roiled, igniting her, and she would have to know that place again and again. Everything would change because of it, and she would be completely different.

A long pause followed the final notes. Charles and Patrick lowered their instruments, and Reenie's bow hovered. Her hands, releasing their grip, began to shake, and she heard herself breathing heavily. Then someone pulled the curtains to keep out the glare, and Arthur named the passages he wanted to repeat as they paged back to the more difficult sections. Whatever he said made the music better. She'd played in ensembles at the conservatory, but never at this level with other musicians who transformed her playing. When finally the rehearsal ended and someone opened the door to the patio, she heard the ocean and felt like she was waking from a long sleep.

Arthur gathered up his music and walked outside. She pictured him still playing the notes in his head, caught up in the music of his own making. While she put her instrument away, Patrick was talking about a woman he'd tried to interest Charles in.

"You are hopeless," Patrick said. "Even after the introduction I gave you, it didn't work out?"

"We met, we dated, we laughed and entertained one another, and then we parted, ill fated, like Tristan and Isolde."

They stood close, facing each other. Patrick laughed and stepped closer, and Charles stood completely still as if he didn't dare move, his head lowered. They were both large men with wide shoulders and waists that would thicken as they got older. Their bodies were mirror images of each other, but Charles wore his clothes sloppily while Patrick was overly neat with straight creases in his pants legs and starched shirt collars. His blazer fit snugly across his shoulders, and he had thick brown hair, cut stylishly, while Charles's was already starting to thin. Patrick's eyes were dark brown and piercing, while Charles wore glasses with thick lenses that made his eyes hard to see. They went on talking about the girl, but it was just a way to stand close and say something very different. Reenie saw all this, and because she didn't know that such an attraction was possible and to be loathed, she accepted it at face value. They wanted each other. They would have each other.

She closed her cello case and stepped outside. Several musicians were on the lawn. She looked around for Arthur, but he wasn't among them. The music they'd played was still in her ears, and silent explosions flashed in her brain as she drew closer to the ocean where the wind blew steadily, lifting the edge of her skirt.

She found him standing below the lawn on the wooden steps near the ocean, his hands stuffed in his pockets, looking out at the water. Remaining behind him, unseen, she examined the length of his legs, the slope of his shoulders, and the tautness with which he held himself. She saw the darkness of his straight hair. Delicacy and softness lay side by side with his wiry intensity, and she felt suddenly alive looking at him, more so than she'd ever felt, even while playing music.

Then as she stood there, not fifty feet behind him, he turned his head, gazing out at the ocean. She wasn't in the perimeter of his sight, and she couldn't know what he was staring at, but she felt like she knew. She felt like she could see that view herself—the spot where the waves broke near the coastline, just beyond the rocks. The waves glimmered because they were breaking apart. For a second before they dissolved, they were full of light.

His eyes were focused on this. His skin had darkened since yesterday. She observed the color and the sharp angle of his nose, the curve of his chin. In one moment, she committed all this to memory.

A few hours later, it was evening and fog had blown in off the ocean, climbing the cliffs and drifting across the wide lawn into the Great Hall. She sat in the hall's back row, near the misty windows.

"Fog is perfect for Beethoven," Charles said. "They've engineered it especially for the performance."

"Drink too much tonight and you'll fall into the ocean," Tom Baxter said.

"That could be less dangerous than falling into bed, depending on who you're with."

"Less enjoyable though," Charles said.

A man's voice sputtered, "I would never."

Even more chairs had been set up than the night before, and the room was quickly filling. She didn't see Arthur and Patrick anywhere. Maybe they hadn't come in yet. Next to her Charles was saying there must be a room available at the Jameson's.

"I heard there's nothing."

"Even since George Shields left this morning?"

"No room anywhere. Every one of them is full."

Tom said, "There's a party afterward down by the water. Harry went to a liquor store and bought up all the gin." He tapped Reenie on the shoulder. "You should come."

She said yes, she would. She'd had a couple of glasses of wine at dinner, and now it softened everything. Colors blended together, a flash of gold jewelry mixed with the glittery sheen on the paintings above her. As everyone settled into their chairs, the room filled with a pleasant hum, and then the hall grew silent as the performers walked to the stage. They took brief bows and seconds later Beethoven's string quartet poured from the gilded walls. Reenie knew the piece, had studied it, and she followed the themes and variations, feeling the change in emotion from the allegro to the adagio. The emotions built from one movement to the next. When the quartet ended, she had to wipe her face before standing to applaud. The two hours had gone quickly past.

As everyone left the hall, she followed Charles out and crossed the lawn with him, still hearing Beethoven's final notes. They were magicians, those who could make music like that. Suddenly she saw herself as part of a select group of musicians who would end up playing important performances. Great musicians centuries earlier had played the composers of their time, and she would do that as well. She would master Arthur's music and become part of something new and unprecedented. Below them, the waves were loud and Charles was describing what they would do when they got back—he had a bottle of bourbon and they would find somewhere to sit and drink it—but she was thinking of what she would accomplish. She would be the first woman cellist to embrace the new classical music, the sort that Arthur was composing without predecessors. She would become expert at performing it and would find that she was meant to play this music.

As they walked away from The Breakers, the fog dispersed, as if what Charles had said was true and nature had engineered it especially for the concert. When they reached the Jameson's lawn, she spotted the rocks above the wooden steps that went down to the water.

"Climb down there with a bottle of liquor and break your neck climbing back up," Charles said. "Patrick and Arthur are below us with the others. Let's sit on the cliff edge above them. We'll listen in and spy. We'll see who leaves with whom."

Someone was laughing and she heard Arthur's voice. Charles pointed with the flashlight. "That tall shape is Patrick. I can just make him out. He's the one over to the right and that's Adele next to him. She's wearing his jacket."

Reenie peered down. The voices were indistinguishable, except for Arthur's. She heard his above the others.

Charles found a place on the rocks, and she sat down as he opened his bourbon, drank, and passed it to her. The liquor spread across her tongue, flashed for a second, and when the taste was gone her mouth still burned. She took another sip.

"Have you had bourbon before?"

"No," she said.

"Do you like it?"

"Yes."

They settled back on the rocks, but she hardly noticed the hard and jagged surface. It felt smooth like stones under the water. Charles handed her the bottle again and she took another drink. The cool dampness of the air fought with the bourbon's fire. He offered his jacket, but she said she didn't need it and stretched out on her back, not caring that she'd have to use the bathroom sink later to clean her dress. One minute the voices below them sounded far away, the next close up. She kept listening for Arthur's voice. She could live off that sound.

"Patrick's good at courtship," Charles said. "You should have seen him earlier, inviting Adele Jameson to join their party. A woman who's married to wealth can afford to flirt. People expect it. He's got his arm around Adele. When she's with us, she acts like she doesn't mind sitting on rocks or drinking cheap booze, which you know she would normally never touch. It's a game to her. She thinks it's what artists do. Patrick says she might finance another concert. I hope you'll continue to play with us. Les is unreliable and a female would distinguish us, especially one playing the cello. I think it would set us apart."

"Yes," she said. She would be the one to set them apart. High above them, the clouds had been swept away. A crescent moon was rising.

"Patrick and Arthur are criticizing those who laud Beethoven, even though I've heard Arthur put Beethoven on a pedestal. Now the two of them are knocking him right off. Do you hear them? They're doing just what I said they would do, pairing up to laud the avant-garde. New music that breaks with tradition is exciting, but it will soon be old. The modern is always being replaced."

She said she'd hardly studied the modern composers.

"Learn about them from Arthur and Patrick. They're experts and they like holding court. They are suns, while you and I are orbiters."

She asked if they had girlfriends, spoke her question to the sky. She'd been wanting to ask about Arthur and now she'd drunk enough that she could.

"I believe so, here and there," he said vaguely. "But Arthur's not the type to want a wife managing his career. That's what Patrick claims he wants. He knows how to torture me. When I first arrived, before I drove to the train station to pick you up, he took me down here to the ocean, and he described

42

the first time he heard me play. He said listening to me he felt I had newly invented the violin or even music itself. He was so moved, he was nervous about coming up afterward and introducing himself."

"But he did," she guessed.

"Yes, and we went out to a fancy bar for a drink. I was trying to impress him, and I drank and talked too much. Afterward, I worried I'd never see him or hear from him again, but then he phoned me and we met for lunch. He and Arthur were forming this quartet, and he asked me to join."

"Maybe he got you drunk on purpose," she said. Down below, Arthur was listing composers—Boulez, Christian Wolff, Earle Brown—names she'd never heard of. She could lie on the rocks all night listening.

Charles said, "They'll be up late. Arthur will talk on and on. There was speculation before you arrived. I guessed you'd be engaged. Patrick and Arthur said you wouldn't be."

"You discussed me?"

"Speculated, merely."

The bourbon made her feel unsteady, and she found she loved feeling unsteady. "What else did you say about me?"

"I guessed you would be pretty, and I was right." He glanced over at her. "After you arrived, Patrick said pleasant looks at a performance would help draw attention. The audience likes a pretty bird. Then we heard you play. One expects a woman's looks will be in inverse relationship to her talent. Instead, you enchanted us."

"What relationship would talent have to someone's looks?" she asked. Then, "Did Arthur comment on my playing?"

"I don't remember. Why do you ask? Did something happen?"

"No, not really," she said.

"Tell me. You're making me jealous."

"We had a heated discussion about music is all, after the first rehearsal."

"Arthur likes to argue and when he says something, you completely believe it, as if he owns exclusive rights on the truth."

"He's an expert on composing."

"Yes," he told her, sounding discouraged. Close by, she heard footsteps, then whispering and a woman's laughter. "Patrick's walking Adele back to the house. He'll say good night and then perhaps come back down. The others will think I'm trying to get you drunk. I hope I haven't. I hope you're not too drunk to walk me back. Arthur will stay up half the night. I've seen him hold court until late and then perform the next day as if he's fully rested. That cottage he's staying in at the edge of the property is so pretty, small but nicely appropriated, with a baby grand."

He took a long drink. Reenie glanced up and saw Patrick close by at the edge of the lawn. "Plenty of bourbon still, if you'd like some," Charles called out to him. "It's only Reenie and I drinking it." He paused, but Patrick didn't say anything. "Did you hear me? The bottle's not half empty."

"I think I'll go back to my room. We have an early day tomorrow. We need to be at our best. There's just one day left to rehearse."

"We're at our best when we've relaxed."

"Not if you've had too much to drink." Patrick turned and faded into the darkness. She heard his steps retreating as he walked back toward the house.

"I'm a lush," Charles said. "That's what he means. Last winter I had too much wine before a performance, and later he and Arthur told me my playing was off. I thought I'd played more stunningly than ever."

"We should go back," Reenie said. "I have to rehearse that duet in the third movement with Arthur in the morning."

"When the four of us met in New York to discuss the piece, Les had a few words to say about that duet between the piano and cello. 'Uninteresting' was one and 'impossible' was another. Les called Arthur a hack, and Arthur said something like he only had to glance up to see if Les's bow was moving to know he was out of tune. By the end, Les had described the entire final movement as bombastic. He said, 'You throw in every innovation you can think of and call it new music.' A week later when he called to say he'd broken his arm, we assumed he'd invented the story, but I did hear from someone else that his arm was in a sling."

"I should review that duet again before I go to bed. It's long and difficult," she said. Then she described the odd markings she'd noticed on that part of her score, notations she'd never seen before.

"That duet is the hardest part of the sonata," Charles said.

"I'll manage it," she told him. "Somehow." She stood up and peered over the cliff edge.

"You are truly heroic."

Down below, Arthur was elaborating on the relationship between history and music. If he looked up, he would see her.

"Wait for me. I'll go with you," Charles said, fumbling with the bag and his bottle.

"Are you two leaving?" someone called up from below.

"Yes," she told them.

"So early?" Arthur shouted.

"I'll leave the bottle for you," Charles said.

She turned around and peered into the darkness. The lawn was up ahead with its burning torches. Somewhere beyond it lay the house, like another continent, and they had to climb over the rocky ground just to reach the lawn. She started out and Charles lagged behind. After a minute or so, he dropped down onto all fours, and she heard him huffing like a steam engine.

"Damn," he called out, stopping suddenly. "There's a thorn in my scalp and these trousers will be ruined."

"What happened?" she asked, circling back. "Are you hurt?" He was lying on the ground next to the wild roses.

"No. I've just had a run-in with that bush. I drank too much of the bourbon. Patrick detests me when I get like this." He curled up with his hands over his face. "Earlier this summer, we spent the night together. You wouldn't have guessed, would you? He was so amorous, then afterward he acted as if we'd never been together."

She dropped down beside him, thought maybe he was crying. She patted his shoulder, wanting to say yes, she'd guessed, meaning to say it, but unable to. She could hardly stand how sad he seemed.

"I'm so tired, I can't move," he murmured. "I'll stay here for a little while and rest."

She stroked his rounded back. "We're almost to the lawn, and then it will be easy. You'll see. We'll quickly be in our beds."

He glanced up at her. "Thank you," he said. "You do enliven me so with your optimism."

She helped him turn onto his back, and when he lifted his arms, she grasped his hands and pulled. There was resistance at first, but then he rose suddenly. He let go of her hands and reached one arm out, as if pointing.

"We need to go in that direction," he seemed to be saying. He stayed in the pose for a few seconds, and when he lurched toward her, there was a moment when she could have stepped to one side but didn't, so that as he fell, he crashed into her. She hit the ground hard, and he landed on top of her. Her back and head hurt. His weight took her breath away.

"Oh Lord, have I knocked you out? Have I injured you?" He didn't move at all when he spoke. The words just seemed to erupt out of him.

Down below someone called up, "Are you two enjoying each other, or should one of us come up and help you?"

"We're just turning in," Charles called back, trying to lift himself. "I've left you the bourbon. You'll find it when you climb back up."

She felt his weight on top of her shift. She could hardly

breathe, but it didn't seem to matter. Everything felt suddenly ridiculous. He was heavier than he looked, a giant disguised as a human.

"Are you hurt?" he kept asking, again and again, but she had started laughing and couldn't stop. It was all an eruption— his falling on her, his words, her laughter.

From down below, she caught pieces of the conversation. "Good thing they're not taking the bourbon with them," someone said, and there was speculation about what 'turning in' meant.

"Just roll off me," she told him, still laughing. "Can you? That would be easiest."

"Sounds like a party up there," someone shouted.

"Perhaps you should go up and check on them, Arthur," someone else commented. "You can't afford to lose another musician."

She pushed him then, hard, and Charles rolled off her. "Come on. We have to give it another try," she said, pulling herself up. Charles stumbled to his feet, and she got him to drape his arm over her shoulders. Together, they took a few steps toward the lawn. In the distance, she could see the lit torches near the house.

"Charles is reliable," she heard Arthur say. "He'll get her to bed."

She wanted to know what he meant, but Charles leaned in heavily. "Steer me, Reenie," he said, bumping against her hip, and she took his arm and directed him.

Chapter 4

She felt nervous and giddy whenever she saw him, even though she was normally sure of herself. She didn't know what to say and said things she hadn't planned on—that images had floated across her mind when she'd heard the Beethoven concert, that she'd never heard such music played.

Arthur asked, "What do you mean by *such music*? What makes music, music?"

"Melody, harmony," she said.

"No," he argued. "Sound, pure sound."

"But what is pure sound?"

He said it couldn't be described with words or narrowed down to a few qualities, but one recognized it immediately when one heard it, and she accepted his answer, didn't question it. She wanted to know everything he knew. When they met to practice the difficult duet the morning after she sat with Charles on the rocks and heard what Les thought of it, she said how remarkable it was, difficult but innovative. Then she asked about the notations she hadn't recognized.

He told her they were microtones. "Play them a quarter tone sharp," he said. "When you play slightly off tune against my notes, it'll create a shimmer in the sound waves. Play it that way and you'll hear what I mean."

"But it will seem like I'm just playing out of tune."

"No, it won't. When you play them with my notes, it'll be obvious that the dissonance is on purpose."

She didn't see how anyone would know it was on purpose, but when they began to play she tried it.

"That's right," he said, but she couldn't tell if she was a quarter tone sharp or three-quarters. The notes just sounded wrong. She glanced up for direction, but he stayed bent over the keys.

When they reached the end, he told her, "Go back to the beginning," not looking up.

They played the duet again, faster. She heard wrong notes, or thought she heard them, felt her fingers slipping too far in one direction, then too far the other way. She couldn't find the right positions, and she couldn't hear if she was more than or less than a quarter note out of tune. Playing that way went against all her training. He kept going and they played the pages again and again.

"Keep up with me. You'll get it," he said.

"I won't," she told him, but they played it through several more times. Then just when she couldn't go any farther and had no idea what she was playing, she saw she couldn't stop. She was lost inside a maze of notes and there was no stopping place, no tonal center. She was too sharp, then not sharp enough. Her ear lost perspective. She paged back to the opening measures, poised to play, then leapt as if from a high place and fell without seeing what was below. He glanced up at her nodding. Somehow, unexpectedly, she had slipped into place beside him. For several pages, the two instruments raced along together, and it felt like she'd climbed inside him and knew how he was hearing the music, knew even how it had sounded to him in his mind when he'd first written the notes down. Between their instruments, something new was coming to life, something that hadn't existed. She leaned into the action of bowing, playing the notes but listening as well. She was producing the sound, but it was also producing her, tipping her out of the container that moved the bow and watched the page of notes. She heard Arthur, not the piano, but Arthur himself—swooping, crackling, and singing. They turned together. They spread something throughout the room. Wind on a brown-gold field. They played to the end, including the final lines of music where Patrick's viola and Charles's violin would have joined them. Afterward, she stayed bent over her cello, as if she'd absorbed the instrument into her body. Her hair had fallen forward and her back was rounded.

Arthur said, "That's what I wanted. That was the sound I was after. It was better even."

He went to the glass doors and opened the drapes. Bright light invaded the room. She had to squint because of the glare. "You asked what pure sound is," he said. "That was it." Their eyes met for moment, and something passed between them. It was like the brightness of that light, but not like it. It had to do with the music, but it wasn't the music. It felt like something far away and not yet visible had dropped down into them.

He glanced away. "I won't see you at the dinner or the concert. I'm meeting others there."

She was confused. Why would they sit together at the concert?

"After it's over, wait for me by the cliff path and I'll walk back with you."

"You'll walk back?" she said.

"Yes," he told her. "I'm staying in that cottage, but it isn't far from the house, just down the road. I keep late hours. I can't sleep when we've been playing music all day."

She sat back and leaned her cello against the chair.

"I'll see you then after the concert?" he asked.

"Yes, by the path."

He nodded and then he was gone. She saw him quickly walk off the patio and across the lawn as she closed her score.

She had to get through the dinner and the concert before their meeting. She sat with Charles and said little, not noticing what she ate and not interested in hearing Brahms' *Jerusalem Quartet*. A chair was being pulled across the floor of the Great Hall, and Charles said, "Patrick is still outside talking with someone. He and Arthur know everyone, while I have a select group of friends, one that chiefly includes you."

The concert room filled gradually, and she paid no attention to the audience or the musicians when they came out, bowing to brief applause. She looked for Arthur, spotted him, then watched to see if he would turn around. When the concert began, she ignored the program and didn't hear the instrumentation. She and Arthur had played pure notes, and he'd insisted on the ones that were slightly out of tune, those sound waves that shimmered. What did that mean? A new piece of music written now could reverse the centuries old conventions embraced by Brahms. She sat listening but not hearing and didn't follow the shift from the allegro to the adagio. It was old music, she told herself, dead music. Brahms did not matter anymore. His music could teach her nothing. The performance tomorrow by The Modern Strings would outshine this one and all of the others before it.

She went on thinking in this way and did not bother to listen, but during the adagio a shift happened in her perception. It came without her conscious intention as if Brahms himself had pushed away her thoughts, demonstrating his music was very much alive. The quartet was playing the second movement when she found herself listening intently. She heard the sounds coming from the instruments as if she was approaching something unknown but enormous at the center of Brahms or maybe at the center of all music. As soon as she focused on it and tried to follow it, the sensation disappeared. She had no word for it—the thing that mattered inside the music being played and all those ideas about music, the hours spent learning notes and perfecting technique, and the opulent room filled with men in evening dress and women wearing evening gowns and jewels. One of the women in the next row actually wore a tiara of diamonds. Ridiculous ornamentation. Yet inside this and inside her desire to have Arthur turn and look at her when he passed back through the hall after the concert was over, was something bigger, a presence there in the Adagio. She slipped down, feeling nearly asleep but not asleep, hearing more and more and deeper and deeper, and then there it was suddenly in front of her—beauty. There was no other word for it. Beauty—the reason for the performance, for all this, including an enormous mansion built on the sand and the hundred or more people in the audience. It was the reason also for the chance of a broken arm, and for Arthur and her meeting, and for her performance tomorrow evening with The Modern Strings. Beauty, which it turned out was so great a sensation it overwhelmed everything else, including arguments and politics about which music was better, the old or the new, and including even the future and what would end up happening. Beauty was so great a sensation, she could barely perceive it.

The feeling disappeared when the concert ended, but she sat for a few minutes as the others were leaving, waving to them to go on ahead, still listening for the echoes of the notes. Charles was gone when she rose to leave, and she walked out onto the lawn alone. She didn't see Arthur anywhere.

"Reenie, are you coming with us?" one of the other musicians called to her.

"No," she called back. "I'm waiting for someone." She angled away from them and walked at the edge of the crowd that lingered on the lawn.

"Are you staying till the end of the season?" someone said.

"Yes, unless of course the weather changes. Last year there was that hurricane."

She walked past them all, toward the back of the lawn near the ocean. White flowers shone in the torchlight and Charles caught up with her. He handed her a flashlight when she said she was staying behind to walk with Arthur and then went on ahead. She continued walking alone past the torches and through the thick grass until she reached the cliff path. She made out the row of hedges at the back and the hulking shapes of rocks. She smelled salt water and a hint of gardenias and heard laughter, farther away now. Arthur was possibly back there still, near the mansion where a crowd still gathered. Maybe he won't come, she thought switching on the flashlight, and then she saw his shape walking toward her.

52

"You have a light," he called out. "Good. I'm without."

"Yes," she answered, and the air felt suddenly alive, trembling as she turned toward the path. Rocks came into sharp relief under the flashlight. She walked ahead of him, swinging it, unable to keep it steady. She'd worn a pale blue skirt with a white sleeveless top. She guessed it made her easier to see in the dark. The flashlight picked up silvery blades of grass poking through the sand. The island was dark where there were no houses or where the houses were empty, then lit, suddenly, where the houses were full of people. She heard music, snatches of a popular tune. She had to concentrate on the beam of light to avoid tripping, and all the while she felt him behind her, heard his footsteps.

"Slow down," he said, and when she turned, he pulled her toward him. He was warm, the sleeves of his shirt soft and billowy. She kissed him and when he grasped her hand, she kept hold of it, even though it was awkward, and they couldn't walk side by side on the narrow path. As they drew close to the Jameson's, the flashlight picked up white flowers, floating in the dark bushes. They reached the wooden plank stairs that led to the Jameson's rocky beach and stopped suddenly. The air was warm and close. Down below, she heard laughter and voices. Charles and some of the others had gone there. Something important was happening, sweeping down like the sensation of beauty she'd experienced listening to Brahms. That feeling of beauty made whatever happened now seem larger.

Arthur wrapped his arms around her, and a sensation moved between them, rare and pleasurable. "Get your swimsuit and come back down. You have to swim at least once while you're here."

"But we won't be able to see."

"The moon will rise. Swimming is best at night. The water feels warmer. I'm going in. I need a swim."

"All right. I'll change and come back down. Aren't you going to change?"

"I'll swim in my undershorts." He released her and called down to Charles below on the rocks. "What have you got in that bottle?"

"The bourbon left from last night," Charles called back. "I thought Patrick might come down here, but I don't know what happened to him. Where is Reenie?"

"She's going to the house to get her bathing suit. We're planning a swim. Do you want to come?"

"No, I'll just sit here and watch for you to come back. Have you met Felix and Robert? They've just arrived from New York."

Reenie walked across the thick grass. She went upstairs quickly and changed into her suit, then wrapped a skirt and a long-sleeved blouse over it. Henry Jameson stood by the opened doors to the patio where a small group had gathered and several men stood on the lawn, but she walked past them without speaking. At the edge of the lawn, Arthur called to her from below. "We're down here."

He and Charles were sitting on the flat rocks near the water with Felix and Robert, a cellist and violinist whose wives she'd heard were staying together at the nearby inn. She walked down the wooden steps and climbed over the rocks, sliding down to sit on one near Arthur. In front of them was the ocean.

"Drink," Charles commanded, handing her the bottle from the night before.

She up ended and swallowed a little.

"Have more. You'll need warmth if you're going in—and courage."

"Reenie doesn't need courage, Charles," Arthur told him. "She has that."

"She's mortal," Charles said. "Like me. Entering the frigid Atlantic at night demands courage. Am I right, Reenie? I think you're brave."

She handed the bottle to Arthur. "I haven't gone in yet."

"We shouldn't sit here too long, thinking about it."

"I heard Harmon Rothschild went in earlier and cut his foot on something," Felix told them. "It wasn't a bad cut, just the sort that needed iodine and a small bandage. Someone up at the house had a first aid kit and fixed him up. He swam too close to the rocks."

"That's more the danger," Arthur said. "It's safer to swim farther out, past the breakers. If you get hurt, it'll be going out or coming in."

"That's enough to keep me here, looking out over the water and feeling the delicious spray. I could sit here all night with pleasant company. It's wonderfully beautiful and dreamy. Reenie knows what I mean. The two of us sat on the cliffs up there last night, and the conversation below us faded in and out with the sound of the waves."

"I heard you stumbling back to the house," Arthur said. "Everything seems beautiful when you're part way through a bottle."

"Not everything," Charles said, a vague uncertainty running beneath his effusiveness.

"I'd better go up to the house before I get to that point," Robert said, rising.

"Not yet, please," Charles said. "These two will go out into the water, and I'll be left alone. Stay and talk. We'll plan an entire season for the Philharmonic. We'll design the list of composers."

Arthur nudged her. "Ready?"

"The sooner you go in, the sooner you'll be out," Charles said.

She slid off her skirt, folded it, and placed it a few steps above her, then removed her blouse, realizing she'd forgotten to bring a towel. She'd be cold when she came out. She'd have to run back to the house to change clothes.

"Come right back," Charles said. "Don't let him convince you to stay in the deep ocean. That's what he'll try to do. He went in the first night we were here. You had already gone to bed, but I sat here with Patrick, and we waited and waited for him to emerge. I worried he'd drowned. Except that Patrick kept saying he was certain he could still make Arthur out or hear him, I would have alarmed the household. Then, of course, Arthur rose up from down below, like a dark seal."

"I wasn't gone that long, Charles. It only seemed that way because you were drinking."

"I hadn't even had anything that night, and I'm injured that you think any concern I have for you comes from drinking. I would have mourned if you hadn't come back, and I wouldn't have recovered. Patrick might have. He's less emotional. He would have begun searching the next day for another composer he could pair up with."

"Thank you, Charles. I'll remember that when we're playing together tomorrow."

"Not that he would be able to find a replacement. Not that anyone would measure up."

Arthur stripped to his shorts, and they scooted down the steps, stopping just above the water.

"Is the tide in?" she asked.

"Not for another hour or so."

A flock of gulls wheeled toward them, and a wave broke against the steps. Arthur slipped in silently. At first, she couldn't find him, but as her eyes adjusted, she saw where the line was that separated the sky from the ocean, and she made out the shape of his head.

"Just push off the step," he called out. "You do swim, don't you?"

"I've had lessons, if that's what you mean, while growing up."

"You'll be fine."

"Don't let him convince you, Reenie," Charles called down. "Not if you don't want to go in. You can sit here with us and watch. You can wait for him to have his nightly excursion."

She forced herself into a low crouch on the step and pushed

off. The water felt shockingly cold, and almost immediately a wave broke over her head. Water rushed into her ears as she fought to reach the surface, and her foot hit against something sharp.

"You need to get farther out, past where they're breaking," Arthur called.

Above them she heard Charles. "Reenie, Reenie...."

"Dive under now while it's calm and swim out."

She plunged beneath the ocean's surface, then rose gasping. When a wave swelled up, it carried her high on its surface, before dropping her down as another one slapped her face.

"I think we're too far out," she shouted.

"No, we're not. Reach your feet down. You can still touch."

She tried to drop her feet, but another wave washed toward her, churning and spitting. She dog-paddled and shook her wet hair back from her face. Water streamed from her ears and nose. Underneath her, the water roiled, pulling one direction and then the other. Arthur dove under and surfaced farther out. She saw his dark head above the water.

"Swim out here with me and you won't get knocked around. The water's calm when you're past the breakers."

She dove and swam straight through the next wave, and in an instant, as she broke away from it, the water settled. She was right next to Arthur. She could have reached out and touched him. The water was calm and it felt warmer somehow. They swam side by side, turning one way and then the other, in rhythm. A piece of seaweed slipped past. Reflections of stars spread across the ocean's surface, as far as she could see.

For a while, she just swam, pairing her movements with Arthur's and not thinking about the shore or how far out they were going. The water grew cold again and the ocean felt vast, as if she'd entered the thing that had swept down earlier to lift her up. It was larger than she was, this thing that contained beauty; it was so large it couldn't be named but was directing her. She was swimming in it. Then she slowed. She glanced back and listened but didn't hear voices.

"Where's Charles? Did they go to the house?"

Arthur drifted beside her. He dipped his head backwards into the water, and his wet hair streamed away from his face. "Felix and Robert did. I saw them walking up. We're down toward the point, out of sight and earshot by now."

"Should we turn around?"

"In a few minutes. We're swimming with the current, that's why it's so easy. I could do this sort of swimming all night."

They took off again, staying close together. She rolled when he rolled, reached when he reached, and the water felt thick and warmer again. It felt weighted with warmth. It bathed them.

"Keep going," Arthur called out, whisking his tail. Her legs slid through his, her scales touched his scales. In their fishes' bodies, they circled one another. Stars streaked the sky with patches of milky light. Their reflections gleamed everywhere on the water's surface.

Eventually Arthur slowed. He turned. Lifting his head from the water, he said, "We should start back," and she noticed suddenly that the water had grown very cold. Her legs drifted downward. The ocean felt bottomless.

"How far out are we?"

"Farther than I thought. We must have been pulled more than I realized by the current, but we'll head in. We can cut back at a diagonal."

She peered into the darkness, looking for the shore. "This way," he said as he struck out, and almost immediately she lost sight of him. How did he know which way to swim? There was no indication of a shoreline. They had reached the middle of the ocean where the water's black surface was endlessly uniform and rippling with waves. She dove, following him, and the ocean rose up, then wheeled down, pulling her under. She tried to see where she was going but couldn't. Even a ship would get lost out here, she thought. It would be a mere toy. It would have no more chance than a piece of flotsam.

Up ahead, Arthur had slowed, waiting. "It's harder swimming back. Will you be all right?"

She said yes without considering. If she thought she might not be able to swim back, she wasn't going to acknowledge it.

"I can help you if I need to. I can pull you along."

"Just swim," she told him.

Moving against the current made everything that had seemed easy impossible. The water slapped her face, and when she pulled with her arms, the water pulled back harder so that she wobbled, shifting back and forth, swimming first to one side of Arthur and then the other. She tried not to lift her head, swimming for whole long minutes without breathing, then gasping and sputtering when her lungs clenched.

"Slow progress," Arthur said, stopping to tread water.

"How much farther?"

He pointed. "See the shoreline? There."

She stared but couldn't see what he pointed toward, even when she narrowed her vision, concentrating on one spot.

"Have you had enough of a rest? We should keep swimming. We don't want to lose our progress."

They struck out again, throwing themselves against the water. Her muscles were tiring, but she didn't allow herself to notice. When we're close enough that I can see the shore, I'll rest, she told herself.

Arthur slowed again. He treaded water waiting for her. "Keep going," she said. "Don't stop until we're close enough to touch bottom."

"Better to not tire ourselves."

"I won't be able to start swimming again if I stop."

They threw themselves at the water in order to keep going, and just then a sound came from somewhere behind them. She couldn't tell if it was far away or close. It rose up off the ocean's floor—a long hollow note like the foghorn of a far-away ship. She glanced back, watching for the outline of a huge creature against the water—winking eyes, glimmering portals or spot-lights—but all she saw in the darkness was shadow on shadow. She listened and the sound came once more, great and deep.

She began to swim as hard and fast as she could. Arthur stayed behind for a moment, listening, but the sound didn't come again. Instead a force came from out of the ocean's depths. All around them, waves rose higher, breaking over them. They had to ride in the pitch of those waves. They had to fight to keep from being knocked under. She was pummeled, ground into the ocean floor, crushed and kicked, then pulled back again to the water's surface, sputtering and coughing. Water churned through her ears. She swallowed gallons of it. After a few minutes, she couldn't see or hear Arthur. She couldn't see or hear anything except the water. At one point, she was spun under, like a wheel, and for a long moment, her body couldn't find which way to turn to get to the surface again. Finally, when it felt like her lungs would implode and she saw she would have to give up and be turned in one circle after another all the way to the ocean's bottom, she spurted into the dark air. Her lungs seized and her head exploded. It was a few minutes before she realized she was close enough to the shore that she could stand. Then the waves died down for a second between breakers, and she was able to stagger forward against the undertow that pulled the bottom from under her feet.

Arthur had washed up nearby. He raised an arm to signal just as a wave knocked her under again, pitching her to the ocean floor. It ground her into the muddy silt, then spit her back up. She managed a few more steps before another wave pushed her under, and when she came up again, she crawled to the shore where she lay down in the shallow water. Every now and then a wave washed gently over her. Nearby, she saw the outline of the trees and rocks along the coast.

"Are you okay?" he called out.

"Yes," she called back.

They lay a few feet apart in the shallow water. Waves rippled over them, then retreated, leaving a bubbly foam. She felt the sandy silt under her harden with each retreat. Both the air and the water felt cold, but she was still warm from the hard swim. Her muscles began to let go, her heart and breathing slowed. Arthur crawled toward her, collapsed beside her.

"Sorry. I misjudged. That current was much stronger than I thought."

"Some currents develop suddenly," she said. "Rip tides."

"Yes. Maybe." He was still breathing heavily, lying so close she heard each breath. "Sorry," he said again. "I shouldn't have dragged you out."

"You didn't drag me."

"If I'd looked at how far we were from shore..."

"When I looked, after we stopped to turn back, I couldn't even see the shoreline. Not until we were almost here."

A more vigorous wave washed over them. She felt the jagged surface under her scrape her side. He moved closer, reached out and pulled her toward him, where the water was shallower. The large amorphous thing that was beauty was still there, all around them. She thought, I will not forget this.

"The tide's coming in," he said as she settled back against him.

"Yes." She felt his ribs against her ribs, his belly against her back.

"That may have been what changed the currents. We'll get cold lying here. Do you need to start walking?"

"No," she said. "I can't move." The water washed between them and she sighed. "It feels good now."

He chuckled. "When there's just an inch or two, it feels good."

Her muscles released. They gave way into the container of his muscles. Her exhaustion felt wonderful.

"Did you hear that sound when we were swimming back? It had to have come from the same thing that caused those swells."

"I thought they'd drown us," she said. "It must have been a fishing boat."

"We would have seen lights or heard a motor."

"Maybe not."

"A whale, deeper down and farther out would do that."

She said yes, believed what he said. She was certain and was swept along by her certainty. His hand slid over her hip, and the air and muddy sand and water mixed together. Her spine was malleable, could bend however it needed, and behind her, his heart hammered steadily. He tugged at the top of her suit, pulling it down and kissing her shoulder, then her ear and along her neck. His hand spread across her breast. She didn't move, didn't want to risk that he would stop or acknowledge where they were going. Her mind turned off. She felt his fingers dig into the soft flesh and instantly grew warm there, hot even. The shore they'd landed on was uninhabited and rocky. There were no lights except for the stars and the moon that was beginning to rise, a thin white sliver. The water had carried them far enough. Everything felt amorphous.

He kissed her shoulder again. "There's a path before we reach the Jameson's that leads to the cottage. We could try to find it," he said. "Even if Charles and the others are still outside on the rocks, they won't see us, and you could stay the night. In the morning, if you left early, no one would know. If anyone saw you walking back to the house, it would just look like you went out for a morning swim."

She agreed readily, said only that she wished she had her skirt and blouse which were down on the rocks in front of the Jameson's, but that she could wrap instead in a towel. He said if Charles and Patrick questioned what happened, they should say they'd taken the road back after coming to shore past the island's point, and she'd gone straight to the house, feeling exhausted. "We'll tell them our nighttime swim together was a disaster."

"Well you did try to drown me," she said.

"Yes, tell them that."

She didn't question him, saw the need to say whatever he suggested, and they went on lying together in the shallow water, their breathing slowing. She felt that thing that was so much larger than her—beauty. They were both inside it.

"You are a such a surprise," he said. "I hadn't expected any of this."

"No." She turned toward him, turned into him and felt that as well, the fronts of their bodies pressed together. This new thing. She pushed herself into him just as a wave broke, and seconds later they were sitting up, laughing and spitting out water. She shook water out of her hair and attempted to knock it from her ears, as they struggled to stand up. Her legs felt wobbly when she walked into the ocean again and dunked under to rinse away the sand and shells. She pulled her suit back up into place and said it might be easier to walk along the shoreline.

"Yes, I don't even know if the cliff path extends this far."

"How far are we?"

"Past the point, I think."

They focused on figuring out the easiest path. They had a long way to go and they walked together, side by side, at the shoreline until they had to drop hands to scramble across outcroppings of rocks. What she knew, her new understanding, kept expanding. She felt warm still and flushed. Beauty was guiding her. It was her whole self, and it was so much larger than anything she'd ever known. Nothing else mattered.

They came to a pool of water and she stepped down next to him, against him. They began kissing and didn't stop. "Where is this going?" he asked but she kept on, didn't answer, felt herself move closer.

He said again that she was a surprise, then added, "I wasn't looking for this. I wasn't expecting it, anything serious."

"This is serious," she said, knowing.

He said yes and went on then talking about difficulties. She felt him pull back a little, but she was still warm and flushed.

This close, his profile was clear even in the dark. "I'm not looking for anything permanent. I can't do that," he said. Broken shells and stones covered the ocean floor, and the cold water numbed her feet. "I travel so much. I'm working with an ensemble in Philadelphia this winter that's performing a piece of mine. I'm making up for lost time, ever since the war ended when I got back and returned to my studies. There's so much pressure."

"How long were you overseas?" she asked.

"Less than a year, but it felt like forever. Before that, I was studying to be a pianist, but when I came back I knew I had to compose. I know that sounds weird."

"Not weird," she said.

"It feels like I've been charged with creating this new aesthetic, but I don't know what that aesthetic is. I'm in the dark with it, really. Only time will show if my music is valid or not. I can't see into that."

They stepped apart and began walking again. They were headed toward the cottage if they could spot the path that led to it. She felt she'd been waiting for this for a long time, maybe all her life, and she was not disturbed by what he'd said. The other thing, beauty, felt too large. It governed everything.

"But surely your music's valid," she said.

"I don't know. I can't tell. Sometimes I feel certain, like I've been given a divine order even, and the music I'm writing is a sacred text. That sounds presumptuous, I know."

"No," she assured him.

"Other times, I have no idea what I'm doing. I'm trying to combine all innovations. That's what Beethoven did. It's the work of those composers who come after the composers who have brought in new aesthetics and techniques, changing how we view music. Those who come after are the ones who write great music. Some say Aaron Copland's doing that, but he's not and neither is Bernstein. They're not writing anything new. They're writing for Broadway. Schoenberg, Pierre Boulez,

George Antheil—they had courage. I know so much, but I have no idea what I'm doing, not really. No fucking idea."

"But how do you compose? You must have a method. You must have learned methods."

He said he was schooled in Schoenberg, a great innovator, and he used Schoenberg's twelve-tone technique. "But I don't start with it, and I need to break free from it if I want to do something new. I don't yet know myself what that means. To a certain extent, I rely on my own ear. Technique enters into it, but it's secondary. I start with a handful of notes, which I keep playing together in various ways. I might love the way they sound together, that's the main thing, like with those microtones. I began composing that duet with them in mind. Once I have a group of notes, I build on them, going on from there, moving the sounds around in my mind first, sometimes for weeks at a time before I write them down. There's no real reference point when I'm doing that."

He said that while most of his training was in classical music, he loved other types of music, including jazz. "I first heard jazz, really listened to it that is, when I was in Paris just after the war ended. A few of us wandered into a club. They were playing this incredible music even though all around them, the city had been destroyed."

"I've heard so little jazz or any other type of music than classical," she told him.

"You need to hear jazz and learn about it. Listen to as many different types of music as you can. Train your ear to hear all of it," he said, and then he went on for a while talking about what a good musician she was, especially given her age and experience. He said she had real talent, he had heard that, and he was a good judge. She mustn't short change herself. She should be performing and pushing herself to excel and to learn more and more music. He said she was meant for that, and she felt like he was the first person to really look into her and see her, including her deepest desires and her fears that if she ever had to stop playing music she could not live. Everything he said opened up a new place inside her and those places kept opening. There was no stopping this from happening, and the more he talked, the more the place at the center of her opened up. That place inside her, underneath everything else, felt enormous and full of possibilities, and she was sucked up by it, couldn't have prevented it.

They came upon another outcropping of rocks, and she couldn't see the end of it, even though the moon was higher now, brighter, and her eyes had adjusted to the dark. The rocks were black, solid shapes. They focused on climbing. She cut her foot and felt blood there when she touched it with her hand. They kept climbing and she held on and didn't let go or step away, and the feeling, her knowledge that a large amorphous being contained her and was directing her, did not leave her. The certainty of its existence kept expanding.

"What is music?" he asked.

"Notes," she said. "Tone, harmony."

"Yes, it's all those things. Put simply, it's an arrangement of notes or sounds. Two hundred years ago they would have added, an arrangement that's pleasing. Then pleasing was replaced by expressive. But now there's no modifier, and with the freedom to make music be absolutely anything comes the possibility that one will create nothing, or even that one will create babel."

They stopped walking for a moment and rested on a rock. She looked out at the black sky and the ocean. His task seemed impossible. "How do you do it?" she asked. "How do you compose?"

For a moment, he didn't answer and when he did, when he said, "Intense concentration," he sounded tentative, frightened even, and she had the sense of a lone person surrounded by influences and imperatives, trying to make sense, to make meaning out of the chaos.

"Sound lies underneath all of it," he went on once they were moving again. "The history of music is important, and all the earlier composers showed the way. After many centuries of composing music, we've pared music down so we finally know what lies underneath all those efforts. Real music is based on pure sound, I'm sure of this and I'm determined to write real music, even if I have to give up the successful career my education promised in order to do it."

"What is that," she asked, "*real music?*"

"I don't know," he said after a while. "I haven't heard it, but I would give up everything else in order just once to hear it. That will be my life's work, even if it leads me to compose music that ends up in a box in an attic somewhere."

"That won't happen," she said. "You'll become well known for what you're doing. Your work will be played and remembered." She felt certain, as if the future was being directed by that large being that lay at the center of everything else and held them.

"Sometimes when I compose, I see things, simultaneously," he told her. "It's like there's a separate world layered on top of this one, because of the music, the notes. If the notes are right. I see a yellow rectangle. Then at some point if I keep watching, listening, the rectangle becomes a field of grasses. I start out in the music, hearing that color from far away, and then gradually as I hear and write more notes, I see the grasses up close. I'm inside a world that feels apart from everything else."

She remembered what she'd seen when they were playing together and felt completely connected. As they climbed over rocks and waded through the water that reached higher than their knees, he told her about the fields surrounding his grandparents' farm where he'd spent summers growing up, seemingly endless fields of golden grasses.

She listened and imagined everything he saw, and the large new presence she felt all around them continued to grow, fed by anything they said or did. It would never stop but would keep growing now that she had found it.

When they reached the inhabited part of the shoreline,

the change in the landscape felt sudden, as if they'd crossed a barrier, not realizing, and had journeyed from a far-away place back into the ordinary world. They stood on a narrow strip of sand where the shapes of houses loomed above them and lights burned in the distance.

"We're close to the Jameson's," Arthur said. "That's the cliff path above us. We must have gone right past the place where you can climb up to the cottage. I didn't spot it in the dark."

"We'll have to swim out around those rocks in order to come to shore in front of the Jameson's," she pointed out. "I left my clothes on the steps there earlier."

"Hopefully not too far down. The tide is exceptionally high."

They waded out into the water, then dove under one last time and swam around an outcropping of rocks until they spotted the place they'd pushed off from. "There," he said, and they swam toward a pool that had formed in a curve of shoreline. The water grew warmer close to the land. Arthur came up beside her and she heard voices above them. She felt things snap back into place.

"Is that Charles on the rocks?"

"Yes. He's with Patrick. We've no choice now but to go up. They may have already heard us."

She heard Charles up above, louder now, heard him say, "But you indicated that while we were here...."

His voice trailed off and Patrick said, "We *are* spending time together. What do you call this, right now?"

"But we're arguing."

"I can't help that."

"Ready?" Arthur whispered.

She nodded and they moved through the shallow pool to the shoreline and the rocks where they'd entered.

"Who's there?" Charles called out. "Is that you, Reenie and Arthur? I've been waiting all night for you to come back."

"Yes," Arthur called back.

Reenie felt for her clothes along the rock edge but couldn't find them. I'll just have to walk back in my bathing suit, she told herself, but then as a wave receded, she spotted her sodden skirt. Just the blouse was gone.

She felt for a foothold and pulled herself up, then crouched on the rock to wring out the skirt. Arthur climbed past her, and after she'd pulled the wet skirt on, she followed. On the rocks above her, she could make out Charles and Patrick. Arthur had reached them, and there were three outlines, dark shapes in the darkness. As she approached, she heard Arthur say, "It took a while because we had to walk back. Reenie isn't much of a swimmer."

"She didn't claim to be a good swimmer," Charles said. "You talked her into going with you, the way you always talk people into things. She never would have gone for a swim at night on her own."

She climbed past them and sat down just above them, folded her legs together under her skirt. "The current was strong. We got washed up shore quite a way."

"A night swim is always romantic," Charles commented. "Don't you think so, Patrick?"

"No," Patrick said. "Not always."

"Not when you have to fight to get back to shore," Arthur said.

"Were you awfully angry, Reenie?" Charles asked.

"Why would she be angry? She agreed to the swim," Arthur said. "I didn't talk her into anything."

It was silent for minute and then he added, "You can't count on the ocean to be peaceful, and even if it is, it can change in a minute. Currents and high waves can come out of nowhere."

"Yes," she agreed. She twisted her hair, squeezing the water out.

"We got too far out, without noticing," he went on. "Then we turned to come back, and a group of rough waves came from nowhere. Something huge that we couldn't see was out there."

"That's why I don't swim at night," Charles said. "There is too much out there that can't be seen. And I'll only go in during the day if conditions are perfect. I don't like being pushed around or carried by unknown forces."

They sat in silence for a few minutes, with just the sound of the water. Then Patrick said, "I spoke with Adele earlier. She arranged to have a music critic at the performance, along with a society reporter. One of the Kennedys is said to be attending—John Kennedy and his new wife. They got married here last summer. Jacqueline, his wife, is said to be a champion of modern music."

"Wonderful," Arthur said.

"Yes, we owe Adele a lot. She's arranged everything."

"Now we just have to pull it off and play stunningly," Charles said. "Too bad she can't arrange for that as well."

"Stop sounding morose, Charles," Patrick told him. "You'll jinx everything."

"I won't. You always say that, but my moroseness isn't a jinx. It's just me."

"Well, cut it out. The rest of us don't need dire predictions."

"They're not dire. I'm just saying it will be tough is all. It's difficult music."

"The earlier rehearsal between Reenie and me went well," Arthur told them. "The final part, that duet, is stunning—to use a descriptive word of yours Charles."

"Reenie is stunning," he said.

"Yes," Arthur agreed.

Patrick shook out cigarettes and passed them around. "Lawrence is driving up tomorrow for the performance."

"Really?" Arthur said.

Charles said, "Who is Lawrence?"

"A musician friend from Yale."

Arthur leaned back into a rock ledge behind him and

stretched out. He hadn't put on his trousers and his legs were visible in the darkness. Lit ashes scattered from his cigarette. "Where is he staying?"

"At the inn in town. I phoned and got him a reservation. He wasn't sure when he would arrive. He has a performance tonight. I think he told you about it."

"Yes, I didn't expect him to come up at all."

"He wasn't going to, but he decided to leave right after his concert is over and drive partway and stay with someone he knows. He hopes to be here by tomorrow afternoon. Then he'll stay over tomorrow night."

"That's something," Arthur said.

"Yes."

Reenie drew the wet skirt more closely around her legs, shivering a little. When she closed her eyes, she felt herself swimming inside of beauty, that thing so much larger than all of them. She heard what they were saying without hearing, without paying attention.

Patrick threw the last of his cigarette over the rocks. The orange tip fell toward the water. "It's late. We should go on up and get a good night's sleep."

Charles said, "Wait. First, we need to talk about the quartet, with Reenie here, with all four of us. You said we would."

"I said we would at some point, not now. It's late."

"But we're performing Arthur's new sonata again in a few weeks in New York."

"We all know that, Charles," Arthur told him.

"We should talk about it while we're all here, when we have Reenie with us who already knows the cello's part. You yourself just said she played it stunningly, and it's the most difficult part in the entire sonata."

Arthur tossed his cigarette as Patrick had done. "Right now, Charles, we're just focused on the concert tomorrow. We'll plan for the next performance after that."

"If Les refused to learn your piece for this concert, why

would he learn it for the next concert? He'll probably still have his arm in a sling."

"We'll talk about it after the concert's over," Arthur said. "By then we'll know more."

"What will we know? How it came off?"

"We have to contact Les," Patrick said. "You can't just cut someone out. There has to be a decision and a conversation."

Charles nodded. "But we'll need to have a replacement. I'm just saying that while we have Reenie here, there could be a discussion."

"We know what you're saying, Charles," Patrick told him. "Wait until after the performance. Focus on being prepared."

"Oh, I forgot. We have to survive the performance, which means first surviving the dress rehearsal."

"What are you saying?" Patrick asked.

"Nothing. I just hate dress rehearsals. They're always terrible, much more so than the performances."

"That's as it should be. The performance is meant to be the pinnacle."

"I'm talking about the experience of playing in it."

"You're exaggerating, Charles. The dress rehearsal has to be stressful. It's the final chance to iron out difficulties. But you could see it as exhilarating instead of dreadful. Come prepared and you'll be fine."

"I'm always prepared."

"Yes," Patrick said, although his voice implied a question, and with that he stood. "I'm going up to the house to get some sleep. I'll see you all at nine a.m."

"The rest of us are coming," Arthur told him.

"Yes, just wait while I gather my things," Charles said.

"What things?"

"Well the bottle for one, unless either of you want it. There's a bit left."

"Not me," Arthur said. He stood and quickly stepped into his trousers, pulling them on. "I'll walk with you as far as the

72

house, Patrick. Are you coming, Reenie?"

"No. I'll just sit another minute and then I'll be up," she said.

Charles and Patrick started out ahead and Arthur lingered for a second, but then Patrick called to him and he turned and hurried after the other two. She watched him go, thinking he might wait for her up ahead, after the others went into the house. In the moonlight, the white rocks were glowing and the torches were lit on the lawn. She could see these things when she stared hard into the darkness, and she saw Arthur's shirt, held carelessly in one hand, and the shape of his back, bent as he climbed. Then gradually he faded so that for a while she seemed to watch his form, but she wasn't sure if he was still there or if he'd reached the house and was waiting for her somewhere or circling back to the rocks. In the darkness, there were shadows on shadows. Some could turn out to be rocks or bushes or beds of spiky flowers. Others might be illusions.

She went on sitting near the water with the waves crashing below and the warm air drying her skirt and suit until gradually she stopped shivering, and the steady tug of her heart slowed, and everything felt purposeful, even though she didn't yet know the purpose. It had yet to be revealed. A door had opened. She couldn't see what lay on the other side. It hadn't yet come into focus. Eventually, she would fall or jump or be taken by the future. She would know how everything had turned out. But now she was perched, waiting, and the doorway felt so important that nothing that had happened before in her life held any significance. Her years of cello lessons and her graduation from the conservatory—all that felt like preparation.

She stayed very still, sensing the things that would come, and when she stood on the flat rock and climbed back up the stairs and walked across the lawn, she thought Arthur might be there, waiting at the edge where it was very dark, but he wasn't. She walked quickly despite the darkness and told herself he must have gotten involved in a conversation with the other two.

She imagined living in New York and going out after rehearsals, the way that a quartet might easily divide into two, the likely math. He had influence, would tell Patrick more about her performance that afternoon. She heard this being said somewhere in the darkness, perhaps in a room of the house, and the future flashed in front of her, quick images of herself with the three of them in New York playing in performance halls.

From behind her came the sound of the ocean. She went on climbing, past the dark hedges to the house. She crossed the lawn, and as she approached the house, she heard music above her, a violin playing. The notes were faint at first and not all of them reached her ears. She couldn't identify the piece or tell where the music was coming from. She got closer to the house and looked up, searching the lit windows. In one of them, Charles stood in profile with his violin. She had walked all that way from beyond the point and up the cliffs and had reached the top where a great musician was above her, playing beautiful music. Such music was a pinnacle, it could not be contained. She saw the movement of his arms and imagined the bow made of a polished sliver of wood and hundreds of threads. She stood still listening until he stopped. Then his figure disappeared from the window, and she walked across the stone patio with her bare feet which were bruised and tender and went into the house and upstairs to her bedroom. She didn't pause to talk with Tom Baxter on the stairs or to listen when she passed Patrick's door and heard voices behind it. She went into her bedroom, closing the door, and the sound of the violin started up again, heartbreaking and mournful. From farther away came the high, ghostly sounds of a flute. It was late at night, but music still poured from the many rooms of the Jameson's house, a labyrinth of sound.

She took out her cello, paged through Arthur's piece, and began to play. She had always, would never. It was her life's work. Such music was the pure absolute of beauty.

All around her the music of other instruments resonated. It pointed through her like an arrow, from the earliest moments when she'd first heard music and on through what she thought of as her long career ahead. It held her whole life, and she saw and imagined what that meant, a life filled with playing beautiful music. Her fingers pressed the strings and her bowing arm tilted. She thought, *this will endure. Beauty will endure.* She went on and didn't stop, and her music filled the night.

Second Movement:
The Development

Chapter 5

Let's sit you here by the window.
Let's get you back in bed.

She was in the memory unit and she heard what they said, heard knocking and tapping and voices in the hallway. Orchestra music coming from somewhere. Her ears translated all vibrations. She heard wind outside her window and air blowing through the vents, heard music, pieces she'd performed and studied and music that had never been played. It played in her head. She thought in music and music was the thing she believed in. She heard music everywhere and heard what all her life she had missed hearing. Her consciousness was expansive. It swept her along. Someone was humming a tune and then came the applause. She heard what they told her, heard outside her room and past hallways and in concert halls and down long hills. She heard beyond these things, heard something larger and louder, a sound that rose from the basement and blew through the hallways and rooms of the memory unit.

At night she lay wide awake when everyone was sleeping. She confused days and nights. Evenings mixed with mornings and afternoons. She lost time, couldn't say, couldn't know. She was on stage with her instrument, waiting in the wings, seated with an orchestra. The program was lovely but she couldn't stay to the end. There was music playing and she hauled her instrument up a hill. She played better, played with distinction. They said she had accomplished so much and gave her an award. Pages turned and blurred. It all happened at top speed and afterward there was plenty of applause.

Many sounds fell all around her. Music fell, filled the air, filled her head and soothed her. She listened to jazz recordings. She heard folk music from the Balkans and understood Bartok. She bought many albums and played them late into the night.

She heard beauty and heard past beauty, heard many pages of notes. She heard time itself and heard God in the notes. Bach's cantos. Beethoven's requiem. She knew for a second what God knew.

Come now.

Lie back down.

Have a little of this.

Why don't you rest?

Your daughter's here.

Why don't you sit up?

Judith brought papers with her from the lawyer's office. She said, everything is taken care of. She said, don't worry about any of it.

Images blurred, her daughter's face, the mound of blankets on her bed. Sounds fell on top of each other.

I've arranged for a concert of the sonata Arthur Cohen wrote for you.

In just a few weeks, Mother.

The concert would take place and Judith would drive her to it. They would travel by car and then by boat and by train. It was on the other side of the city. She climbed a staircase and couldn't go any farther. She heard a tune, a cello playing. The notes came from her. She found the right path and hurried along it. It was a very long way to go but there was music up ahead and she would get there in time to hear it.

The morning before The Modern String's concert at the festival, they met in the Jameson's living room for a dress rehearsal. They weren't wearing formal clothes, it was too hot that day they'd all agreed, but Patrick asked about Reenie's gown—was it full length and black? He said, "You'll need to blend in. You shouldn't stand out."

"Yes," she said. "Full length and black." She didn't think it would stand out.

Charles said he forgot his pages, ran to his room for them, then hurried back in, dropping them. "Damn," he said. "I'm all thumbs."

"Then how will you play your instrument?" Patrick asked.

"I'll be fine, once I'm set up."

It was a hot day and sunlight poured through the glass doors and windows. A white glow filled the room. Arthur sat at the piano waiting on everyone. "Did you sleep all right?" he asked Reenie. "Were you okay after the swim?"

She couldn't place his tone. Was it mocking or serious?

"It's unwise to go so far out if you aren't a skilled swimmer."

"I was fine," she told him.

"She never claimed to be a skilled swimmer," Charles said. He was setting up his music stand.

"I don't need you to tell me what was said, Charles."

Reenie thought, he's trying to make sure the others think nothing happened between us, but she wasn't sure. It felt like he was claiming something else.

Patrick lifted his instrument and played a few notes. "Can we get started without rehashing last night?"

"I'm ready," Charles said, still fumbling with pages.

They played the sonata straight through as if it were the evening concert, and the run-through went well, Reenie thought, until they reached the final movement where everything sounded off for several measures. Reenie listened but couldn't tell how or what was wrong. She tried to adjust her tone and timing. When they finished, Patrick walked to the glass doors and stood looking out at the glare while Arthur suggested they play the last movement again. "It's the most difficult section," he added.

"It sounded awful," Patrick told them. "By the end, we weren't even playing together."

Reenie was about to ask what she'd done wrong, but before she could say anything, Charles said, "Sorry."

Patrick turned to him. "I don't understand. What's your

problem with those measures? You count to seven, you count to six, you count to three. I don't see the problem. And your instrument's out of tune. Arthur, play him a note."

Arthur played the note and Charles played it back, making a slight adjustment to his strings. "I wasn't that far off," he told Patrick. "No one but you would notice it."

"But I did notice it."

"I didn't want to stop midway and it was slight. I wasn't even sure…"

"It wasn't slight."

"I didn't even hear it until the ending."

"I heard it well before."

Charles bowed across his strings, intently focused. "Not everyone has perfect pitch."

Patrick walked back to his music stand. Arthur said, "We'll play the third movement through again, from the top. Reenie plays a few microtones in the finale, as well as in the duet."

"I know that," Patrick said. "But Charles does not have any microtones. He's supposed to play in tune."

Charles held his bow up and signaled he was ready. "It's last minute nerves. You know how I am."

"You mean falling apart before a performance, so that no one you're playing with knows if they can count on you? I'm sorry to have to say it Charles, but if you didn't know the music, you should have been upstairs in your room last night practicing it instead of down by the ocean."

"I get butterflies beforehand. That's all it is. This rehearsal is ill-timed. It's bad luck. No good comes of beating yourself up several hours before you stand in front of an audience." He glanced at Patrick and Arthur, then at Reenie. "We should be relaxing beforehand and saving ourselves for tonight."

"Given the limited rehearsal times and the fact that this music was brand new to us all and especially to Reenie, we had no choice. Sometimes you have to be flexible if you want to carry it off. The beauty of a quartet is that you only need four performers, but that means one person can ruin everything. We are completely dependent on each other."

Charles gave him a long stare. "Are you saying..." he began, but Arthur cut him off.

"We all know how important each of us is. We don't have to discuss it. Let's play the last movement until we've got it."

They began. Patrick's timing and articulation were precise. He had an excellent ear and was always prepared, but Reenie saw he could be a bully, calling out mistakes no one else noticed, speaking loudly over the music. Some of the critiques were aimed at her, but most were directed at Charles.

"You're off again. Can't you hear it? Maybe you should try playing those notes on the D string," he told Charles.

"It's my instrument. I think I can decide what string to use."

They went over and over the same pages, adjusting timing or slicing off an eighth or a sixteenth of a tone, such small increments even a trained ear wouldn't notice. The heat in the room rose as light poured through the windows and glass doors. "Can we close the drapes?" Reenie asked at one point. The light was blinding her.

Patrick didn't even glance up. "We need more light, not less."

"Let's play the entire movement through again, this time without interruptions," Arthur said, pushing them forward, even while Patrick held them back, forcing his critiques.

Charles stood closer to the windows than Reenie, directly in the sun's glare. His face was motionless, flushed and lit by the stark light. He held his body stiffly in the correct posture of a performer. She couldn't imagine how he could see the music.

By the end of the rehearsal, Patrick was seething and Arthur was tight-lipped and darkly serious. Reenie expected an argument to erupt between them, but instead they withdrew to a corner of the room, talking quietly together. Charles put his violin away and went directly outside onto the patio.

"We'll ride over together at five," Arthur said.

In her mind, Reenie still heard the notes they'd played. For two hours she had bent over her cello, furiously fingering the strings and drawing her bow. She'd pushed herself harder than she could have imagined, and it had both exhausted and exhilarated her. She'd hated the constant, biting criticism, but she also knew she'd never produced a more resonant sound.

She put her cello away and followed Charles across the lawn and down the wooden steps. He was sitting on the flat rocks near the water. No breeze came off the ocean, reducing the waves to a rippling line of foam. Gulls glided lazily in the heat, suspended above the water. Charles sat facing the ocean. His jacket was off and his damp shirt clung to his back. He was still, so still he was trembling with the effort not to move.

"Now you are truly one of us, having witnessed our pre-performance ritual," he said. "The closer we get to the performance, the more enhanced Patrick's radar is for any imperfection. He doesn't care how nervous he makes me. He thinks good music depends on anxiety."

She lifted her hair off the back of her neck. God, it was hot by the water. "I thought he and Arthur would argue after we finished, but when I left, they were in close conversation."

"They're close all right. They played together at Yale and got along famously."

"They *did* push our performance to a new level," she said.

"Yes," Charles agreed miserably, glancing over at her. "But I hate the way it's accomplished. They thrive on a punishing and driven rehearsal. Les would ignore them or make jokes when it got tense. He gave exaggerated apologies, and once he arranged to have a toad inhabit Patrick's case while we were practicing. I sensed something was up—Les was unusually quiet. Then at the end of the rehearsal, Patrick flung his case open in a fury over something, and the toad—it was quite small—jumped out."

"He didn't appreciate the humor," she guessed.

"No. Patrick put his instrument in the case, closed it, and walked out without a word. Later Les and I wondered if the creature had defecated while in there, potentially damaging Patrick's instrument because he was too angry to stop and inspect it. But if the inside of the case was soiled, Patrick never mentioned it."

He raised his head and glanced over at her. His face was bright red. "Last night after I went up to the house, I stood by the window in my room looking out at the moon. It was so slim and bright, like a curl of white paint. Did you see it?"

She nodded.

"So you know what I mean. The sky was a piece of cloth, and the stars were tiny torn places in it. The moon was a larger tear. I was so moved I had to play something, and I took out my violin and began to play a Vivaldi concerto, lesser known but it fits certain moods. Patrick heard me. He knocked on my door on his way to his room. When I left him with Arthur on the lawn, they'd been talking. They stood close and spoke so privately, it was like they were part of a world that was very serious and professional and important which excluded me. But when Patrick knocked on my door, he was alone and he said how he loved hearing Vivaldi as he ascended the stairs. I should have simply embraced him or asked him to spend the night, I don't know, but instead I asked what he and Arthur had been saying to one another and if it was about the group's future because that affected me also and with Les leaving or threatening to leave, I can't stand it if the whole thing falls apart. I said perhaps you could move to New York City, and he agreed that being as how there are so few female cellists, a woman would distinguish us and that you would certainly be more committed than Les was. There are quartets that last forty to fifty years, they outlive marriages. I told him that this was a crucial time and tried to argue my point again, but he dismissed me. He said, what is this really about, Charles? It's not about the quartet, is it? Then I accused him of giving mixed signals. I told him I couldn't know how to respond when one minute he says how much I move him and the next he ignores me. He interrupted and said, so you're upset that I haven't given you enough attention."

"That's what you think he was doing just now, giving you his attention?" Reenie asked. Her mind went in many directions, wondering about the conversation they'd had about her.

Charles picked up a stone and flicked it toward the water. "If I believed it was love unrequited, I'd force myself to drink heavily and obliterate him from my mind. But he'll say something awful, then moments later ask me to meet him privately. He did that when we played in Philadelphia. I went to his hotel room. I was so nervous, I almost couldn't knock on his door."

"That happened last night?"

"No, he left in a huff and I went to bed alone. If I confront him about how he treated me during that rehearsal just now, he'll tell me I need to separate my private life from my professional life. He'll say something like, perhaps I shouldn't be in both."

Reenie stared at the water, squinting because of the sun. She imagined Patrick and Arthur discussing her and the group's future. She tried to picture herself moving to New York, but the image was dim and half formed. A blur drifted in front of her. It was Charles's face.

"Let's stay here all day. We can lounge by the water and watch the sea gulls. Later we can choose whether or not to leave our abode and head over for the concert. We'll devote the day to us."

"It's too hot next to the water," she said.

"I think I'll attend our concert instead of performing in it. It will be even hotter inside the Great Hall, especially standing at the front. We could sit at the back and listen to Patrick and Arthur play. There are several large fans at the back of the ballroom. Perhaps they'll turn them on."

"Maybe, but they'd make it hard to hear the music."

He sighed. "You are the voice of reason. But let's refuse

to play tonight. If Arthur and Patrick are so sure of themselves, then they can carry it off, just the two of them."

She smiled. "But I'd miss my chance to perform with you. Even before Patrick telephoned to ask if I could substitute, I'd heard of you. My music coach once talked about a new and unusual, but very good, quartet called The Modern Strings."

Charles smiled and his eyes brightened. "How wonderful to be inside your notice when I hadn't yet met you and to know your mentor admired us. You would be the perfect fourth member. I do hope we're able to keep you."

She stood and reached down to help him up, and they started back to the house, climbing the wooden steps to the lawn. The air shimmered. Wavy lines of heat rose up from the ground, or were they pouring down from the sky? She couldn't tell. She walked through them and felt the stones and the thick bristles of dry grass under her thin-soled shoes. Groups of musicians had gathered on the patio, holding small plates of sandwiches and drinks. The future appeared in front of her. She saw lit stages and snatches of a life in New York with a walk-up near Charles, so they could meet for breakfast. She climbed the steps to the top of the cliff, and the pictures kept appearing, a future that didn't exist but felt real, based on last night and what Charles had just told her.

They reached the top of the cliff, and she turned around to look at the ocean. Below her, a pool of water had formed between the rocks, and inside the pool was something bright red on a white background. She stared at it for a minute before realizing what she was looking at—her white blouse, lost the night before, caught in the rocks with a brilliant red sea creature on top of it. It was so colorful. She read it as a portent of good fortune.

"Aren't you coming?" Charles called to her.

She turned to the house. Arthur was hurrying toward them. "Charles," he called out. "Patrick is looking for you. He thought you'd gone inside."

He and Charles met on the lawn and conferred, then Charles continued toward the house. Arthur turned to the ocean. "Come with me," Reenie told him. "I want to show you something."

"What?" He looked puzzled.

"Something. It's down on the rocks."

He reached her and she touched his arm. "It's a little way down."

"How far?"

"Not far," she told him.

They climbed over a group of rocks off the path, and she bent and squeezed through a tight opening. He crouched down. "It's hotter than hell down here. The air isn't even moving."

"It's not much farther. There, see it?" she said, pointing at the niche in front of them. She pulled him into the shaded overhang. Just below them within arm's reach, the sea anemone glowed like a strand of red lights above her white shirt in the small pool of water.

"I saw it from up above. It's my shirt from last night under that creature."

"Beautiful," he said but he sounded remote, troubled even. "And I'm glad you've found your blouse."

"Are you worried about Charles?" she asked.

"Not really. He'll be fine. He always is. It's just that this is the first time my music's had such a large premiere. It's the most important concert we've played as a group, and it'll be a long day. We've got to get through the dinner on the lawn later, and then go straight into the performance." He glanced behind them. "Lawrence, a friend of ours who's driving up to hear the concert, will arrive anytime now. It's so hot. If he wasn't coming, I'd go for a swim."

"What's Lawrence's instrument?"

He hesitated but it was brief. She hardly noticed. "Cello, like you. He plays with an orchestra in New Jersey, as well as with a group of Yale musicians. I told him about the performance a few weeks ago. I wanted him to hear my piece. He originally said he couldn't make it, but he squeezed the trip in."

She was leaning back against the cliff face. The rocks were wet and hard against her back. Later she'd find a hole where a jagged point had cut into the thin rayon of her blouse. "I should go back." He started to move away, then turned quickly toward her. "Lawrence will be here until after the concert. I don't know yet if he's staying the night or if he'll drive straight back."

"Okay," she said. His arm went around her, and she turned into his chest. She felt his hand pressing into the damp place between her shoulder blades.

"When you play, these bones right here push out." He rubbed his palms against the bony points. "I can see them moving with your arms."

He backed away from the shade and into the light. "You did fine in the dress rehearsal. Patrick is a real perfectionist, but don't worry, your playing is strong. The mistakes you've made are just from a lack of experience. Once you catch on, you don't flounder, and you produce a full, rich sound. Then the next minute you play with such transparency and color. Patrick said that just now, after the rehearsal, or something like it. Everyone is curious about you. The women will all want to see your gown."

"Hopefully, they'll also want to hear my performance."

"Well, the performance will not just be yours, will it?" He turned to go. "Aren't you going to get your blouse?"

She knelt by the pool, intending to reach her hand into it, but saw that she'd have to touch the sea creature to get the blouse. "I'll just leave it," she said. "When the tide comes in, the anemone will be released."

Arthur didn't hear her. He'd begun scrambling over the rocks and was already near the top. She stood and followed, but he was well ahead of her. The climb took longer than the descent, and she was just halfway across the lawn when Arthur reached the patio. He stood with Patrick and a man she didn't recognize. The man was quite tall, taller than either Patrick or Arthur. He wore a light-colored summer suit. The jacket lay over his arm, a concession to the heat. He had dark hair, cleanly cut, and his face was tan and handsome. There was nothing noticeably similar in the three men's appearances. Arthur was slight looking next to the other two, and his hair was longer. Patrick was huskier, with broad shoulders and an equally broad waist. But there was something about the three men standing together that made them look like a trio, a closeness conveyed by similar postures. They looked comfortable with each other.

When she reached the patio and walked past them, they were too engrossed in their greetings to notice her. She went inside, through the cool back hallway and upstairs to her room, not stopping in the dining room where platters of sandwiches and glasses of lemonade were laid out. Charles called, "Reenie don't you want lunch?" but she didn't respond, not having heard him.

Chapter 6

Quarter notes hung in the air, whole notes dropped toward her. Arthur's face swam in the bright sunlight, and then all at once everything turned dark. She looked for an endpoint but couldn't find one. There were no boundaries, nothing that could be measured. The darkness spread out, broad and immense—a solid presence.

Play someone said but she couldn't lift her arms. Her cello balanced between her legs, soft like a human body while her arms were stiff as wood.

She didn't know, couldn't. She heard a note, A in the scale of C major, and after a long pause another note. They swelled up from her vibrating cello—a new piece of music, something she'd never heard before. Was she playing the cello or was the cello playing her? Notes spilled out. They boiled over and split apart.

Before her, the audience sat unmoving. Her father sat among them in the front pew and when the congregation rose to sing he stayed seated listening. He tipped his ear. She pressed her weight into her instrument and played. A new thing had come. The darkness opened like an eye. Inside was a golden field and inside that a myriad of grasses. She saw their many shades of color—browns, tans, russet gold, white and silver. Countless stalks. The music poured from them.

It's nighttime. Lie back now, someone said. It was her daughter's voice.

I need to say....

I need to tell you....

Hallways connected with other hallways, each with many rooms. "I was in love with you even when we were children," Benjamin said smiling, abashed at his confession. The tables were so close together and the waiter was slow.

"I can't think," she told him. "I'm not sure." Panicked. Outside she tried to find a taxi, but couldn't and ended up walking several blocks.

She went out to a party and Cheryl was singing, wearing red lipstick. A group of them walked back together and the night air felt chilly despite her coat. She waited by the door for Benjamin to pick her up.

She had always, could never. A sound came from underneath the building. It blew through the rooms and hallways. She heard it in the light and in the darkness.

Let me tuck you in.

Let me get your feet covered.

The sound had a beautiful resonance. A thrumming sound that expanded and contracted all around her. It absorbed all other sound. It was all other sound.

Don't you remember?

Can you hear me?

Someone else was there, standing by the bed.

She can hear you, that person said. *It's just her mind that's going.*

Yes, her mind was still going. It hadn't stopped. And it was everything.

Outside, the air was still hot and the sunlight hurt her eyes. She stood alone in front of the Jameson's house, sweating in her full length, black gown, the one with the folded pleats at the waist. Earlier she'd gone downstairs and walked out onto the patio just as a parade of musicians came up the lawn from the ocean. The men wore towels over their shoulders and opened bathrobes, their pale legs showing under their swim trunks. Several of them, including Charles who was in the middle, wore straw hats. Charles's trunks ballooned out around his thighs. Adele Jameson was at the end of the parade in a red, strapless swimsuit, heels, and a sun hat.

Charles spotted Reenie as soon as he reached the patio. He

stopped next to her, dripping onto the large, flat stones. "You missed the deliciously cool water. Not a single wave. You could wade out and splash around with no trouble. It was like lounging in a cool bath." He shook the water from his hair. "Oh, sorry," he laughed. "I've sprayed you."

The drops of water dried immediately on her skin and clothes. "Patrick and Arthur weren't with you?" She'd searched the parade but hadn't seen them.

"No. They took Lawrence—did you meet him? —down to the hotel in town so he could get a room. They said they wouldn't be long, but that was two hours ago so they must have ended up in the hotel bar, even though Patrick says he never drinks before a performance."

"I'll shower and then come back downstairs," she told Charles, but she'd spent the rest of the afternoon preparing her music and dressing. Eventually she'd come outside to wait. They were supposed to drive over together at five to set up before the dinner. The sun was still plenty hot. It bounced off the windshields of the parked cars. Another car drove up and four men, one of the quartets, got out and walked toward her. One of them whistled. "You look very pretty." They slowed, waving at her, then went quickly inside, and she stood alone at the entrance next to the bed of bright gardenias, her heart beating fast and light. Her nerves felt unrelated to the upcoming event. Instead it felt like something unknown was coming at her full speed through the heat, about to slam into her.

Just then, the front door burst open, and Patrick and Charles appeared with Tom Baxter and Harold Simmons, all four dressed for the evening—Charles and Patrick in tuxedos, and Tom and Harold in dress slacks and blazers.

"Oh good, you're here," Patrick said.

"You look lovely in your gown," Tom told her.

Charles was already halfway down the semicircle of parked vehicles. "Do you have room for all of us?" Patrick called to him.

"Yes, of course. If those in the back don't mind being squished."

Tom took Reenie's elbow. "You should ride in the middle on the backseat. That way, no one in the back will complain."

"Oh, that's why you wanted me to drive, Tom," Charles called. "So you could sit next to Reenie."

Charles pulled the DeSoto up to the entrance and got out to open the trunk. "Where is Arthur?" Reenie asked. Would they cram him into the car as well?

"He's driving over in Lawrence's car," Patrick said, as he began loading their instruments.

Reenie climbed into the back while Patrick fit her cello in with the smaller instruments. Tom and Harold wedged themselves onto the seat on either side of her, and Patrick got in the front with Charles. It was very tight. Reenie's feet rested on the hump in the middle of the floor. She hiked her dress up and folded it over her legs.

"Everyone cozy?" Charles asked as he started the engine.

He shifted into gear and the car lurched onto the drive. They drove slowly down a tree-lined side road through dappled light, past tall hedges and large homes—white two stories and rambling capes. Shade trees opened like umbrellas over the road. Hot air blew through the windows and pieces of conversation drifted over the front seat, something about a concerto the group might perform later that year. "Of course you will," she heard Patrick tell Charles.

"I'm nervous is all, and I can't do anything when I'm nervous."

"Relax. Driving is a good distraction."

"The misery of anticipation loves a distraction."

They passed more large homes and trees heavy with apples next to a field of Queen Anne's lace. A tall iron fence enclosed The Breakers mansion and grounds. The gate was open. Behind it was a small, brick building for a guard or attendant, but no one was present.

"This is intimidating. Do I just drive through the gate?" Charles asked.

"Yes, of course," Patrick said. "We're the performers."

He shifted the car back into gear, and they drove slowly through the imposing gate and up to the main door. Deep green hedges towered over them. Large planters of ferns and wide-leafed, tropical looking trees surrounded the mansion's front entrance.

"Just leave the car here," Patrick told him.

"Are you sure? It's blocking the front doors."

"We have to carry in our instruments, don't we? Leave the key in the ignition and someone will move it later if they need to."

"Leave the key?" Charles repeated doubtfully as he slid it back into the ignition.

"Yes. And think about something else other than the performance. We'll all have a drink after it's over. Back at the Jameson's. We'll sit on the rocks by the water. Think about that."

"The four of us?"

"Yes, and Tom and Harold and Lawrence and whoever else wants to come. Think about sitting on the rocks with all of us and a bottle of champagne."

Reenie pushed herself across the back seat, and Harold was quick to offer his hand and help her out. She straightened the pleated folds on her skirt. In another few years, the pleats would lose their folded edges and the skirt wouldn't hang right, but now it was still new.

Someone opened two ornately carved front doors, and they entered a spacious hallway. A few minutes later they had left their instruments in a small alcove and were walking through the Great Hall, a large, empty ballroom filled with rows of folding chairs, and out onto the lawn. Down by the water, a crowd gathered—men in summer suits and blazers, and women in sleeveless, pastel dresses with sunglasses and straw hats. Tables were set up at the far edge of the lawn next to the tall dark

95

hedges, with crystal bowls holding floating hydrangea flowers. Evening light folded over the lawn. Adele and her husband were talking to Arthur about seating arrangements.

"You're at the head table with us, Reenie," Patrick told her.

Down near the water, there was no breeze and the waves were calm. The head table sat closest to the ocean, under the shade of a large chestnut tree with a wide, gnarly canopy. Nearby, clusters of rose-hips the size of grapes covered the bushes. She found the card with her name next to Charles's seat.

"You didn't come back downstairs earlier," he said, coming up beside her.

"I was getting ready for tonight."

"You look splendid, doesn't she, Patrick?"

"Radiant," he answered generously.

"You're the belle of the ball," a woman dressed in sequined gray commented.

Patrick and Arthur sat with Lawrence, opposite Reenie and next to Adele Jameson, whose husband sat at the table's end. Three other couples filled out the seating.

"Reenie, this is Joseph Strand and his wife Bernice," Adele said, introducing her to the woman in sequined gray and her husband. "They're neighbors of ours, music enthusiasts. Tonight is Reenie's first professional performance."

"I've never met a woman cellist before," Bernice Strand said.

"She's very brave," Charles told her, leaning across Reenie. "She's withstood our male company for four days."

Bernice raised her glass. "I think we should toast this girl. Everyone—listen. We're going to toast Reenie." She lifted her champagne glass higher to demonstrate. "To Reenie and her first concert."

All those at the table lifted their glasses. "To your success," Bernice said loudly. "Beginning with tonight."

Arthur glanced across at her with a wry, half-smile, as if to say, "We already knew you'd be a success, didn't we?" Pat-

96

rick and Lawrence were smiling as well, and Adele and Henry Jameson leaned in, so that everyone's glass met at the center, just in front of Reenie. Twelve glasses shimmered in the light filtering through the shade above them. There was a moment of silence as they drank, and then she heard the hum of conversation starting up. Nearby, gulls dipped toward the still water, and she saw a group of cormorants farther out stationed on a rock.

"Oh look, geese," someone said as several swooped low and settled on the lawn, their long necks bending in impossible curves, like water pipes, as they poked through the grass for grubs.

"They shoot a gun off each afternoon to keep them off the lawn," someone else said. "Picturesque but messy."

They ate steaks with baked potatoes, a tomato aspic, and green beans. Across the table, Arthur talked about Stravinsky between bites, music's answer, he said, to Ravel. Henry Jameson wanted to know if there were plans for Arthur's sonata to be recorded. "But if it's deemed worthy, it has to be recorded," he said.

Adele said something about Yale conservatory being the pinnacle of musical study. Its graduates would shape the new direction of classical music. They passed baskets of soft, round rolls and bowls with pats of butter. Charles took several for his potato. "I'm always ravenous before I play a concert." He ate quickly and adeptly. Reenie thought he hardly seemed nervous anymore, and he kept up a conversation with the woman seated on his other side, explaining about musicians who played in shows in the city. "I'm someone who loves Rogers and Hammerstein, side by side with classical music. I would die to play a Broadway show."

"*Die*, Charles, really?" Patrick asked.

"Oh yes."

They passed the food again and ate and drank more champagne. Arthur caught Reenie's attention and introduced her to Lawrence, who said he was impressed she'd learned Arthur's sonata in four days.

"With lots of practice," she told him.

Then Patrick leaned over to get their attention. "As soon as we finish eating, we should walk up and get our instruments in place."

"But you must wait for the desert," Adele told them. "It's coming in a minute, a peach cobbler."

"We'll have to forgo it, to be ready by seven," Patrick said. "You stay and enjoy. Don't encourage the others to come up to the hall too soon."

Reenie rose as Bernice Strand lifted her glass and tipped it again in her direction, as if to say, "to your success," one last time, and Patrick told Lawrence to come up with them so he'd get a seat in the front row. The bowls of cobbler were arriving as they left the table and walked across the lawn. It was full evening now. The sun had dropped low, and a smooth, clear sky washed everything dense with color. Some of the guests were milling about on the lawn or walking up toward The Breakers, and around the front of the mansion, the larger audience was beginning to arrive.

"There's a bathroom around the corner," Patrick said as they reached the back entrance to the Great Hall. Reenie found it, used the toilet and splashed her face with water, then glanced in the mirror. When she returned, Lawrence had disappeared and the others were removing their instruments. Minutes later, they entered the staging area and set up their music stands and Reenie's chair. Everything happened quickly, and it seemed like the other three read her mind, turning her chair just enough that she would be able to glance up and see Arthur when she needed during the performance. They brought out their instruments and tuned, then walked back to the alcove and stood waiting for the ballroom to fill.

"How big do you think the audience will be?" she asked.

"Two hundred or more," Patrick said. "They're prepared with more chairs in the back."

Reenie stepped out to the hallway that connected the alcove to the ballroom. The lights had not been switched on, but sunlight still permeated the room. She stood in the shadows, watching the audience grow. There were at least fifty people in the room already, with seating for well over two hundred if you counted the extra chairs that could be quickly set up in the back. Not Carnegie hall or the Metropolitan, but the largest audience she'd ever played for, including the audience at the conservatory, which had numbered considerably less.

The concert goers flowed down the aisles and into the rows of chairs. Sunlight shone gold on the cream-colored walls of the hall, and everything blazed with evening light. Charles came up behind her. "Oh, there you are. We all thought you were in the restroom."

"I'm just watching the room fill," she said.

"I don't recommend that. You can't tell yourself you're playing to an empty hall if you've watched it fill."

"I don't want to tell myself I'm playing to an empty hall. I want to know what I'm playing to, and if the audience is large, if it's two hundred, I want to see it so I'll remember it."

She peered at the front rows. "Who is that?" she asked as an elegant couple walked down the second row of chairs and took seats at the center. He wore a classic black tuxedo, a white shirt and black bow tie. Her sleeveless, peach-colored gown had simple lines with a slightly gathered waist formed by a single pleat at the front marked with a bow.

"That's the two Kennedys Patrick spoke of," Charles whispered. "They were married last year in Newport. Did you read of it in the papers? What a gorgeous dress, what style."

The audience found seats and settled as the heat cast a spell of lassitude and stillness. Women fanned themselves, men removed their jackets, while the Kennedys went on looking impossibly cool and unaffected. Charles left to go back into the recess of the alcove, but Reenie stayed at the edge of the hall. The rows of chairs were nearly full—so many faces, so many colors, they bled into one another. She'd never seen such an audience. Then Patrick stood behind her. "Reenie, are you ready?"

She nodded. She felt Charles and Arthur behind her also, waiting as the sound of the audience faded and six large chandeliers turned on. Impossibly, they washed the hall with more light.

"The better to see you with, my dear," Charles whispered.

She looked at the chair where her instrument lay twenty feet or so from the first row of the audience. The other two stood behind her, assessing the situation. "A few more minutes until everyone is seated," Arthur said.

They waited, not speaking. Then Patrick told them, "Let's go," and moving quietly, as smooth as flowing water, they walked together onto the stage, where they stood in a line and bowed. Reenie looked out at the audience. On the small stage the lighting was even brighter, but her glance was too quick to take in more than the fact that the ballroom looked full, all the way to the back by the windows. She took her seat as the brief applause died. Arthur waited for silence to descend before signaling them to position their instruments. They tuned again, quickly, and then the music began.

The festival in Newport took place at a time when classical music was at its height in America, with Leonard Bernstein's orchestra program and large concert audiences. Just ten years later, the audiences would shrink dramatically, but now no one knew that future, and it was easy to believe audiences would keep growing and composers like Arthur Cohen would achieve Bernstein's status. This was the pinnacle, but the musicians thought they were still on the upward trajectory. They saw themselves someday at the top, high above themselves.

The quartet played the first two movements, and Reenie didn't look at the other three. She listened for her cues, and the others' notes wove in and out between her own as she followed the complex patterns and difficult, changing rhythms.

Patrick's intonation and timing were impeccable. Charles

100

played with a range of emotion she'd never heard from a stringed instrument. He made the violin speak—one minute through a harsh, jagged attack, the next through a smooth and sorrowful decrescendo. But Arthur was the center of it all. He led them forward through the difficult passages to the end of the first movement. He plunged and dipped and squeezed sounds out of the piano, then slowed everything to a near halt, allowing the soft whistle of the strings to merge with his notes.

They finished the first movement, and for several seconds she stayed seated, bent over her instrument, her bow hovering above the strings. Those in the front were the first to begin to clap. She stood, smoothing her gown, leaned her instrument back against the chair, and walked with the others to the center of the stage. Sweat glistened on her back and arms. Outside, the winds had shifted and the smell of the ocean blew through the back windows and doors. She felt its coolness against her skin.

They left the performance area for the intermission together as if on cue, even though none was given—Charles first, with Reenie directly behind him, then Arthur and last of all Patrick. A pitcher of water and four glasses had been placed on a table in the alcove. The men removed their jackets, and Charles loosened his cummerbund. Patrick was asking how he was handling the heat, and Charles answered that he was fine, more than fine. He said he had hardly noticed the heat.

"I noticed it," Arthur said. "My hands were sweating." He went out to use the rest room and returned several minutes later with a white towel, which he used to blot his face.

At one point, Adele entered the alcove to tell them how wonderful the first movement had been. Patrick and Arthur followed her out into the small niche, where a whispered conversation was held. After several minutes when they returned, it was time to prepare to walk back to the stage. The audience was returning to their seats, talking in whispers and fanning themselves with their programs. Reenie re-checked her score to make sure the pages were in order. As they walked out, she

101

slipped them onto the music stand before stepping to the front to take a quick bow with the others. They went to their places and quickly tuned. They waited another moment, then Arthur gave the down beat and began to play.

Reenie listened, her bow hovering, as she waited for her entrance. The piano's notes broke the silence, and within seconds the music climbed toward its attack. Then, just as suddenly, lighter, softer notes replaced the harsh sounds, as the others entered with the suggestion of a melody.

Reenie's cello followed the music's thread. It developed in the first measures, disappeared for whole lines, then reappeared, suddenly rising to the surface, bobbing there for several measures before coming into full view. The melody lay mostly beneath her grasp, even with the repetitions and the coda, but in the moments when it surfaced, a world unlike any other composer's unfolded.

The sun was setting in the windows at the back of the hall—tiny and orange and glittering. Arthur and Charles's high notes ended the second movement, then after a brief pause, Reenie entered the music again as the final movement began. The tempo increased, and next to her Charles bowed furiously. It felt impossibly fast, and for a second, she was afraid she'd lose a note, but she didn't. Her instrument had its own life. Waves of sound swept above her. They were coming from her cello, but the sound felt bigger than that, as if it was its own entity, rising.

They played on and on, and the music stopped making sense as phrases became disconnected and hard to follow. Then all at once, everything snapped. She played a wrong note and had to focus completely on the score. For a second, she lost the others, stopped hearing them, but then suddenly she was with them again, right where she should be in the music.

The four of them were communicating, creating something substantial and new between them. Her playing became more assured and vigorous. Colors materialized out of the notes—tangible and real, having nothing to do with the colors from the audience or the setting sun. She saw purples and blues, crimsons, tawny browns. Each musical phrase built upon the others. She felt her body vibrating with the cello. Her arm pulled back and forth on the bow. Her chest could barely stand the pressure. Any minute, her heart would explode. Then the tempo changed again, and the notes howled. They pushed her into another dimension. Every nerve switched on and in a cacophony of sound, time spread out, diffuse and unmoving. What the four of them were making was beyond understanding or language, beyond reason. Music *was* time, and tempo demanded precise counting, but they had exploded time's boundaries. In that moment, she knew absolutely what she was meant to do for the rest of her life—perform like this.

Gradually, the tempo slowed again, and the cello and piano began their duet. Light from the setting sun suffused the hall, falling over the audience like a colored net. The two instruments played together, crossing and fighting with one another, then finally intertwining, in sudden harmony. This was greatness, if only for a few pages, communing so completely with another instrument. Her cello became heavier, more weighted, even as her body became light and insubstantial. They played faster and the notes rose effortlessly, separate from her. The music swept through her, swooping down and lifting her, and she stretched out over the Great Hall hovering for a long second. Then a volley of sound detonated and burst her apart. It did this over and over again. Even after the last notes of the duet were played, she felt the vibrations of sound flashing.

The final difficult passage of the last lines followed. All four instruments entered at once, and the sudden dissonance was sobering. It brought her back down to earth, but mystery lingered, brilliance flickered. There was a purpose behind everything, and music made you know that, made it possible to feel the authority of that purpose. Life wasn't orchestrating music. Instead, music was orchestrating life.

For a moment after the last notes sounded, she continued

to hold her bow against the cello's strings. The rows of chairs came into view, and she saw the hall with its high ceilings and gold trim. She felt the stickiness of her hands and the sweat dripping off her forehead. She didn't hear the applause beginning. Until it filled the hall, she still heard only the echoes of those final measures.

The other three were already walking to the center of the stage when she stood and joined them. Heat radiated. The applause washed over the room, built to a crescendo, then faded and built again, rising around them like a tide.

They bowed, then Patrick swept his arm toward Arthur who stepped forward and bowed again. The applause swelled as Arthur rose from his bow. He brushed his hair back from his eyes. Sweat coursed down their faces. She was out of breath as if she'd run a marathon. Patrick signaled and they followed him off the staged area.

For a moment, they stood at the edge of the alcove, close together, almost touching. She heard the four of them breathing and felt the heat pouring off their bodies. Then they walked back out, grasped hands, held them high, and lowered them still linked as they bowed. Finally, Arthur stepped forward, taking another bow. Applause swarmed the Great Hall, gradually climaxed, then lessoned. They had no encore prepared, as playing one in the event of a standing ovation would be unseemly at a festival where no other group had played one. Instead they waited until the applause died and exited the stage.

They reached the alcove together, and for a second they were still fused, still one instrument. Then they broke apart, congratulating each other—the three men beating on each other's backs, then embracing Reenie. Charles wiped his face with a handkerchief, looking flushed and happy.

"We pulled it off," Patrick said. "It's a stunning sonata, Arthur. Prepare yourself for the praise."

"Or for the attack," Arthur said, glancing at the opening to the hall, but he didn't sound nervous. He sounded as if he expected greatness.

Reenie went to the restroom, filled a sink with cold water, and washed. She straightened her dress, re-pinned her hair, and put on more powder and lipstick. When she returned, Patrick and Arthur had already gone, and she followed Charles out into the hall.

A crowd had gathered around Patrick and Arthur near the front of the hall. She and Charles stood off to the side where those from the audience who had not pressed close to the other two quickly engaged them.

"Were you dying up there with the heat?" a woman asked her.

"How is it that you can perform such difficult music?"

"Do you like the moderns?"

"What did you think of Arthur Cohen's sonata? What was it like from a musician's perspective? What was it like playing with him?"

She answered, was cut off, then asked another question. Nearby she heard Charles's melodious voice claiming that playing inside The Breakers mansion was the peak experience of his career. His voice rose and fell as he explained the different movements of Arthur's sonata from the point of view of a musician, and said that yes, the hall was hot, but he hadn't noticed the heat at all when they were performing. One wasn't affected by anything like that when on stage. And yes, he'd felt nervous about the difficulty of the music beforehand, but not when he'd seen the audience. He delighted in playing before an audience of music lovers, and he'd had absolute confidence in Arthur's piece and in the quartet.

Gradually, the four of them moved with the audience toward the back of the Great Hall and out onto the lawn where they stood surrounded by more people. Every sensation felt heightened. Whatever she saw was luminous, thick, and vibrating. The sounds of the crowd mixing with the ocean were almost hypnotic. Large torches lit the lawn, and tables of food and drink were scattered about for the reception. Sequined dresses, necklaces, bracelets, and earrings glittered in the torchlight.

The air had changed, she could feel that also. The temperature had dropped as winds brought in a cooler air mass. Nearby, she glimpsed Arthur standing at the center of a group, explaining his music. Someone had given him a glass of champagne, and he held it in one hand, lifting it to emphasize a point. His black tuxedo was perfectly creased. His hair swept back from his face, unaffected by sweat or heat, and his dark eyes flashed, like mirrors for the torchlights. He projected an unnameable quality—an excitement or authority. It was kinetic. Those closest to him grew flushed and animated.

"How long did the sonata take you to compose?" someone asked.

"What about the finale? Was that difficult?"

"What will you do next?"

"Where will you perform?"

"What are you working on? Will you compose something longer?"

Arthur said he had a symphony partly finished and was composing another sonata. He also had an idea for an opera. There was so much you could do with opera. He loved the pageantry, the grand scale. He'd write one eventually. Any major composer had to do that. All his music, he said, would embody the future that was quickly arriving. His music would point the world toward that new direction.

"They should quote you," someone said. "Where is that reporter?"

Arthur went on answering questions about his work. Nearby, Patrick was also answering questions, saying he'd recognized Arthur's piece from the first time he'd heard it as a fitting finale for the festival of concerts. The women around Reenie were remarking on her dress. They asked her to turn so they could get a better view, and then she heard a strongly accented, measured voice that ten years later she'd recognize. John F.

Kennedy was saying, "Thank you, Mr. Cohen. We very much enjoyed your music."

Those around Arthur had parted, and the Kennedys stood directly in front of him shaking his hand. Jackie Kennedy had on white gloves, even in the August heat. "Oh Mr. Cohen," she said. "It was truly amazing."

"We will look for your recordings," John Kennedy told him. "Let us know next time you perform."

They stepped away and Reenie watched them slide through the crowd as they moved toward the front of the building where their car would be waiting. She saw the crowd ebb around them and heard the way excitement surged then dissipated with their passing.

Someone lifted a glass to Arthur, and then he lifted one to the Jamesons. Smaller groups began to gather in front of the tables of food, and couples walked along the edge of the lawn, looking out at the ocean.

Reenie watched the crowd fan out into the darkening air. Behind her, the Great Hall was still lit like a lantern. Then Charles found her, said he was famished, and convinced her they should plant themselves in front of a table overflowing with shrimp and cocktail sauce.

"I'm not leaving this spot until the platter is empty," he said as he scooped up half a dozen shrimp. He didn't remove the shells and instead chewed them whole.

Tom Baxter came over with glasses of champagne, and Reenie drank hers quickly. Everything was moving fast, building toward pinnacles of congratulation and praise and then away from them. The lawn still seemed full, though half the crowd had left. It didn't feel like anything had ended.

They finished off the shrimp platter and moved on to a table covered with truffles and strawberries when a reporter approached her and Charles. He wanted to get their opinion, he said, of Arthur Cohen's sonata.

Reenie acknowledged that she'd found the music hard to

play at first. "On the cello at least," she qualified.

Charles put it more effectively. "From a musician's standpoint, difficult. From the audience's, brilliant."

Minutes later, when the critic had gone, Charles announced his view that they should return to the Jameson's. "We can raid the kitchen before the others get to it. Have you seen the refrigerators? There are three of them—each one larger than any appliance I've ever seen. I was told two are rented. They're like the ones found in restaurants."

He convinced her they should drive back and quickly found several other musicians who filled up his car. They crowded into the two seats with Reenie's cello and Charles's violin stowed in the trunk. When they reached the Jameson's, the others went upstairs to change while Charles led Reenie to the kitchen. He gave Reenie a tour of the cupboard where breads were stored, the pantry which was full of delicacies and canned meats, and the three refrigerators, lined up as he'd described. Inside them, they found a bowl of the crab paste from lunch, sliced meats, cheese, peaches, melons and dozens of eggs.

"A feast," Charles declared, filling two plates with quickly made sandwiches. They cut some of the fruit, opened boxes of crackers, and finished off the crab paste. Before they escaped to the lawn, Charles located a bottle of champagne and a box of petite fours, which he tucked under his arm.

They walked down to the edge of the lawn, overlooking the ocean, and spread their picnic on a tablecloth they'd found in the kitchen. The others climbed down the steps, laughing and calling out, exclaiming about the water's temperature.

"I could sit here all night, eating and drinking," Charles said.

"When do you think Arthur and Patrick will come back?" Reenie asked.

"They were still thoroughly engaged when we left. It could be an hour or more."

"We were going to have a drink together," she said.

"And we will, sometime later," he said vaguely. He glanced

out at the water. "You must come to New York," he said. "You must come visit or move there. We'll live off crackers and truffles. We'll eat cheese and jam with the crackers if the cost of crab paste is too high."

They went on talking about the bars and clubs they'd go to. Charles promised to show her every haunt. The sounds of the swimmers rose up from below the cliffs, and eventually their plates lay discarded on the grass along with an empty box of petites fours and the glasses. A breeze blew steadily off the ocean, making Reenie shiver in her sleeveless gown. She'd find it badly dirtied later, and the pleats would have to be professionally ironed back into place, but now she didn't care. She lay back on the ground and pictured New York, a place with many music events like this one, and life stretched ahead of her with no endpoint.

When the others came up from their swim, Charles told them about the stash of champagne, and they brought down a few more bottles, along with more crackers and a tin of caviar.

"When are the rest of them coming back?" someone asked. "I thought that party at The Breakers would have ended by now."

"They'll arrive at any moment, along with a contingent of guests," Charles said. "I heard Adele talk about leading a group back along the cliff walk. That could have proven unfortunate, given the amount of alcohol at the reception. Imagine if we've lost a music critic to the Atlantic."

They talked for another hour or so, waiting for Arthur and Patrick to appear. "Maybe they've gone into town for a drink," someone said.

"No," Charles told them. "They promised we'd drink together, here. It's the final night."

But when it grew even later and the other two didn't return, Charles and Reenie went up to the house to shower and change. They went to their separate rooms with a plan to meet in a short while outside, but she didn't see him again, not until the next morning.

Chapter 7

Upstairs in her room, Reenie showered and changed into a skirt and her blouse with the scalloped neckline. She brushed her hair. Her performance gown lay across a chair, her skirts were piled on the bureau, and the bed was unmade. A tube of lipstick and a cake of powder sat on the edge of the sink. She'd have to get a ride to the train station in the morning, but she did nothing to prepare for her departure. When they were sitting down by the rocks, Charles had compared her playing favorably to Les Carmichael's, calling it lively and full of color. Earlier when they'd all stood together in the alcove, Patrick had talked about the concert being a great performance, and Arthur had thanked them for learning his difficult music and giving it such a good first showing. She'd felt flushed and excited, and everything had moved ahead so fast it made her giddy. Even later, when she'd come back with Charles and they were having their picnic, the evening had felt portentous. She was high up, skimming the top of a great wave and could see far out. There was nothing specific out there, just a feeling. *This is what life is for*, the feeling said.

It was close to midnight now, and the house was largely silent, the air warm and weighted. No one had lit the torches on the lawn, and when she looked out the window at the lawn, all she could make out were the gray shapes of furniture. For the first time in a week, clouds had swept in, and they moved about ghostly in the sky. There were just a few stars and no moon.

She'd thought the four of them would be having that drink by now. She'd assumed they would celebrate together, and she wanted to know if she'd proven herself. Her window was wide open, but there were no sounds except the ocean waves, no lights in the darkness. She walked back downstairs, unable to stay in her room packing or listening at the window for voices. She told herself Charles might be there or Arthur and Patrick, but when she reached the rocks, she found just a handful of the other musicians and few of their wives and girlfriends.

"Have The Modern Strings deserted you, Reenie? Join our party. We've nothing to pour a drink into, but if you're not averse to drinking out of a bottle, we've got a little of the champagne."

A group of women sat together nearby. Reenie heard something about evening gowns and Mrs. Kennedy as she tipped a bottle to her mouth and swallowed the warm, sweet fizz. Another cellist praised her performance. "The piece sounded difficult," he said. "I couldn't have learned it so quickly. You must have been up all night."

She said yes, she'd been practicing without a break, but that was what happened when you were called in at the last minute. Someone commented on Patrick's luck in finding her. It *was* Patrick who found her, wasn't it? Yes, she told them.

Another bottle of the champagne came around. Someone made a joke about sleeveless gowns and women performers. "That's not true," she said, not following the joke but determined to deny it. The conversation changed to upcoming music events and guesses about who would be featured. By then, Reenie was hardly listening. She watched the lawn, hoping to see Charles or Arthur and Patrick walking toward them, but both the lawn and the house behind it were dark and she spotted no movement. Then suddenly Arthur appeared, standing at the edge of the group across from where Reenie sat, materialized out of nothing. He'd taken off his jacket and cummerbund, but he still wore the pants and shirt from his tux. His shirt glowed white and she could see the shininess of his shoes from where she sat. He raked his hair away from his face and moved his hands to his pockets and then out again, rubbing his bare forearms.

The others called him over and tried to pull him into their

conversation, but he was difficult to talk to. He gave a long description of the similarities between classical music and jazz when someone said that jazz was too much its own art form to be transformed by classical composers. He had no attention for listening, no patience for Harold and the others who wanted to know about possible plans for another festival next summer. He didn't sit down but remained standing at the edge of the group, and when Harold tried to pass him a bottle, he didn't take it. Was he already drunk? Reenie couldn't read him.

Then he looked down at her, or at least it seemed that way. It was too dark to see his face, but he seemed to be staring at her. His look bore into her. The others were trying to convince Wilson into jumping off the rocks into the ocean, even though Wilson was steadily refusing as Harold hypothesized about how much champagne it would take to lose one's sense of perspective.

Arthur was silent. It seemed like he was still looking at her. She felt as if he could see straight into her. She glanced out at the ocean and down at the rocks. He saw something in her, some quality she possessed but wasn't aware of.

"I have to get out of this monkey suit," he said. "I'll be back after I change."

He turned to leave and Reenie stood. Her body did this automatically, as if her mind wasn't directing it. She followed him part way across the lawn, and when he glanced back at her, she said, "I'm going to knock on Charles's door. We said we'd meet later, and then he didn't come down."

"I think Patrick went up to find him," he told her.

They walked on for a minute, not talking. His white shirt was the only thing visible, and she couldn't gage if he was walking fast to get ahead of her or slow to allow her to catch up. The night felt dense and warm.

"Come back with me," he said. He spoke without turning around, and she wasn't sure she'd heard him right. They were close to the house, which was suddenly ablaze with light. Then he added, "Bring your cello. I've been hearing the theme in my head from our duet in that last movement ever since the performance."

"All right," she said.

They reached the house. Through the opened doors, Reenie heard people returning from The Breakers. Adele was talking to a few of her guests, telling them to stay there tonight and that there were empty bedrooms upstairs.

Arthur gestured to the side of the house. "I'll walk around and wait out front."

She nodded and went inside, stopping on her way up to the bedroom only for a moment when Adele passed her with a couple in the hallway. "What fun," the woman said. "To be staying here with all these musicians."

She went to her room, quickly got her cello, and headed downstairs so that Arthur was just coming around the side of the house when she walked out the front door. She met him on the drive.

"Shall I carry it for you?"

"No," she said. "I'm used to it."

They walked next to each other without talking or touching, and when they reached the end of the drive, everything turned quiet and dark. She could hear their footsteps and her cello occasionally hitting up against her leg. The road wasn't lit, but she could still see him, and the pavement was easy to follow.

"You're very quiet," she said.

"I'm very exhausted. I'm always like this after a performance. I can't sleep even though I'm exhausted. I might not sleep until tomorrow."

They turned onto the dirt drive that led to the cottage, and she stumbled a little on the uneven surface. "Let me carry that." His fingers touched hers for a second as he took the cello. He led the way up to the cottage, climbing the steps and opening the door without needing any light. He set her cello on the floor and went into the bedroom.

"There's a lamp in the front room," he said. "I'll just get changed first."

She switched on the lamp by the door. In the pale-yellow light, she saw wicker chairs by the front window next to a small, overstuffed sofa with extra cushions. Across from them stood a baby grand piano, which took up much of the space. On the walls were watercolors of the sea and shoreline. Shells lined the window sills. The rooms were small, like a ship's interior, and the doorway to the kitchen was crooked. The air was warm and slightly damp with the ocean breeze that came through the windows.

He came back fastening his pants. She took his music from her case and glanced around for a makeshift stand, finding a small tray table beside the couch. He was barefoot and she watched his feet on the wood floor as he went to the piano.

"Patrick and a few of the others dropped me off here on our way back," he said. "But I walked down right away to the ocean. I wanted to see who was there." She thought he meant he'd been looking for her, but then he said, "Tom must have already gone inside. I wanted to hear what he thought of the concert."

"I saw him earlier," she said. "He was very complimentary. Someone said a few of them were driving up the island into town. There's a bar that's open until past midnight."

"Complimentary—what does that mean?"

She hesitated. "I don't know. He said he liked it."

"What did he like about it?"

"He said it was a fitting finale."

"That sounds like the kind of thing you'd say if there was nothing particularly memorable about it." He spoke without looking at her as he played a few notes. "I want to play that last movement again with you. I'm thinking about changing it."

She went into the kitchen where she found a jar of instant coffee and a cup. She lit the gas burner and quickly heated some water. In the other room, Arthur began playing the last movement. She noticed some changes in the phrasing.

"Are you listening?" he called out. "Do you hear the changes I'm making?"

She tasted the coffee, burning her mouth. It was bitter and there was no milk or sugar anywhere to cut the taste. She went back to the other room and set the coffee on the table next to the sofa. Arthur was still playing. He watched the piano keys intently as she took out her cello. He was playing the middle section of the last movement, talking as he played, above the piano. "This was the spot where you clammed, do you remember? You lost it for a second, but then you recovered quickly."

She stared at him as she sat down on the couch but said nothing. She felt like she'd been punched. As she sunk deeper into the cushions, he went on playing without even looking at her. He'd made changes in the music and expected her to perform them for him.

"Get rid of the legato," he said. "Take out the crescendo. And change the A to an E in this passage. Change the E to an E flat." He reached across and handed her a pencil. "Write it down. Once we start playing, it will all make sense."

He flung his hair back from his forehead and drops of sweat sprayed the air. Numbly, she took out her copy of the score. "In the third line when I play this, you play the notes I just gave you." He played his notes on the piano. "Ready?"

"No," she said trying to write out his changes, but he had already gone ahead and started playing. His face was tense with excitement. He reached the end of a phrase, glanced at her, and went back to the beginning again. She watched him for a moment, then pulled her cello toward her. Once she was set up, she came in late but somehow caught up.

"Keep going," he said without looking up from the keys. "Figure it out."

She kept playing, but nothing was in sync. She tried to concentrate on the changes he'd made, but even in the measures where she got the notes right, it didn't sound right. She felt like she was cut in two, so that the hand playing the strings was arguing against the hand moving the bow.

Then, just before they reached the duet and for no apparent reason, Arthur stopped playing abruptly and signaled to go back to the beginning. It seemed he was giving her another chance to play the music with his changes, but her playing only worsened. Each note felt completely disconnected from the others. She had no grasp of the music anymore.

Meanwhile Arthur kept playing, even though she knew he heard her making more and more mistakes. His head stayed bent toward the keys. "What's the problem?" he asked. "Why can't you play it?"

"I keep getting lost."

"Figure it out. Music is malleable. You have to be malleable as well to perform it."

"But what about staying true to the music?" she asked, remembering what he'd argued that first evening.

He paused for a split second and glanced up at her. "I *am* the music, Reenie. I composed it."

They played several more measures, and then he stopped again. "Forget it," he said. "Let's just play the duet, and then to the end. That's the part I really want to hear. In the performance, the duet was perfect. I'd never heard it like that before. The performance taught me, Reenie, how it should sound. Hearing you taught me. The microtones were even more beautiful than I'd imagined."

She paged through the score, but he was already striking the first notes, and she felt behind before they started. It sounded like he'd changed something else. "Wait. Explain what you've changed first. I can't read your mind."

"But that's what I want," he said not slowing down or glancing in her direction. "Read my mind. Hear what I'm hearing."

He played the measures of the transition a second time, and

with an effort she slipped into the new tempo. For a few measures, she struggled to keep up and remember the note changes at the same time, but then she stopped feeling her finger pads and her bowing arm, and the changes he'd made to the notes began to come to her automatically, as if by an act of sorcery that had nothing to do with her ability or knowledge. She was too exhausted to think, but that didn't seem to matter. She didn't even have to concentrate to get the notes right. The new notes felt natural, part of the lager sound they were making. It was as if she'd done as he commanded, climbed inside his head and read his mind. Gradually, she even forgot how exhausted she was. Instead she heard what they were inventing—something new and strange.

Arthur didn't look at her. He didn't nod or say anything or give her any signals, but the music spoke, and the story it told erased everything, even the remark he'd made just moments ago about her mistake during the performance. The notes from their two instruments rose and fell, they twisted into a knot, then unwound into two streams. There were no barriers. Her notes were the lower register, his the higher. She forgot the uncomfortable feeling of not knowing what she was doing. She played without any thought. She passed beyond reservations.

When they reached the silence before the coda, she could hear his breathing and feel the cramped intensity of his posture. They were twined so tightly together, they couldn't unravel.

Then came the burst of cacophony, a splatter of notes. She heard the groan of the cello and the crashing notes of the piano keys. She squeezed the neck of her instrument and pulled the bow back and forth with several quick, strong strokes. The sound filled the silence that followed. It went on and on filling the silence.

"That's what I meant," Arthur said, sounding triumphant. "That's how the duet should sound." He wiped the sweat off his forehead with the back of his arm. Large areas of dampness puddled on his shirt. "You have this amazing ability. I've never heard anything like it before. Play it again. Play it that way one more time."

Her arms and ribs hurt, and her legs were trembling as she lowered her bow and straightened up in her chair. She was hot and sweating, and she'd arrived at the edge of something. Everything pulsed with it.

"I can't," she said.

"What do you mean?" He flung his damp hair back from his eyes.

"I just can't play it again." If they were to play it again that way, she couldn't say what would happen. "Just leave well enough alone," she added, unable to explain herself.

She placed her cello in the case and gathered the music. Her legs and arms were still shaking. Her feet and hands felt unsteady. She'd never felt this tired or this wide awake, and a feeling she couldn't understand rushed through her, unnameable.

"What are you doing?" he asked. "I'll stop in a minute. Don't go. I just want to play you something else. It's new. I've been composing it while I'm here. I want you to hear it. You'll know how to listen to it."

He leaned heavily into a string of cords, then his hands moved up and down the keys, suddenly light and quick. The music had a strong rhythm, and he changed tempos seamlessly. "Patrick couldn't hear what I was doing with the rhythm," he said, speaking above the music. "The tempo is *supposed* to keep changing. It's unpredictable. I *want* it to be confusing."

Sweat dripped from his face, and his opened shirt sleeves flapped against the keys. He had to fling his hair back, but the movement didn't challenge him. His eyes had narrowed, his brow was furrowed. If he reached an ending measure, he went back immediately to a starting point. In this way, he played on and on, repeating passages. She thought he would never stop, and she sat on the small sofa thinking *he is possessed. I could never both perform with him and be with him.* For a second, these thoughts penetrated.

118

Eventually, when she gave up trying to understand what he was saying, thinking he might play himself to death like the dancer in Stravinsky's ballet, he became silent and the notes faded. He played with one hand for a while, listening closely, trying out different combinations of notes. "What do you think?" he asked.

"Incredible," she said, not knowing how else to respond.

"It's fairly new still, but we're supposed to perform it in a few months, so I have to finalize it. You could play it—the cello's part. You're able to grasp my music." He looked at her, but it seemed he hardly saw her. He was looking through her. "I'll write something great for the piano and cello, a sonata. We'll play it together. I'll write it for you."

He went on experimenting with a few notes, tilting his head, listening with his eyes closed, and then suddenly he stopped and pushed the bench back and stood. He stepped away, stumbling. She stood also, as if to catch him, but her body hit up against his. They had moved toward each other simultaneously, but it felt like he'd fallen and she'd caught him, or they'd slammed into each other. His shirtfront was damp and cool, and he tried to unbutton it, but his fingers slid over the buttons. His eyes were unfocused, lost looking.

"I'll stop," he said. "Tell me." And she didn't know what he meant—that he'd stop playing or stop this. She didn't tell him. She held on and he said something more, murmuring words, *You should. I should.* She didn't let go of him as they fell, lowered onto the floor.

She pulled off her skirt and it stayed under them, a makeshift sheet. The air was very damp, and every surface felt sticky. He moved over her, and at first, he seemed too much to hold up, but then after a few minutes, he didn't feel heavy at all. He seemed almost weightless. Sweat dripped from his forehead, and his hair brushed across her eyes. She felt this, felt also his hand on her shoulder.

"You scare me," he murmured. Or maybe he said, "This

scares me."

"How?" she whispered.

His pulse beat in his temples. His face was close and his eyes were dark and unfocused. She wrapped her arms around him and lifted up to meet him, holding on. She didn't know where this thing between them had come from or where it was going or what would happen afterward, but she held on as tight as she could and kept going without knowing. She didn't stop even though she was exhausted and couldn't see an endpoint. Nothing else mattered—not his insane playing and rambling monologue, not his remark earlier about her performance, and his comment the night before that he didn't want anything serious. None of that mattered. She raced ahead with him, exceeding all rhythm until there was no stopping, and then she followed farther, still playing. By now, she was outside herself, and it seemed her feeling of being without boundaries and high above everything else would last forever. Beauty was here and something else she couldn't name or describe. It was herself—a large reservoir that held everything else.

Afterward she came back into the room again slowly. She descended, but the feeling of racing ahead with him stayed with her, even as she rose from the floor and went to lie on the bed beside him, so that though he fell asleep immediately, lying completely still on his back, she curled around him, her arm resting on his chest, not able to fully sleep until the early morning hours when a dim haze crept into the room. She had reached a pinnacle, but there was nothing clear to be seen. She was poised to leap into the next part of her life. In several hours, she would return to Boston, and then she would know. What came next would reveal itself. The next part.

In the morning, he rose early, and when she woke, she found the note he'd written telling her he needed to meet with Patrick and had gone over to the main house. He had no idea, the note read, when she was leaving, but would see her at the house after she was up.

She dressed right away, trying to remember if there was a later train, knowing there wasn't. She would just have time enough to pack and find a ride with Charles or someone else driving to Providence.

She walked back by way of the road, then part way there, remembered her cello. I'll leave it, she thought, wanting a reason to go back later for it.

When she reached the main house, all was quiet. She saw no one in the downstairs rooms and went upstairs first before looking for Arthur. She pulled her suitcase from the closet and set it on the bed. She was about to change her blouse and put on a pair of slacks for the train trip, when she looked out at the patio and saw Arthur, Charles, and Patrick. They stood in a tight cluster talking.

Quickly, she brushed out her hair, straightened her wrinkled skirt and blouse, and went directly downstairs without changing. "Reenie," Charles called out when she came out onto the patio. "I missed spending the rest of the evening with you— one of my few regrets. Did you sleep in? I just now woke up and found these two out here. I could have slept all day if we didn't have to depart."

"What time is your train?" Arthur asked her.

"One o'clock, out of Providence."

"We'll get you a ride. I think Tom Baxter's leaving soon, and he may have room. I'll go find him."

Arthur moved, as if to break away, but Charles said, "Wait. The four of us need to talk before Reenie's gone."

"There's not time for that, Charles," Arthur said.

"But you said we would after the concert, and we have to talk now, while we're all still here. We've agreed we'll likely need to replace Les permanently, and now the performance is over and it went well."

"Yes," Patrick said. "But you and Arthur and I haven't had the chance to discuss the situation together yet."

"But I'm saying we *should* discuss it now. We might not

get another opportunity while Reenie's present, and over the phone is never preferable. Reenie would have to move to New York, but if she's willing, we'd be getting a fresh face along with someone who has a genuine feel for our repertoire. And she already knows your sonata, Arthur, for the September concert."

"Charles, you're jumping ahead," Arthur said.

"I'm not. I'm merely stating." Charles stopped abruptly, looking from one to the other. Reenie didn't say anything. She heard what was being implied, but she couldn't keep up with what it meant. "We'll need a cellist and Reenie could do it, couldn't you Reenie? You'd be able to move to New York, wouldn't you?" he asked her. "We three know the city. I could help you find a flat."

"Of course," she said.

"Good. And Arthur, we're performing your sonata again in less than a month. Reenie knows the music. She's just performed it. Doesn't this make sense?"

"I suppose," he said, but he shook his head. His face was inscrutable.

"We should talk about this at another time," Patrick said. "There was a discussion last night, Charles, which you weren't present for."

"A discussion? What do you mean? With whom?"

"With Lawrence before he drove back to his hotel. We talked about the possibility of his joining us. Arthur had spoken with him a few weeks ago to see if he might be interested, but it didn't sound like he would be, given his commitments in New Jersey. After the concert, we were able to convince him."

"He thinks he can start fairly soon, in several weeks," Arthur said, focused on Charles. Reenie stood off to Charles's side like an observer. "He said he'd give notice to the orchestra in New Jersey and eventually move to New York. Living there will be advantageous for him. He'll find other groups to play with. You know, he played in our original group at Yale, and we asked him to join us back when we first formed the quartet, but he wasn't able to."

Charles glared at Arthur, then at Patrick. "I don't see why I was kept out of all this. It's a major decision."

"Because you weren't there last night is all, Charles," Patrick told him. "Nothing personal. You came back here after the concert, instead of staying on. Important discussions occur at gatherings, and if you want to be part of them, you have to be there."

"But you could have said you planned to try to convince him. Then I would have stayed. This is all because I wasn't part of the original group, because I wasn't at Yale with you. Next, you'll be replacing me."

"That's not true, Charles We didn't know in advance about Lawrence, and we were actually surprised by his readiness to consider the offer," Arthur said. "We weren't even sure he was coming until two days ago when we got his phone message. Before that, we had no way of knowing. It's just coincidental, a good coincidence, that he can see his way clear to move to New York right when we have the need for a new cellist."

"But it sounds like you offered him a position days ago."

Patrick and Arthur exchanged looks. "That offer was given before you joined us, Charles, when Arthur and I were first forming the group," Patrick told him. "Don't take everything so personally."

"You've been deceptive, both of you." Charles looked at one and then the other. "You could have told me last night, Patrick. You came to my room, and you didn't even mention it. And Reenie had no idea either," he said, glancing at her. "You set up false expectations."

"Late last night was not the time, Charles. And nothing was ever said, was it Reenie, about your joining the quartet?" Patrick asked turning to her. "You performed beautifully. We're all immensely grateful that you took this on with such short notice."

"And put up with us for four days," Arthur added.

"Of course," she said, not wanting to say anything at all.

"If we led you on at all, I'm sorry," Patrick told her. "But I can't imagine that we did. You'll have to come to New York for one of our performances. You'd like Lawrence. We could all go out for a drink afterward."

"Yes, I'll try to come," she told them.

"And we'll use you again if we need a substitute," Patrick added. "That is if you'd like to play with us again. In fact, it's very possible Lawrence won't be able to do the concert coming up, and if he's not, we'll be in touch to see if you can do it. As Charles pointed out, you already know the music."

She nodded.

"Good," Arthur said. "We should find Tom and ask about that ride."

"He's probably out front," Patrick told them. "I'll run and see."

"I could drive Reenie to Providence," Charles protested.

"But you're driving us back to the city, remember. You'd have to leave in the next hour to get Reenie to the station in Providence on time, and we won't be packed by then."

"But I'd rather...." He followed Patrick to the house, and Reenie couldn't hear the rest of what he said.

Suddenly she was alone with Arthur. He wore a fresh-looking shirt and looked well rested and as if he'd showered. She said, "I'd better see about riding with Tom. I have to get my things together. I've got to finish packing."

He looked at her regretfully. "Reenie, I would have told you about Lawrence, but I really didn't know it was possible until last night."

"It's okay." She glanced up at the house. "It's gotten late so quickly this morning. When I came through the house a half hour ago, it seemed like no one was even up yet."

"Oh, they've been up. Adele had breakfast downstairs earlier for her guests before they left. I got over here just in time to have a pastry and coffee." He smiled. "I'll miss having my meals prepared."

She said yes and that she had to get packed and get her cello from the cottage, then she turned and hurried toward the house, walked quickly across the patio and through the hallway and empty rooms to the front entrance, then back outside again and down the front steps. Tom's car was pulled up to the top of the drive where he stood arranging things in the trunk.

"I hear you have a one o'clock train," he told her. "I'm happy to drop you off. I've got Harold and his girlfriend who have a train at noon. We'll all fit nicely."

"I'll be right back with my bags."

"Do you need help?" Tom asked her. "I can carry down your suitcase."

"No," she told him. "I'll get everything. I just need a few minutes."

She made a quick exit and ascended the stairs. When she reached the bedroom, she threw her clothes into the suitcase, not slowing to fold them or arrange anything. The shoes went into the main compartment without any effort to clean them, and she bunched her underwear and stockings together. Her performance gown went in last, laid on top, and she leaned heavily onto the case to secure it shut. She was glad to be moving, glad for the need to rush and not think about anything except the task of gathering her things.

She brought the suitcase out into the upstairs hallway. Several doors down, at the far end, she heard Patrick's voice, then glimpsed him stepping out of Charles's room. She heard the sound of Charles's laughter, and Patrick leaned in toward the open doorway where she saw their faces close together. She turned and hurried down the stairs with the suitcase just as Patrick stepped back into the room.

When she reached the front entrance, Tom Baxter was bent over the hood of his car, checking the oil, and Harold was talking with a couple of other musicians standing next to another car farther down the drive. She left her suitcase next to Tom's car, said she'd be back in a few minutes, and darted down a side path, away from the house.

Minutes later, she reached the cottage, hot and out of breath. She threw the door open after knocking, but Arthur wasn't there. The rooms were cool and dark and silent. Her cello lay propped against the end of the small couch where she'd left it. Last night when she'd first stepped into the cottage, it had looked so pretty, like part of the seascape with its watercolors and the baby grand piano and the windows that opened to the ocean. Now the place smelled damp, a little moldy even, not fresh like the ocean. Arthur's clothes were still on the floor where they'd landed last night, and through the opened door to the bedroom, she glimpsed the unmade bed and towels lying everywhere. She didn't stop to look at the rooms any closer.

She packed up her cello and left as quickly as possible, hurrying up the drive with the case bumping against her hip. Her skirt was dirty. There was a streak across the middle of it, that showed up darkly against the golden, mustardy color. She brushed at it, but the mark stayed.

She reached the circular driveway and noted that many of the cars were already gone. In front of the house, Tom and Harold were fitting her suitcase into the trunk. "Here's Reenie," Harold said. "And she's got her cello. It will take up more trunk space. We'll need to re-arrange."

"No problem." Tom took her instrument from her and set it on top of the other luggage after removing a couple of the smaller items. "We can put these on the back seat." He glanced at Reenie. "Have you made your goodbyes? We'll need to be off in a few minutes."

"I'm all set," she told him.

At that moment, Charles burst through the front door. "Are you four leaving already? You must wait a minute. I'll go and get Arthur and Patrick. Patrick is just upstairs, and Arthur said he was going to walk down to the water. He thought maybe you'd gone there, Reenie, for a last look."

He would have known I was going to the cottage for my cello, she thought. Harold had climbed into the front passenger seat, and Tom fit a few of the smaller bags onto the back seat between where Harold's girlfriend and Reenie would sit. Before Charles could go off looking for the other two, Reenie threw her arms around his neck. "Say goodbye to the others for me, Charles."

He patted her back. "I can't. I must find them. Wait a minute and I'll search."

"We really don't have much time," Tom said as he opened the door to the driver's seat. "I told Patrick that when he first came out and asked me about taking Reenie. Harold and Stella have an earlier train, and as it is, we'll just make it if there's no traffic."

Tom started up the car as Reenie and Harold's girlfriend slid into the back seat on either side of the bags. Reenie opened her window and leaned out to wave. "Good bye, Charles," she called as they pulled away from the curb.

"It's been lovely," he called back.

Chapter 8

The drive to the train station felt much shorter than the drive to Newport five days earlier with Charles. Tom's car glided under the shade of the tree-lined streets, then through the small harbor town. Reenie stood on the deck of the ferry as they crossed to the mainland and watched the string of mansions on the island's coast shrink to small specks and then the island itself turn into a mirage. When they drove on the coastal road toward Providence, sunlight glinted off the passing cars and the patches of water. She saw small roadside shacks and scattered cottages. These things flashed quickly past.

When they reached the train station, Tom dropped Harold and his girlfriend at the entrance, and then found a parking spot along the road. He insisted on carrying Reenie's suitcase into the terminal. "You've got time to freshen up and get your bearings. Shall I get you a newspaper? I'm buying one for myself. There should be a review of the festival in it."

"Thank you," she said, quickly extracting a quarter from her purse. He took the change from her and moments later returned with the newspapers. They sat together flipping through the sections. "There's an article about the festival on the front page of the entertainment section," Tom said. "Oh, and listen, there's a description of your performance last night: Arthur Cohen's new sonata breaks music barriers. We never know what to expect from these modern composers. The performance received a standing ovation from the audience of Newport's finest, which included John Kennedy and his new wife who wore a cocktail length dress of pale orange satin. The quartet will give a second performance of the sonata in September in New York City, and I recommend attending. You will find the music excitingly unfamiliar. Besides pianist Arthur Cohen, the Newport performance included Patrick Dempsey on viola, Charles Breedlove on the violin and newcomer Irena Siesel who gave a strong performance with her cello."

Tom looked up from the paper. "Fabulous, Reenie, you were mentioned. You'll need to clip this article out when you get home and save it for your scrapbook."

She glanced up from the article, which also included a listing of the other chamber groups as well as a lengthy description of The Breakers mansion. "I haven't got a scrapbook."

"Time to start one." He folded his paper. "You did well. Just remember that. I've seen many young musicians at their first or second gig who don't have your poise or ability. Being called on to perform at the last minute, that's the hardest, and many musicians would have turned this down because the music was so difficult. But you did right to come. The Modern Strings is having a lot of success, precisely because they're playing music no one else is attempting. The group I'm in has a much harder time finding performance opportunities. You're just getting started, and you've already had this great experience."

She nodded, embarrassed at the praise. "Well, your performance of Bach transformed the ballroom."

"Or the room transformed us. We perform mostly in churches, and once in a while at events like this one. The Modern Strings aims for larger halls and conservatory audiences where people are composing and studying new music. I was a guest violinist at Julliard last spring, and the Modern Strings performed in Julliard's concert series. That's where I met them." He stood, getting ready to leave, then added, "You were lucky it was Les Carmichael who broke his arm, versus say our cellist."

She agreed, yes, she was lucky, and he said she might not have the chance again to play a debut, especially something written by a composer like Arthur Cohen.

She stood when Tom rose to leave, and they briefly embraced. "You're very talented," he said. "You'll have to work hard, that will be the main thing. It may take a long time—

sometimes success takes years—but I think you'll get there. I really do."

She watched him leave the station, stopping to speak with a fellow violinist who'd played Friday evening. Then she sat alone on the bench waiting to go outside to the tracks. Travelers milled about, and whole crowds arrived in waves, gathering under the timetables at one end or the clock at the other, then dispersing.

A musician she'd seen earlier in the ticket line waved at her, before hurrying off to catch his train. As she stood up and carried her cello and suitcase down the hallway toward her track, her thoughts went round and round. She only caught pieces—*music was beauty but it was a long way. There was no stopping what would come, and she had to work hard, practice, couldn't stop.*

The staircase to the tracks was long and steep. "Can I offer you a hand," someone asked.

"No, thank you," she said and began climbing with the crowd of travelers. She had left without saying goodbye, and Arthur had wanted it that way.

She walked quickly following the signs to Track 2 and set her things down on the platform when she reached it. A businessman stood nearby, reading a newspaper with a small suitcase beside his briefcase.

She saw dirt on the concrete platform and rust on the tracks. Down below between the tracks was a crumpled piece of newspaper and what looked like a small red ball, a child's toy. Above her, pigeons roosted on a wooden beam. A few loosely formed clouds dotted the blue sky.

The air was warm and still. As more passengers drifted up the platform, she hardly noticed and was suddenly so deeply fatigued, she felt like she was only partially present, watching a dream. The passengers spoke but she didn't hear the words. One waved an arm. Another hoisted a large bag. Then the train arrived with a sudden roar and the screeching of metal, and she

130

gripped the handles of her burdens and was carried as if by a great wind to an opening in the train car, then helped across the gap at the edge of the platform.

She gave the conductor her ticket and was bounced forward when the train departed as she made her way among the seats. Passengers sat reading books and newspapers. They leaned against windows and stared out at the city buildings. Two children sat by themselves eating something from a paper bag.

She found an empty seat at the back of the car, and a young man helped her stow her suitcase on the rack above it. "Where are you going?" he asked.

"Boston," she said, and she sat down remembering suddenly that those were the last words she'd said to Arthur in the cottage early that morning. She'd woken when he'd stirred. She'd rolled close and for several minutes lain with him. He was warm and she was cool, having slept without the blanket beneath the sea breeze that came through the open window. He got up from the bed and she asked, "Where are you going?" Now she couldn't remember if he'd answered. She'd fallen back asleep, but in those few moments when his warmth matched the coolness of her body, she'd felt awake and the future with him had felt palpable. Before falling back asleep, she'd read that future, and she'd assumed when she first heard the three of them talking beneath her window that they were discussing how to help her move to New York.

The train left Providence quickly behind and gathered speed. She turned and stared out the window, where the coastal landscape flashed past. It became a blur of colors—the bright water mixing with sand and grasses and worn wooden fish shacks. Before they reached Boston, they passed through a brief storm. Sudden gray clouds pressed together, and rain trickled down the window in streams.

She would never, couldn't imagine. None of it had mattered in the end—the performance, her mastery of the difficult music, all the practicing. A door had opened and shut again. Or there had not actually been a door at all, and she'd just imagined it with a life on the other side. That life with Arthur and The Modern Strings had felt so real. She'd wanted it badly, and for a moment she'd felt herself step into it. But one couldn't expect, couldn't know. What she had thought would happen. It had not, would never, and a stab of disappointment cut through her. She kept her face toward the window and sobbed, couldn't help it, then sat staring at the rain feeling numb, as if in shock.

Just before the sky cleared, she saw a quick jagged line of lightning. He had known last night when she'd come to the cottage, had already made up his mind about the future. He'd determined that future and her place in it. He'd known and hadn't told her.

The train sped along the coast toward Boston. It rattled across the tracks, and as they neared the city, buildings flashed past. They sped briefly underground through the darkness, then pulled into the station where she had to gird herself to stand and lift her cello. Many people pressed toward the exits, and she was just one more person, part of a moving crowd. Someone handed down her suitcase, and she walked off the train and through the terminal, outside to the curb. She had many emotions at once and she didn't try to stop them, couldn't. She sat her things down on the sidewalk beside her. A stream of traffic passed in front of her on the busy street. She stood staring dumbly at it, watching for her mother's car.

Third Movement: The Recapitulation

Chapter 9

She must, would never. Couldn't know but saw. She watched the train appear suddenly, then disappear again with its passengers. What he'd said, his damp shirt front, that yellow skirt, which had been so stained, she hadn't worn it again. They'd praised her performance but hadn't hired her, wouldn't have. She'd worn the gown with the pleated waistline for a decade or more, letting the hem down, later taking it up, and sewing small tears until the material was too worn to be repaired anymore. Her next performance gown had been sleeker, with slits up the sides to her knees. The problem with finding a performance gown had always been that to play her instrument she had to open her legs.

Here's your lunch.

Let's crank you up.

Are you ready to lie down?

Judith brought musical recordings and sometimes she brought the young woman called Kia who was Irena's granddaughter. They held her hands and rubbed them with cream, massaging the palms and the knuckles that were knobby with arthritis. They helped her into the wheelchair and pushed her down the hallways.

Let's sit by the window.

Let's try a little dinner.

It's gotten colder outside and very windy.

The nurse thinks this will help.

The doctor thinks. He hopes.

They pointed out the window for her to look and Judith said she'd arranged for the concert at a university. Deborah Cohen was going to play the part of the piano and a woman in the music department would play the cello.

We'll drive to it, she said.

Did you hear me, Mother?

Did you understand?

There was a red car down below, Judith's car, a splash of color beneath the trees moving in the wind.

It's a performance of the music you received in the mail, the one written by the composer you once played with.

It will take place in a few weeks and it will be a premiere.

The concert will be given in your honor.

She'd played in many concerts, performed in grand halls, sparsely filled auditoriums, symphony halls, and all those churches. For twenty years or more, she'd performed with minor unprofessional groups, donating her time to church services and weddings, settling for opportunities to make music without pay and playing popular pieces like Clair de Lune so often she couldn't get the notes out of her head. After hearing what was possible, after stepping into Arthur's world.

Benjamin and her mother and brothers had attended her concerts, even the ones given on an odd Tuesday evening in a church somewhere that was hard to find across town. After their mother died, her brothers had stayed devoted, coming to hear her play. One summer she and Benjamin had gone with them and their wives to Germany where they'd ridden on a train and walked through churchyards looking at gravestones for family names. At the house on Cannes Street, Robert and Samuel had sent her down a snow-covered hill in a sled. She flew off the high drifts and each impact shook her harder as she went faster and faster. But she never fell. She always felt assured as if someone was holding the sled's rope the whole way. When she reached the bottom she hauled the sled back up to the top and did it again.

She'd lived on Cannes Street and then in that house with the screened-in porch. Later there'd been the house on Hickory Street where she'd taught music lessons. After Benjamin died Judith had carried boxes with piles of sheet music along with

Benjamin's aquariums up from the basement, and someone had come in a truck and hauled everything away. They took her cello to auction and later told her it went to a younger woman who played in an orchestra.

Tom Baxter eventually acquired a position at Julliard where he stayed for many years, teaching and performing. He'd said nice things about her abilities but ignored the obvious about her being a woman when he talked about the difficulty of achieving success, as if the difficulties she faced in performing were the same difficulties he faced. That was how it was and no one said it would be hard or impossible because you were female even though orchestras didn't audition women and important paying gigs went to men without question. No one pointed that out. They were the facts of existence and you needed to work hard and place your music above everything else without making excuses. The Modern Strings had never intended to hire her to be a permanent member of their quartet. She'd been naïve to think it could happen. Except for Charles, they hadn't even considered her.

Eventually she'd gone on without them. For many years she'd taught at the local music academy and played with a non-paying civic orchestra. It was only later in life that she'd performed with a major orchestra, played solos and achieved those awards. In a way, Tom had been right. Her success had taken a long time but had come about in the end. When she retired from the city's symphony orchestra as the first female cellist, they'd already taken on two more women cellists.

Those were the facts. There was no denying. She couldn't change them.

Mother, I'll come early tomorrow.

I'll be here when the doctor visits.

Did you hear, Mother? Tomorrow.

I've had the pages from the music book Arthur Cohen sent to you copied for the performers. I've arranged everything for the concert.

The concert, it would happen. They said it couldn't. What they meant. What had happened. Arthur said he was always composing in his mind, no matter what he was doing. His mind was made up of notes, and music meant more than anything. It counted for more. "Come with us, Reenie," they said, and she said, "yes, of course."

A week after the classical musical festival in Newport where she'd performed with The Modern Strings, Patrick phoned and asked if she could come to New York and perform the same piece at a theater before a different audience. She'd agreed, knowing it would likely be the final time she performed with them, and a couple of weeks later, she took the train down. Something had seemed one way but was another. That fact lay at the heart. She remembered rain falling on wet streets, a car splashing water on the hem of her gown, and walking on the rainy sidewalks at night with Arthur, close together under an umbrella. In the early hours of morning, she'd stood in the rain waiting for a cab, and in the hotel room she'd hung her wet clothes over the shower rod to dry them.

When she first arrived at the theater in New York, Arthur kissed her cheek. "How good of you to play with us again." He took her hands in his, not letting go until Patrick came over, and even after he'd dropped them, he went on looking at her and didn't glance away until she met his gaze. They sat and talked for a while and gradually her hurt feelings dissipated, and she felt hopeful and allowed herself to be carried forward by that, did not protect herself from it.

By the time of the performance, the rain had begun to fall, hitting the building in a steady roar, and the house manager warned they'd need to stop playing and evacuate if the electricity went off. She had a box of Kotex with her and she wore one for the performance, feeling a pressure low down as if her bleeding would start at any minute. She was just a couple of days late by then. Someone had told her it was impossible to get pregnant the first time. Someone else had said it was very possible, but if your cycles were irregular, one missed period was no reason to panic. At the conservatory, late at night in a dorm room, her friend Gloria had said she knew someone who'd gotten pregnant and ended it. Everyone had worried, but it had come out all right in the end. You couldn't predict, needed to be careful. Still, one missed period meant nothing. Two was different, but one that was late or didn't come, you could ignore that.

"There's a plan underfoot to go out afterward," Charles said before they went on stage. And then, "wonderful," when she answered yes, she'd go with them.

The performance of Arthur Cohen's piece felt easier than it had in Newport. She knew the music by now and slipped effortlessly into place beside the others, sliding through transitions, working hard but not feeling anxious about tempo changes and dissonant notes. When she played the duet with the piano, the music felt so effortless that even when she lost her place for a second it didn't matter. The cello remembered perfectly, and suddenly the music conjured what Arthur had told her he'd seen when composing it. The sight of this happened quickly—a large field of grasses, a barn and a house in the distance. Music poured from them, his piano and her cello.

"Wonderful performance, as good or better than the premiere in Newport. Thank you all," Arthur said later when they were seated around a table at a restaurant to celebrate. Lawrence was there as well, having come for the weekend to hear the performance and look for an apartment.

"The duet with the piano was extraordinary," he told her.

In the lively, warm restaurant, they ate creamy soups and plates of beef tenderloin, lamb chops, and lasagna. She remembered a large round table with a white linen cloth and glowing silverware, along with a coat check at the front where they'd left their wet coats and umbrellas. While they ate, the four men planned their upcoming year, writing a list of possible performances on the back of a card. Now that Lawrence was joining them, they predicted the group's rise would be simultaneous with Arthur's as a composer.

Later, in a crowded bar they drank fifteen-cent beers and argued that classical music was the purest of all art forms, while someone banged on a table nearby and a crowd gathered at a window to watch a fight outside on the sidewalk. The surface of music and art was made up of color, movement, pitch, rhythm, and duration, they said, and the surface was what mattered, not the nebulous emotional content underneath or the response of the audience, elements that popular music courted. They discussed little known composers, names Reenie had never heard of, and Arthur praised a woman who'd lived in Paris and spent her life composing music never performed.

"I envy her," he told them.

"But why, if her music was never performed?" Reenie asked.

"I envy her *because* her music was never performed," he stressed. "It remained in the purest state."

"But if she couldn't get anyone to perform her music, she never got to hear it."

"She may have been a little crazy, but I envy her craziness," he said.

"Crazy? How? Because she kept composing even though her music wasn't played?"

"Yes," he said with emphasis. He put his glass down a little too hard and beer sloshed over onto the table.

"One minute you claim the performance is the most important thing, the next you say the performance matters not at all," Charles complained.

"He's saying the performance is secondary to the music," Lawrence told him.

"At least for now," Charles said. "Any minute that will change. And how depressing that she lived her whole life never hearing her work performed."

140

Yes, Reenie thought, glancing at Charles. Depressing.

More people gathered at the table, and they called for more beer. A friend of Charles's brought a chair up next to Reenie's. He told her he was an artist and wanted to know whose date she was.

"Be careful," Charles said, "he'll want to show you his drawings."

"What I want is to draw *you,*" the man said.

The five of them stayed until they'd drunk too much cheap beer, then ended up outside in the rain climbing into a cab to go to a club. In the backseat, Arthur had his arm around her. Rain pounded the cab's roof and she saw rows of watery car lights and pools of red and blue neon. Crowds crossed intersections under seas of black umbrellas, and the whole city felt submerged as their cab swam down river after river, with lit corners, bars, and music halls drifting past. She saw neon signs advertising strip joints, including one with the outlines of a woman's body mingling with a human-sized snake.

Charles said, "You must stay longer, a few more days at least. Let us show you more sights. Won't you stay? Say you will."

"I don't know," she laughed.

"Yes, stay," Arthur said, squeezing her toward him.

"All right," she said, sinking deeper into the seat beside him, and it felt settled. They said it made no sense for her to catch a morning train after a late night out, and when they reached the club she stood outside for a while with Arthur, kissing him under the dripping umbrella. When they went inside, they kept together, holding hands until they found a table with Charles, Patrick, and Lawrence at the back.

Towards the front of the room, a topless waitress walked among the tables near the bandstand where four musicians were playing. The music was fast with a racing nervous rhythm. A saxophonist and horn player took turns playing the melody and improvising, and the other musicians followed their leads. Patrick and Lawrence went to the bar and brought back glasses filled with watered-down champagne, and for a while, the five of them just sat and listened, unable to talk much with the music playing. Then after several songs, Charles pulled Reenie up, insisting they move closer. They wove between the tables until they reached a spot off to the side and next to the bandstand. Instantly, she felt the excitement. Nearby, everyone was listening intently and she felt the roomful of people around her, tapping out the same beat. For a while the saxophonist and piano player played together, smoothing everything out, then there was a flash as a horn was lifted and the musician blew a long single note. It howled above everything else.

Smoke hung over them, thick as a curtain, and she felt like she'd been drinking cheap beer and bad champagne for days. The other three musicians backed up the horn player and then the piano player took the lead. He began with the same melody, but the tune quickly changed. She heard a familiar interval and felt a jolt of recognition. Mozart had been a master at improvisation also, she told herself.

Next to her, Charles tapped his foot and nodded to the rhythm. A few others had come to the front to listen, and everyone pressed closer. She forgot about the table where Arthur sat, forgot about going back to it, and instead stayed next to the band. She closed her eyes and felt the music pulse through her. It cranked impossibly louder and pulled her down a churning pool. She kept her eyes closed and fell deeper.

Later, when the set ended, she followed Charles back to the table. "It was incredible," she told the others. "That music somehow just got inside me. At one point I nearly wept."

"It knocked me out, truly," Charles told them.

"Knocked you out, Charles?" Arthur asked. "Really?"

Lawrence started laughing and overturned a glass. It soaked Reenie's slacks. "It's okay," she said, not caring. Every nerve still felt tense. "Up close it was different. Like being invaded."

"They were sloppy," Arthur said. "It sounded like that guy

on piano was wearing mittens."

Patrick left with Lawrence to get napkins to wipe up the spilled drink. "I believe the piano player is a substitute," Charles said, "not their regular guy, but I thought he was good. Besides, they were experimenting. I love it when that happens, when you're hearing them mess with a familiar tune."

"They should save that for after hours."

"You're a snob," Charles told him. "Do you think you're better than that guy?"

"Yes," Arthur insisted.

"You said earlier it was the surface of the music that mattered," Reenie said, still trying to articulate what she'd heard. "But I kept hearing what was underneath the surface."

"Yes," Charles said. "She's right, Arthur. Powerful emotion was underneath that very uneven surface."

"You're an idiot, Charles. You don't know pig slop when you hear it. You can't tell the difference between garbage and solid improvisation."

"What do you mean? What is the difference? That music is as difficult to play as the music you're writing. It's a completely different type of music, not better or worse than what we do. You or I couldn't play it."

"I know plenty about jazz," Arthur said. "I've played it and it's not so difficult."

"Where? When? You and Patrick are just alike. You'd lie about your abilities rather than admit one short falling."

"A few of us formed a jazz band at Yale. We played some of the clubs."

"I don't believe you. Reenie doesn't either, do you?"

He looked at her and she nodded, uncertain. She was still thinking about the surface of the music and what lay underneath it. Part of her was still up next to the bandstand, listening.

"The two of you are missing something critical," Arthur said. "You possess talent, Charles, but you're not doing anything with it. You don't care about precision. And Reenie, you're a beginner. You shouldn't be taking your instruction from Charles."

"What are you talking about?" Charles stood up, shoving his chair back and Arthur rose as well. Reenie watched them, stunned, but they didn't get into a fight. Instead Arthur walked around to the side of the room and up to the bandstand where the musicians were picking up their instruments, getting ready for another set. They were laughing and talking to each other in a relaxed sort of way when Arthur came up to them. The horn player seemed to know him. Reenie watched him shaking hands with the others.

"This is unbelievable," Charles said. "I'd leave, but I don't want to miss the train wreck."

She looked around the room but couldn't find Lawrence or Patrick. Up front, Arthur was sitting down at the piano.

"My god, it looks like the piano player's allowing it," Charles said. "I guess he figures since he's not a regular...."

A few minutes later, they began to play. At first, Arthur stayed in the background. He kept up with the rhythm and chord changes and played impressive runs of scales. Then toward the end of the piece, when they let him take a solo, he ran quickly away with it, playing a million notes so fast it was dizzying and pounding on the keys, as the others fell back, so that after a while only the drummer joined him with a soft roll. It was growing late and more people were leaving, but Arthur played on. The horn player left the stage for a while and returned with a stool. He perched on it, watching. The other piano player brought the drummer a drink.

Finally, the piece ended, but Arthur didn't return to their table. He stayed up front with the band. Patrick and Lawrence didn't return either, and after a while Charles suggested he and Reenie should find cabs out front. The club was nearly empty.

Reenie followed Charles outside, and her last sight of Arthur was at the piano, playing a long run of heavy chords. She imagined him staying on, playing music at the club into the morning hours. Outside on the sidewalk where it was still raining, Charles put her in the first cab to pull over.

"Goodbye and sleep well," he called out before he closed the cab's door. "Have a wonderful trip back home."

On the way back to the hotel, the rain was so heavy she couldn't see anything but water streaming down the windows. She paid the driver and ran inside. Once in her room, she hung her wet clothes over the shower rod and slept fitfully, waking repeatedly to thunder.

The next morning, she was up early enough to catch her train. At the station, she walked past the ticket lines and out to the platform, feeling barely conscious. She'd seen Arthur's world, she'd stepped into it but couldn't stay. There was not even a question of that. He would not, could not. The quartet was complete, something apart, and Arthur was so caught up in his own talent and music that he saw nothing else. She couldn't penetrate that, would never know. She would go back to Boston and teach at the small, local music academy even though it would mean spending hours listening to kids play scales out of tune. The teaching would lead to something better. One had to believe that, one must.

The rain stopped just before they reached Boston, and outside she found her mother's car on the street waiting for her.

"How was the performance?" her mother asked.

"It went very well," she said.

"What a wonderful opportunity you had with that group."

"Yes," she agreed.

She put her things in the trunk and got in the car. It was noon and the streets around the station were crowded with vehicles and a street vendor selling hot dogs and soft drinks that took up part of a lane. Her night with the four men where Arthur had kissed her and she'd felt so moved by that jazz band had already faded, as if a veil had passed over it, and she didn't know, after all, what any of it had meant.

Chapter 10

Irena couldn't say. Didn't know. Everything she heard and saw and felt, whatever he said. All that had happened. She hurried down a hallway. She rode the train a very long way. Clouds blew overhead, they raced across the sky.

She went home again to Boston where she wrote up and followed a strict schedule: practice each morning from 6 to 11. Lunch with Mother, then teach at the academy from 1 to 4. Once a week she met with her music coach and at his prompting joined a small civic orchestra. It didn't pay but the conductor was adequate, and Gloria, her friend from the conservatory, had joined. Irena met Phyllis Wagner there as well, a violist who many years later, would play with her in the large, professional symphony orchestra.

The civic orchestra began holding weekly rehearsals for their holiday concert, and with all these events she was very busy. She flew energetically from practicing, to teaching, to lessons, but felt dull and tired as if a large weight had rolled onto her. Later in life this feeling of working under a weight became familiar and unnoticeable even, but now her disappointment canceled out other things—joy and excitement. The disappointment was so ubiquitous she never talked about it, even with Gloria or Phyllis, who also didn't complain when they took part-time jobs in stores or offices and fit in practicing their music for auditions that seldom materialized.

When she came back from New York, she expected to get her period right away but did not. One minute she thought pregnancy was a possibility, and the next she remembered other times when it had been late, including once when she'd skipped a month. She tried to add up the days and weeks and kept arriving at different answers. Her records were bad, which meant she could have been two or three or even four weeks late. She scribbled possibilities on her calendar, and later when she was teaching lessons or practicing, her mind went on trying to calculate. She woke up in the night adding strange numbers, not knowing what they meant. She berated herself for not being more careful, and she berated her body and tried to force it to comply, as if she could bring on her period with her will, bearing down while on the toilet and pushing on her abdomen. She checked three and four times with the paper after peeing—this became a ritual—and she checked herself for a bit of blood even when she was not on the toilet, certain she'd felt something damp in her underwear. She mistook old stains for new ones and afterwards spent an hour or more thinking her period might have started. She slid her fingers up inside herself but found just a coating of mucus when she pulled them out. At night, she dreamt she sat on strange toilets and open pits. Blood dripped down from her own hole into the other, larger dark hole, but when she woke her underwear was always as clean as ever.

Sometimes she took it for granted that if she ended up being pregnant, she would contact Arthur right away. Other times she knew she wouldn't. But mostly she didn't think about pregnancy as a reality and instead saw the delay in her period as an annoyance or an affront, which caused her more and more frustration. She felt cramping off and on, and once for a whole week she felt tender and sore, as if at any minute actual and prolonged cramping would begin, but no matter how much she believed getting her period was inevitable or how much she berated herself, the period did not arrive, and finally, she made an appointment with the family doctor she'd had since childhood, where she told him that her cycles were confused, due to recent travel and she wanted something that would return them to normal. Later, in the 1970's, she might have gone to a clinic, but back then she knew of no clinics, and at-home pregnancy kits were an invention of the future. It didn't occur to her to find a different doctor, one who didn't know her. She wouldn't have known where to start.

The doctor ran a couple of tests, and a few days later she sat in his office across from him at his desk to hear the results. Piles of folders lay between them, along with a framed photo of his wife and four children. Irena's folder was open in front of him with the page that showed her results.

"You're going to have a baby, Miss Siesel," he said, not mincing words. He glanced at the papers, as the title "Miss" settled between them.

"Oh," she said, surprised despite everything. Then she added, "I'm planning to get married," an automatic response. He'd been her family's doctor for years, and her mother was still his patient.

He wrote something in the folder. "I wouldn't delay," he said, not glancing up.

"How far along am I?" she asked.

"A few weeks, if you're right about the dates of your last period."

She sat for moment, compulsively adding numbers again, as if that could change the outcome, while the doctor talked about the do's and don'ts of pregnancy and handed her a booklet. The cover showed a model who looked very un-pregnant wearing a slim skirt and stylish top. The caption read, "Await the stork in pretty clothes."

"You're a musician, if I remember correctly."

"Yes, a cellist."

"The baby you're carrying is your main job now. Its needs take precedence, and vigorous activity could harm it. That includes playing a large instrument."

She nodded but wouldn't consider and couldn't imagine, had to ask and didn't know where else to turn. "What other possibilities are there?"

His face wrinkled with confusion, and she clarified, "I mean besides having the baby."

She glanced away, down at her hands, but he stared at

her without apology. Finally he said, "I don't know what you mean."

"Since it's just a few weeks." She felt flushed and dizzy.

"There are no other possibilities, at least none I'm aware of, if I understand your question." He returned the papers to a folder and tapped it lightly against the desk. "You'll need another appointment to meet with my nurse who will go over everything in detail. Do you smoke?"

She shook her head.

"Good. There's new research suggesting it's better not to, although I've never seen it affect the baby."

He stood, went to the office door, and opened it. He held it for her while she got up from her seat and walked into the hall. "Better not make it a lengthy engagement," he advised before leading her back to the waiting area.

She left the building quickly and went down to the parking lot and sat in her mother's car. She had Patrick's phone number—he'd given it to her when he'd first called her about the festival—but she didn't have Arthur's number or Charles's. Arthur could presumably get her number from Patrick, but he'd never phoned her. None of them had, except for Patrick those two times when he'd made the arrangements with her for the concerts. She was unsure if she'd see or hear from any of them again. She could call Patrick and ask for Arthur's number, but what would she say if he asked why she needed it? She didn't know how Patrick would react or what Arthur would do, but she sensed the outcome would be terrible and felt sick just thinking about it. She had a few girlfriends still in the area from high school and a handful she'd known at the conservatory, including Gloria who'd told the story about her friend who'd gone somewhere to get rid of a pregnancy. She'd been to Gloria's apartment recently and had seen her just a few nights before at a rehearsal for the civic orchestra, and whereas before she'd debated what she would or would not do if she was pregnant, now that she knew for certain, she didn't waffle or sit in her mother's car for too long considering. As soon as she thought of Gloria, she drove into downtown Boston. The traffic was heavy, and she had to circle the blocks around Gloria's building—a five story brick apartment building on Commerce Ave. with a new awning over the front entrance—a few times before finding a parking spot. She rang up and when her friend didn't answer, waited in her car until five when she remembered Gloria would return from a shop where she worked three days a week.

"I was in the area, and since it was close to five I thought I'd wait for you," she said when she met Gloria outside the building near the entrance, and Gloria said, "wonderful," she was glad for the visit. She led the way and they went inside to the apartment where Gloria made them a pitcher of iced tea and told Irena about a church concert she'd recently played in. They talked about the festival in Newport, and Irena described Arthur's piece as innovative and exciting. She said the audience had included two of the Kennedys and numbered more than two hundred.

"I played the same piece a few weeks later with them at a concert in New York," she said. "But I won't likely perform with them again. They've found a permanent cellist, a young man who also went to Yale."

"Pity," Gloria said. "But something else will come round. We all thought you were the best of our small lot. If any of us has a performance career, it will be you."

Irena denied this and said that all the women at the conservatory had been very good, including Gloria who was sure to find opportunities. Harpists were more often in demand, while cellists were common, and female cellists were not well considered. They talked of the others at the conservatory and what had become of them. Gabriella was back in Detroit, and Shelly had returned to her parents' house in a small town in New Hampshire, where she was teaching violin lessons. They talked about Nina, another violinist who lived not too far away, and Betsy who had been a very good flutist with a clear, strong sound, and then Irena said, "You once told us of someone who went somewhere because she was pregnant. She had a procedure, you said, and it all went well. I thought of it because I have a friend who doesn't know where to go."

"Hold on, I've still got the information," Gloria said, and she went into her bedroom and brought back a small notebook. "I saved the information, in case anyone ever had the need," she said and wrote out directions to a house she said was in the backwoods of Maine, north of Boston.

"Would she need an appointment?" Irena asked.

"No. Tell her to just drive up there, but only on a Thursday. Make sure it's a Thursday and after one p.m. No other day or time. It's a long way, a couple of hours or more, but it's not hard to find. Tell her to leave plenty of time and to get there early in the afternoon. Otherwise, if there are too many already waiting, she could get turned away."

"I'll tell her," Irena said.

"It costs a hundred dollars, but that was a couple of years ago. Tell her to take more money in case he asks for extra."

Irena nodded.

"Call and tell me how it all comes out." She squeezed Irena's hand. "He's a doctor. It's all very medical. If I ever needed to, that's where I would go. I'm certain I would. It hasn't happened to me, but I wouldn't hesitate."

Irena nodded. She couldn't say, yes, I would do it also, and it felt wrong to say no she wouldn't do it. Instead she said, "Play something for me on your harp before I go," and Gloria got up from the couch and took the cover off her instrument and drew up a stool.

"This is something new, a special arrangement I found."

She touched the harp's strings, playing soft, bright notes, and for twenty minutes or more Irena shut her eyes and forgot her panic and why she'd come. The celestial music filled her. When the concert was over, she said how beautiful the arrangement had been, and they hugged before Irena went back out to the street and drove home to her mother's.

She had to wait for Thursday, following her routine as if nothing had changed, and when it came, she borrowed her mother's car again, took the money she'd earned playing for The Modern Strings, and drove north into Maine. The directions Gloria had given her were straightforward. She left Boston and drove along the coast, then headed directly north into Maine on a small, two-lane highway. The roads quickly became less populated, and there were fewer and fewer road signs pointing to fewer and fewer towns. At one point, she drove twenty miles without even seeing a billboard. Partway up, she stopped at a roadside cabin advertising fresh milk and eggs and gave the name of the town where she was going, asking if she was on the right road.

"You're headed there all right," the woman inside told her, and feeling embarrassed that she'd stopped for directions, Irena bought a bottle of milk that she would end up drinking hours later, pulled off on the roadside, on her way back toward Boston.

After checking the directions at the small town, she should have felt reassured, but as she traveled deeper into the countryside, she felt less and less certain. She passed woods, fields, and rolling pastures. The landscape was rural and lovely, but devoid of any signs of human existence. It was October and the car heater wasn't working well and she began to shiver. Low hanging clouds hovered, and the sky looked brushed with milk. At one point after watching for a gas station with a restroom and finding none, she pulled off the road and walked a ways into the trees at the roadside. Leaves had freshly fallen—muted reds and yellows mixed with clusters of pine needles. Squatting, she steadied herself with her hand against a trunk.

It will all be over by tonight, she told herself. I'll find the house, and in a few hours, I'll be driving back into the city. She reassured herself that when it was over, she could forget the entire experience, including Arthur and everything that had happened with him and The Modern Strings. The directions Gloria had given her to the doctor who performed the operations were simple, and the way forward was laid out. Gloria's friend had gone there, and Irena told herself that afterwards she would be fine, but squatting among the trees, she couldn't quite convince herself, and it felt like she would never find her way back out of this place to Boston.

She returned to the car and drove north again going as fast as she dared. She passed overgrown meadows with stonewalls and vast wooded areas that broke suddenly for open fields showing a barn or a house in the distance. Miles of electrical poles flashed past close to the pavement. After what felt like many hours, she turned off the highway onto a narrow, paved road and then onto a dirt one. Trees encroached, so close their branches brushed against the car. The tires spit small stones and clunked into depressions. Houses appeared in clusters. She watched for mailbox numbers and when the number eighty-eight appeared next to a "No Trespassing" sign, she pulled off into the trees to park behind another car.

A small yard lay behind a screen of pines, and as she walked to the house, she saw flowerpots filled with just dirt now that summer was over, along with numerous painted ceramic ornaments. There was a blue and yellow windmill, a pink birdbath, several fawns and oversized squirrels, and one of those ceramic figures, which she hated, of a black person holding a lantern and dressed in the red jacket of a serving boy.

An older woman wearing a headscarf answered the door. Irena said, "I'm here to see the doctor," and the woman led her wordlessly into the kitchen. The room was small and grim, with dark wood cabinets and a scared wooden counter. A small table covered with a greasy oilcloth was pushed against the wall, and the woman indicated Irena should sit in the chair next to it to wait. Nearby, the oven door hung open. This seemed to be the main heating source, but the room was so chilly, she wondered if the oven was lit.

The woman stood at the counter, clearing her throat and sipping from a glass of water. "Have you got money with you?" she asked.

"Yes, one hundred dollars."

The woman took the bills from her, counted them. "It's twenty in addition," she said, and when Irena gave her the last twenty, the woman curled the bills into a tight cylinder and wrapped it with a rubber band. "He's with someone else. You can sit here until he's ready."

The woman said nothing else, and Irena went on sitting at the table, careful not to touch the oil cloth and listening to the clock, a dark wooden cuckoo-clock that made a slight sound as the clapper swung back and forth. She wanted a glass of water or preferably something stronger but didn't dare ask for it. The woman had a tightly puckered mouth and large gray eyes that had likely been pretty at one time but were now dull and washed out like the colors of the walls and the dishes on the shelves. She went about her business of cleaning something in the sink, clearing her throat every now and then but not saying anything. Only a little sunlight came in through the window, and the silence felt dreadful, as if it lay at the center of everything else that was dark and gloomy in the room. Irena tried to think of something to say, but couldn't, and the only sounds were the clock, the running water, the woman's throat clearings, and indistinguishable noises that came from a room deeper in the house—inaudible voices, a metal tapping, and once the sound of something heavy being pushed across a floor.

Thirty minutes or more passed before the doctor came out, an older man, thin and balding. He wore a blue work shirt with the sleeves rolled up and went to the kitchen sink and washed his hands. When his wife handed him Irena's bills, he unlocked a cabinet and took out a jar with other bills. Irena watched as he added hers to the jar, then returned it to the locked cabinet.

"This way, please," he said, acknowledging her for the first time.

She stood and followed him into a hallway, past closed doors to the back of the house, and entered a room that smelled of cigarette smoke and rubbing alcohol. While the kitchen had felt grungy, this room seemed clean even if it was cold like the rest of the house. A wide curtain hung between two beds. Through it, she glimpsed the shape of a woman lying down.

"Take off everything under your skirt," the doctor told her. "Put your things on the chair and then lie down on the bed."

He stepped to the other side of the curtain, and she sat on the chair shivering a little from the cold as she took off her shoes and stockings. She heard him ask the other woman if she was ready to get dressed.

"Not yet," came the answer. The woman's voice was pinched and barely audible.

"I have another patient, so you'll need to lie still and be quiet. Afterward, you'll need to get up and gather your things. Do you have far to drive?"

"Two hours," the woman said.

The doctor gave directions for her care. His voice was soft but firm. He said she would bleed for several hours at least, perhaps for several days, and should wear a thick pad. "Did you bring some with you?"

There was a short pause, then, "I can furnish you with two for the drive. Cramping is normal. Stay in bed once you are at home. Rest. You will return to normal within several days. Meanwhile, you will bleed heavier than you would with a period and any amount of bleeding is acceptable. Don't be alarmed. There will be no reason for you to go to the hospital or see another doctor."

Stainless steel instruments lay on a folded towel spread out on a table near the bed on Irena's side. She saw a thin blade clamp and several rods, one with a hook. The instruments looked clean, and the doctor's voice while firm was kind. He was saying something more about the other woman's drive back and that she would be fine.

The woman whimpered, "But it hurts," and said something else that Irena couldn't make out.

"I explained that it would hurt, didn't I? It will all be fine. You only need to go home and rest."

She said something else, then, "I'll go. In a few more minutes, I'll go," spoken in a schoolgirl's voice that was soft and scared and held the distinct sound of shame.

Through the curtains, Irena watched the doctor stand near the bed and reach down to touch the woman's wrist. "You're absolutely fine," he said after a minute or so, but the girl kept crying. Irena stood as if to finish undressing, but instead she stepped into her shoes and walked swiftly to the door and down the hallway carrying her purse and her wadded up stockings.

She couldn't say why she was leaving. She only knew she had to reach her car. She had not made a conscious decision. Her body propelled her into the kitchen, which was now empty, past the gaping oven and out into the yard where the doctor's wife stood by a fence gathering wood. She wore a large, man's sweater that hung down past her hips, draping over her skirt. At the sound of the door, she straightened and looked across the yard. For a second Irena met her gaze, and she could have sworn the woman smiled a little, even though she said nothing and merely watched as Irena went across the lawn. By the time Irena reached the drive, the woman was walking back to the house, hunched over her armload of split logs.

Without stopping, Irena walked to the road where she'd left her mother's car. Shivering badly, she started the engine and turned up the heater. The other car still sat in front of her, and to turn around on the road, she had to back up, then pull forward several times, sharply cutting the wheels. On her third try, one of the rear tires caught on the edge of a ditch, and for a second she panicked, feeling the car start to slide. She drove forward, gunning the engine, and when she was headed in the right direction, she pulled out fast, spitting dirt and gravel as she bumped over the uneven road.

It was nearly four o'clock, overcast and gloomy. Curls of smoke rose from the houses, all alike, all squat and stubbornly solid among the trees. A large man standing near the road followed her car, the car of a stranger, with his eyes. Trees loomed overheard, growing closer and closer to the road, and when she didn't come quickly to the highway, she worried she'd missed a fork or turned the wrong way. Instead of driving toward home, she was traveling farther and farther into the woods. It felt like she would never escape them. She was about to turn around and head back toward the doctor's house to look for a missed turn, when she came suddenly upon a small paved road. It led to the highway where she turned south, headed toward Boston.

She was chilly and desperate, and her relief from finding the highway didn't last long. Wooded hills pressed in on her and the sun was getting ready to set, but there was no hint of color, just a sickly yellow sheen. At one point, she pulled off the highway and squatted inside the cover of trees as she had on the drive up. Cars sped past on the nearby road as she tried to pee, but though she felt the urge, when she squeezed her muscles, nothing came out. Beech trees towered over her like a crowd of giants. Beyond them, more trees grew even closer together, a dense wood.

She gave up after a few minutes, and rising with difficulty, stumbled to the car. She hit her shin on the running board as she climbed in and slammed the door shut. The engine failed to start on her first try, and a minute later when it did, it gunned suddenly to life. She heard a thud as she drove over a mound of dirt onto the pavement, and the heater turned back on, rattling. She continued south as the sky darkened, a change that happened almost imperceptibly. The dull yellow sun slowly faded, and darkness seeped out of the air, filling the road and the woods.

She had heard of drinking large amounts of Castor oil and thought there were probably other methods, such as drinking poisons or bottles of cough syrup or using enemas. She'd heard of a girl who went to some sort of a home and left the baby for adoption afterward, but she couldn't imagine how she could get an address or disappear for several months.

As it grew darker, she passed fewer cars. The gas gauge dropped close to empty, but she didn't pass a station, and she hoped she was close enough by now to Boston. Hungry and thirsty, she pulled over again briefly and drank the quart bottle of milk she'd bought earlier, leaving the engine running, afraid of turning it off and getting stranded.

She'd fled the doctor's house in Maine without thinking. She'd lost her nerve, botched her opportunity, and she knew she wouldn't drive back up there again, couldn't. She'd escaped that small, cold house with its curtained room and the two beds, the strange doctor, and his awful wife, but her escape gave her no relief. Instead she'd run headlong into greater trouble.

She reached the coast, and businesses that sold gas and food appeared, but still she didn't stop. She couldn't allow herself to. She couldn't eat or sleep or even try to pee again until she knew what it was she would do. The reality of her pregnancy pressed closer, and she sensed how it would take over. It would have its own timetable, its own life, separate from her. She passed more and more buildings and saw she would soon reach Boston, but she was lost still for good with no way out.

It was fully dark by the time raindrops began to splatter the car's windshield, so that she had to turn on the wipers, which made a loud, rubbery squeak. The drops grew larger and fatter as she drove through the city. They thudded against the windshield and spread, forming small lakes.

The storm was coming toward her from off the ocean, pummeling the city buildings, which were closed-up tight against it. The dark city streets were uncharacteristically empty. In the distance, over the ocean, lightning flickered, illuminating a sliver of sky.

Single women did not have babies. It wasn't possible. Some disappeared for a while, and when they came back it was assumed what had happened. People guessed and spoke of it, and you wouldn't know how far gossip had spread. Keeping any job would become impossible, including teaching at the academy.

She passed other vehicles, cars and trucks streaming past in the dark, rainy night. Low down in her belly, the pressure was there still, as if she had to pee. Likely she would have been fine if she'd stayed in that awful house. The man was a doctor for God's sake and knew what he was doing, had probably done it hundreds of times. She had to decide, had to act now before the pregnancy showed. She shifted against the seat, but the pressure didn't ease up, wouldn't. She felt nauseous despite eating nothing since breakfast. She needed to do something and quickly, and she couldn't tell anyone, not even Gloria and especially not Arthur which would mean contacting Patrick who would likely learn from Arthur why she'd called, so that all four of them might find out. She was completely alone.

Impossibly, the rain grew heavier. Her wipers slashed back and forth at high speed but couldn't clear the windshield. The streets filled with water. In low-lying places, it pooled, slapping up against the body of the car. Benjamin lived in an apartment building in Boston with other graduate students, near one of the hospitals where he was completing a research degree. She hadn't seen him since she'd turned down his marriage proposal in the restaurant.

It became harder and harder to see out the windshield. Her headlights did nothing, and the heavy rain rendered the streets unrecognizable. She made several wrong turns before spotting his apartment building, then had to park a few blocks away, jockeying the narrow space between bumpers, pulling forward and back until she felt something catch and heard the scrape of metal. She inched forward again and left the car, not stopping in the rain to investigate the damage with the flashlight her mother kept in the glove compartment.

She didn't have an umbrella and had to pull her sweater up over her head before making a run for the building. She hurried up the steps, then squeezed under the overhang above the entrance. Water poured down all around her. It seeped through the crack between the overhang and the building, falling at an impossible angle, striking her. She had to hold her hand over the buttons to find Benjamin's number so that she could ring up to his apartment, then wait for him to answer. His voice was muffled in the call box. "I'll be right down," he said when she told him who she was.

Minutes later, he opened the door. She was soaked through, and the cold water still ran down her hair and face in rivulets. The cold felt good. There was nothing gentle in it, nothing unsure. Each shiver wrung her harder and each roll of thunder shouted behind her in a sudden burst of wind that howled above the building and drove the rain harder under the overhang.

"What are you doing here?" he demanded. "It's no night to be out. You're soaked." He stepped aside to let her in, but she stayed where she was, rain streaming down on her. Three months ago, he'd looked angry and hurt, and now she stood in the rain for a minute before going in with him, the only time she hesitated.

"You're freezing," he said. "You're shivering all over. Quick, come in."

She stepped inside and followed him up the stairs and down the hallway and into his apartment, then went at his insistence straight to the bathroom to remove her wet things. He cracked open the door to pass her a shirt and a pair of his pajama pants. The pants were so large, she had to roll the cuffs and cinch the waist with her belt. She fit her arms into the warm sleeves of the cotton shirt and toweled her hair, rubbing the wetness from it. Outside, the thunder came in waves, rolling over the city. Each time it sounded, the floor under her shook. Dressed and dried off, she went out to the kitchen where she found Benjamin brewing coffee.

"This is all I've got to warm you, this and a little whiskey." He pointed to the pint bottle, half full on the table. "It belongs to Nicholas, but he won't mind if a little is missing."

She took the cup he offered, pouring a few swallows of the whiskey and drank it down. Then Benjamin filled the cup with hot, black coffee.

"No cream, I'm afraid," he apologized. "That's how it is with research students."

She glanced around, not having seen his apartment before. It would have been suggestive to invite her up.

"You're still shivering," he said. "Do you want a sweater or my bathrobe?"

She shook her head and drank the rest of the coffee down all at once, burning her mouth and throat. "Is Nicholas here?"

"No. He went out earlier with his girl."

She nodded, considering this, then put down the cup with a shaking hand, so that it became unbalanced and rolled off the table, breaking into two halves, with such a neat edge that later Benjamin would glue it back together.

Neither of them moved to pick up the cup. "I want you to hold me under the blankets in your bed," she told him.

He stood a few feet away, at the counter watching her. "Why?" he asked. "What does this sudden appearance mean?"

She was still cold, still shivering, and before she lost her nerve, she turned away and walked out of the kitchen and down the hallway, glancing in doorways, trying to guess which room was his.

"Why are you here?" Benjamin said, following her. "What are you doing?"

She recognized his jacket hanging on a doorknob, went into the room and crawled under the woolen blanket on his bed.

He came and stood in the doorway. "Tell me what this means. I thought I wouldn't see you again. You went off, hardly explaining after you refused the ring I'd got you. You didn't contact me these last couple of months, and then here you are tonight, in a downpour."

The room was dark, only a little light spilled in from the

hallway. The storm was lessening, but occasional lightning still streaked the windows, and each time this happened she saw Benjamin lit by the quick, harsh flash. Then it was dark again and he stood in the shadows. She'd known him since childhood, and he was the only person she'd dated for any length of time. Before that afternoon when she'd refused his proposal, a marriage to him had felt inevitable, and when she'd said no, she'd surprised herself as well as him. She couldn't explain it. She'd just had an undeniable feeling that she had to have something more.

"I don't know what you want," he said.

"I want you to come under the blankets with me." It was a clear request, a simple one.

"Say first what this means. I can't do this with you and then have you drive away and not know what it means. I can't stand that."

She was still cold under the blankets, unable to warm herself. She was shivering harder. "I'm here because I changed my mind."

"About my proposal?"

"Yes."

"Why? What made you change your mind?"

She didn't answer, couldn't think how to explain it, and she couldn't look at him. She wormed deeper into the blankets and curled into a tight ball, her knees drawn into her stomach.

"Are you saying you'll marry me?"

"Yes, of course. That's what I just said, that's why I'm here." She pulled the blankets tighter around her.

He came over to the bed and sat down. He was next to her but turned away, facing the door, slumped over. She couldn't see his expression. "I don't believe you. I can't imagine why you would say no like that and then change your mind."

"I needed time to think. I wasn't expecting it," she said. "You know how I am."

"No, I don't know. How are you?"

162

"It felt so sudden, and I have to decide things myself. I can't be pushed into a decision." It was true. She'd grown up with three older brothers, trying to advise her and give her orders. She'd learned to hold her own. "I needed time to make up my own mind. If you want someone who will just agree to something without thinking about it, I'm not her."

"I never said I wanted that, and I was willing to let you think about it all you wanted and willing to support your cello playing once we got married. I knew you worried about that, and I said I'd support it. I told you that."

"But I needed to think everything through for myself, without you there."

"You didn't say that. You just said no."

"I felt cornered," she said. "And I can't be someone different for you." They were both quiet for a few minutes, and she couldn't see him, but she could feel him, hunched over on the side of the bed.

He glanced over at her. "What guarantee is there that you won't change your mind, once you've decided?" he asked. "On your own."

"We could get married tomorrow if you want, with a Justice of the Peace. If you're worried I'll change my mind, we can do it right away."

"You mean you'd likely change your mind if we waited?"

"No, that's not what I meant. I was only saying that if you want, we could marry soon, and that would be proof that I don't intend to change my mind. All we'd need are a couple of witnesses. Maybe Nicholas could come with us. I don't need a big wedding."

"Your mother would want one. It's her only chance to plan one. She'd want you to have a white gown and go before the minister. She'd want your family there."

She uncurled herself a little and tried to nestle closer against his back. Sitting on the side of the bed, he radiated heat and the strange faint odor she associated with him of rubbing alcohol and chemicals. "That would be a circus," she said.

"Well, a circus worth attending. And I have to say I'd like a church wedding. Signing papers in a courthouse, that doesn't feel real."

She found one of his hands and closed her own over it. "I just don't want to have to make a lot of plans or think about it too much."

"Is the thought of marrying me that repugnant to you?"

"That's not what I meant," she said, and it felt like he was twisting her words, deliberately misunderstanding her.

He pulled his hand out of hers and turned, facing her. "Do you love me?" His gaze was steady, and he looked braced, prepared for whatever answer she gave.

"Of course," she said. The words came out sounding certain, fierce even. She reached up and shook him a little. "I just don't want a lot of fuss. Don't you understand how much I would hate having to spend all that time planning for a big wedding? I'm teaching now almost every afternoon at the music academy, and I have to keep practicing in order to keep auditioning. If I don't find performance opportunities now, when I'm newly graduated from the conservatory, it will only be harder later. I can't afford to lose months preparing for a wedding."

"We could have a smaller affair I suppose—just our families and close friends. Your mother would help, she'd likely take over for you if you wanted her to. I'd do what I could."

She raised up closer to him, hardly feeling the cold now. "Is it so wrong to want to be married quickly and forgo a wedding? We could move in together right away. We could find our own place."

"No," he said. "It's not wrong, if you mean it."

She tried to pull him toward her, but he was still unmovable. "Where would we live if we didn't wait? We couldn't live here. I'd need to apply for graduate student housing or find another apartment. It would take time and the apartment would be smaller than this one, an efficiency or a one bedroom. I can't see us living with your mother."

"She would offer."

He nodded. "Probably, but can you picture doing it?"

"I can't picture enjoying it, if that's what you mean."

She slid her hands around his waist. He didn't respond, but he didn't remove her hands either. "We don't have to think it through tonight," she said, rising from the blankets to kiss his neck.

She felt him nodding, yielding something. Then he began to remove his clothing—his shirt and his trousers. He was still faced away from her, still inside his own thoughts. He turned toward her, wearing just his boxers, and she wrapped the blanket around him and brought him under it. She closed her arms around him, and the fronts of their bodies pressed together. He was heavier than Arthur had been, bulky in build. and she felt his belly push against her own. For a while, they just held each other, getting used to the feeling of their bodies together, and then she reached between them and unbuttoned the shirt he'd given her to put on earlier. His clothes were loose on her and should have come off easily, but she struggled under the blankets, and the pajama bottoms ended up tangled around her legs. He didn't take his boxers off completely either, and she felt the elastic scrape her hipbones. His elbow grazed her side and his hand poked at her ribs, the movements jagged and unpracticed. She stiffened, then rolled onto her back wondering vaguely if he was a virgin.

The thunder softened, but the rain still rolled toward them off the sea, falling over the building in a steady whisper. Benjamin moved on top of her. "Is this okay?" he asked.

"Yes," she said. He was warm, much warmer than she was, and she liked the feeling of his heavier weight. He fumbled down below with his boxers, then his hand moved her legs apart and he raised up over her and pushed inside.

"I love you," he murmured. "I have always loved you."

She sank back into the mattress, and when he raised up and

pushed in farther, she felt her body melt a little under him as the horrible anxiety that had twisted inside her and pounded against her head on that long drive back seeped away. She didn't care if she was pregnant or if she never heard from Arthur or The Modern Strings again. The room was dark enough that she couldn't see his face. Were his eyes closed? She thought they likely were. She was in a warm free-fall and she hit bottom. The mattress under her gave with their weight. She was flattened. Outside the rain went on falling with its steady soothing whisper, and she heard another noise that came from outside the room. It must be Nicholas, she thought, but she didn't worry. She dismissed any anxiety, and it felt like she'd planned this union all along, not as if she'd changed her mind, but as if she just hadn't realized it before, hadn't known her own mind.

Above her, Benjamin clenched. He tightened his hold on her, and she felt his buttocks draw together as a long shudder rippled through him. She was shuddering also, shaking uncontrollably. The relief that had made her feel slack just seconds ago flooded through her with raw power, and for a few seconds she was like a body electrocuted. Then they were quiet, his weight heavy on her. He laughed softly, like a young boy who'd tried something he was afraid of and found it wonderful.

"Nicholas is back, I heard him," he whispered.

She laughed a little also. They were two children giggling.

"You'll have to go quickly. I think he's in his room. The door is likely closed. I'll get up and see, and if that's the case, you should get your clothes from the bathroom and go. You can wear mine. Just carry your wet ones. I'll give you my coat to put on over them."

"But chances are he's been in the bathroom and seen my wet clothes hanging there."

"Good point. I'll tell him you stopped by and we talked and you left in a hurry."

"I am leaving in a hurry."

"I'll say we fought and you stormed out forgetting your

clothes."

"He'll have likely heard us in here."

Benjamin shifted off her. She felt his mouth still close to her ear, whispering. "It doesn't matter. It's the pretense that counts. We just need a story we can all agree on."

For a few more minutes he stayed next to her, under the warmth of the blankets. Rain whispered against the building. Her heart whispered back and exhaustion seeped through her like a tide. He rubbed her arm, moving his hand in a small circular motion. Later she'd learn he was never still. Some part of him was always moving. He twitched in his sleep, tapped his feet restlessly when he sat at a desk or table. The movement of his body was analogous to his mind. He was always thinking.

"I should get up and see if Nicholas is in his room," he whispered, moving away from her as he pushed off the covers and fumbled with his clothes. A moment later, he cracked the door open and slipped out. She felt for the shirt and pajama pants he'd given her and found her way back into them, so that by the time he came back with her wet clothes, she was dressed.

He didn't speak, just handed her the clothes and gestured for her to go out of the room. He took his coat from a closet and hung it over her shoulders as she stepped into her shoes. They walked downstairs where the entrance hallway was empty and sparsely lit. He opened the door and put his hand out, testing.

"It's still raining a little. I should get you an umbrella."

"I'll be fine. I've got your coat. I'm parked close by."

"I'd go out with you, but there's Nicholas upstairs."

"No, go on back up. I'll be fine."

He kissed her quickly, embraced her in a quick hug. "Careful driving back," he said. Then she went through the door, and he pulled it shut behind her.

Outside the rain was nearly imperceptible, just a gentle mist really. She walked the couple of blocks quickly, not worrying about the puddles, hardly feeling the cold water soak her shoes. She found the car and drove to her mother's house, which was completely dark except for a light left on in the kitchen, and crept inside and went to bed.

The next morning her mother said, "Oh, you must have come back early from your girlfriend's place. Gloria, wasn't that her name?"

Her mother didn't notice the paint marks and dents on the back fender of the car for a few days, and by then, it was impossible to say when and how the small accident must have happened. "Maybe I bumped something when I was out yesterday," her mother said. "I hope not. I should have noticed when it happened and offered to pay for any repairs. Or perhaps someone bumped me from behind and didn't leave a note. I hate it when this sort of thing happens."

The day after her drive to Maine and then to Benjamin's apartment in the rainstorm, Benjamin drove with her to the jeweler's, where at his insistence, she tried on several rings, but in the end, chose the same one he'd offered her a few months earlier in the restaurant. The sun had come out and afterward when they walked along the river holding hands, the wet trees glistened. Leaves floated on the water, yellow and red, and a flock of geese rose all at once, in formation. When a little girl said, "Look Mommy, they're kissing," Irena laughed, reached up and kissed Benjamin some more.

That evening, they told his parents and her mother about their engagement, and a few days later when her mother invited Irena's brothers and their families for Sunday dinner, Benjamin asked her brothers' permission, was granted it, and congratulated. The family, with two small children from her brothers' marriages, crowded around the dining room table in her mother's house, and when everyone raised their glasses in a toast, Benjamin looked flushed and happy.

Her mother said she knew the right shop for a wedding

gown, and her sister-in-law, Nancy, gave advice about invitations. Irena said she wished their father was still alive to give her away, but even the moment of sadness that followed was sweet. Her mother noted that because it would be a summer wedding, they could have the reception in the garden behind the house where the rose bushes would be in full bloom.

Irena got swept up, picturing the decorated tables spread across the lawn and the blooming garden, and it was only later, after everyone had left and she was helping her mother to clean up, that the fear which had driven her to Benjamin's doorstep in the rain returned. It was just a thread of fear at first, so that her mother didn't notice and went on chattering about bakeries and cakes, but later when Irena lay in bed, it kept her from falling asleep. In the morning, it was gone, but it would come back again, off and on. She might be practicing her cello, totally absorbed in the music, and suddenly the thread would emerge, for no obvious reason, as if out of the notes themselves. Over the years, that thread would keep appearing, rising up seemingly out of nowhere, so that even after years of marriage to Benjamin, when Judith was grown and Irena had achieved her long held and hard won goal of playing cello with the city's major symphony orchestra, she'd sometimes wake up, feeling an unknowable dread. Then nothing, not even playing music, could make it lift.

"You've been out of sorts lately," her mother said when they were climbing the stairs after drying and putting away the clean dishes. "Marriage is such a big decision, but this is the right choice for you, I feel certain of it." She clasped Irena's hands. "Look how happy you were tonight. That's proof."

Irena smiled and nodded, but as they turned out the hall lights, the wedding gown her mother had described and the five-layer cake that Joseph Steller's bakery was famous for felt vague, impossible to imagine. There was no one she could tell the truth to, and it was just beginning to settle in that there never would be.

Chapter 11

She drove north, then south and everything flashed quickly past. That hat she'd worn. The dress with the lace trim her mother had sewn onto it. The bouquet she'd held made with white and purple irises that her sister-in-law had bought at the florist on the corner, arranging them at the last minute. She had waited at stations, boarded trains and driven for miles. It was a narrow road with few turns, and she passed houses among the trees. The sky turned overcast and later there was a sunset.

Eat a little of this.

Lie back now.

I'll just prop you up.

I'll just help you get that.

She would keep going, had to, couldn't stop, couldn't turn a deaf ear. All around her was a great churning.

Mother, did you hear me?

I'm coming later tomorrow around five. I'll bring Kia with me to see you.

Mother, that concert is all arranged.

It will be in a few weeks.

Arthur Cohen's niece says it will be wonderful.

It will lift your spirits.

She heard what they said, heard voices and steps in the hallway, heard an orchestra playing, heard air moving through the vents, and the sound of a motor beneath everything else. It went on day and night, a beautiful sound, a difficult sound, the sound she'd always known and that was always present. She heard it and knew she had to continue, couldn't stop. She stood on a narrow strip and saw she had no choice. This sound that was larger than her would not let go, and later when she had walked so far and could go no farther she would see how far she'd come and where the end lay.

She resolved not to see Arthur or The Modern Strings again, but then Charles called one evening and said, "You must come to New York this weekend and hear our performance. It's our first one with Lawrence and we're playing Arthur's newest piece. Please come. We can all go out afterward for a drink."

At first she resisted the invitation, but after ten minutes or so, her resolve faded, and by the time they hung up, she'd already planned how she could book a train reservation. When Benjamin heard she was going, he insisted on driving her to and from the station, but she told him she'd be returning late and would get a cab that night back home to her mother's house. It was her last trip to see The Modern strings, and it would be fifteen years before she saw any of them again.

She arrived in New York City an hour before the concert, feeling excited and wide awake. She took a cab partway, then walked the last several blocks to the theater, stopping at a deli for a sandwich. She'd let out the elastic band of her skirt by then, and she wore a green velvet jacket with embroidery on the collar which fell past her hips.

"You look beautiful," Benjamin had said when he dropped her off, and Charles said, "You look so lovely," when he greeted her. "You're different, more vibrant. I can't say why or how, but it's remarkable."

Using the ticket Charles had given her, she sat in the front row, so that when the quartet came onto the stage, they loomed above her, bigger than life, taking their bows and arranging themselves with their instruments. The piano sat close to the edge of the stage, several feet away from her, and she had to look up to see it. From that unusual angle, she watched Arthur arrange his music, test the pedals under his feet and bend his elbows getting ready to play. She saw him signal the others with the nod of his head and watched his face wrinkle in concentration as he played the opening chords.

This piece of music was even stranger then the piece she'd played with them, more than a month ago in Newport. Each instrument had its own melody, and there was little harmonizing. The four themes didn't fit together, an effect furthered by long solos taken by each instrument. The notes of the piano, violin, viola, and cello ran side by side, like four vehicles in separate lanes of traffic, meeting only occasionally, sometimes in a melodious moment and other times in a collision. Musical patterns emerged only to be broken, and random notes sounded, adding to the confusion.

During a short intermission, she used the bathroom—she was using it more frequently by then—and when she returned, Arthur was beginning the final movement with a long solo. She recognized the passage right away. It was the same one he'd played for her in the cottage that night, and he played the notes with the same intensity, his face dropping closer and closer to the keys, his concentration palpable and frantic. Sweat coursed down his face, and he repeatedly shook his hair back from his eyes, with quick, abrupt movements. His figure cast a shadow over the audience, and a strange reality emanated from him. She remembered the field of grasses he'd described, and in a flash, saw many different scenes—a house and barn with music pouring out of them, his music, then the concert halls where he would play, filled with large audiences, and the many recordings of his music. She understood that he would become famous, and whatever she saw felt completely real.

I'll tell him what happened, she thought. I'll explain everything—the pregnancy and the drive up to Maine. She imagined living with him in that house she'd seen. He could continue composing, and they could both keep performing. The child would become a virtuoso.

She was thinking these thoughts or they were thinking her, as the piece ended abruptly, without any concluding notes. The four men walked to the center of the stage and took a bow. Then Arthur stepped in front of the other three to bow again. Some in the audience stood and clapped long enough that the quartet left the stage and then returned. Arthur played his solo again as the finale, and she hung on every note.

Afterwards when she walked to the small entrance hall with the rest of the audience for the reception, she quickly spotted Lawrence and complimented the performance. He said that coming from her that meant a lot, but he seemed distracted, glancing around at the dispersing crowd. In the corner a group of men stood talking, and just as Lawrence excused himself to join them, Arthur and Patrick came out from a back hallway.

"We're being visited by ghosts," Arthur called out, as he and Patrick stopped to talk with the group. "They drove all the way here, and I hope it was worth it."

The others laughed and began pumping Lawrence's hand, and Reenie, who followed Lawrence over to the group, heard snatches of praise about the music. Arthur sounded relaxed and self-deprecating. He commented that the piece wasn't really quite finished, and that he wasn't satisfied with the finale.

As they all began to talk, Charles came up from behind Reenie and pulled her into a bear hug. "Now we'll get out of here and have a visit," he said. He took her hand and pulled her closer toward the others, trying to get Patrick's attention. "Reenie's here. Where shall we go? What shall we do?"

Patrick seemed not to hear him. "Where are you staying?" he was asking the others.

One of them said the name of their hotel.

"That's uptown," Patrick told him. "We should get a cab, a couple of cabs."

Arthur caught sight of her then and came around to kiss her cheek. "You made a long trip to hear us. I hope Charles didn't make you feel obligated."

"No, I wanted to come."

He smiled and held her hands for an extra second. "Did

you take the train again?"

"Yes. I was curious about your new piece. I wanted to hear it after hearing a little of it that night at the Jameson's."

His smile broadened. "Oh, I'd forgotten. You heard my madness, before it found a form."

"It had a form, even then. I recognized the piano's solo as soon as it began. That solo is beautiful."

"What did you think of the entire thing?"

She told him it was brilliant and exciting, not commenting on the strange discordance. "I can't imagine how you composed it in less than two months."

He leaned in close, his mouth to her ear. "I confess. I composed it a year ago. I was still batting some of it around at the festival, but it was mostly finished."

She laughed.

"Except for that finale," he added. "It's still haunting me. I hope your seat was good. We told Charles to give you one up front."

She told him it had been. "I remembered the field of grasses you described," she said, intent on telling him the images she'd seen, but he was glancing over at Charles and Patrick.

"I told you..." Charles said. And, "You said...But why?" Reenie missed most of his words.

"Stop exaggerating," Patrick told him.

Arthur motioned toward the others. "Our cohort," he told Reenie. "They came up to hear us from New Jersey. A couple of jazz enthusiasts are among them, and Bernie who is a great percussionist."

The others nodded in her direction. Two of them shook her hand.

"So you and Charles are going out before you get the train back to Boston?" Arthur asked.

She nodded.

"If we'd known ahead." He gestured at the others again. "But they've already put together an itinerary."

Patrick was telling Charles, "It won't work. We can't just change everything."

Charles went on arguing as Reenie caught Arthur's arm. "It's fine. I'll come again, another time."

"Good." He smiled. "Especially since it means you'll come again. We'll plan ahead for it, and I'm glad you're going out with Charles tonight. He's been moody. Spending the evening with you will be the remedy."

"What are you saying about me?" Charles asked, coming up beside them.

"Nothing. Just that you and Reenie will have a good time together."

"Without the three of you, since you're going uptown for a private evening, and we're not invited."

"It's not private, Charles. It's just that there's so many of us, and Patrick and I haven't seen these guys in a couple of years."

"I shouldn't stay out long anyway," Reenie said. "I've got a train to catch later tonight. Maybe there's a bar near the station."

"It's so good to see you," Arthur said as he leaned in and kissed her. She felt a strand of his hair brush her cheek, and for a second they embraced. He said something else, but before she understood what it was, he had stepped back and was already waving at the others who were moving toward the theater's exit, joking with each other. He followed them, and when the others engulfed him, he laughed, happy to be surrounded.

A few minutes later, Charles had her by the arm. The theater's lobby was nearly empty, and he steered her toward the exit. On the sidewalk, she saw the others squeezing into a couple of cabs, and she moved with Charles toward the door, not quite comprehending what had happened. She would never, could not. There was no way to tell him.

Charles said, "Never mind them. They're caught up with each other. It would have been a bore if we'd gone with them.

We'll have more fun together, just the two of us. We'll go out on the town and forget them."

He watched the cabs pull away still brooding. "I told them I planned to invite you. I talked to Patrick and got your number." He patted his damp hair into place and signaled for a cab. "Never mind. We'll find a club with music. We can stay out all night and have a story to tell later."

"I have a train I need to catch, Charles. It leaves at eleven-thirty out of Penn Station."

"No matter. There'll be plenty of trains in the morning. I've got a couch in my flat. I'll give you the bedroom to yourself. You can rest there after a long night out, if you don't think it would look improper." He leaned closer and whispered, "No one need know."

"That's generous," she told him. "But I can't stay the night. I have to get back." She felt panicked and wanted to be gone.

"Not generous. I want you with me for longer than just a few hours. I know of plenty of places. There's a bar I frequent where I could take you. You'd meet my familiars, and we'd be close to my apartment, in case I get you drunk enough that you change your mind about that train."

"I won't change my mind, and I don't want to go somewhere that's far from the station. There must be a bar that's close."

"But it won't be the one where I would take you," he said as a cab pulled up to the curb next to them. "It will just be another bar."

"It'll serve alcohol," she said. "Which is the main thing. I can have a few drinks and then sleep on the train going back."

They got into the cab, and she told the driver to take them to Penn Station. Charles kept arguing that the area around the train station was no good and that she didn't know New York the way he did, didn't know the neighborhoods.

"I'm sure we'll find a place," she said.

The cab driver didn't turn off course even as Charles kept

listing reasons why this was not a good plan and why she should spend the night. He didn't stop arguing, and after a while she wasn't listening and instead stared out the window, thinking she might forgo the drink with him all together. She hadn't said what she'd thought she would to Arthur, hadn't been able to, and she wouldn't try again, couldn't. She wished she'd never come.

The cab dropped them off in front of the station, and Charles insisted on paying, then instead of complaining anymore about the location, he dragged Reenie up one block and down another looking for the right place. The bar they settled on was small, tucked away on a side street a few blocks walk from the train station. The neon sign over the door advertised "Drinks, drinks, drinks!"

"It was made for us," Charles said.

He led the way inside. The lighting was dim, and at first Reenie couldn't see anything. It was Friday night and a group of men stood three deep at the bar. Charles chose an empty table, then went to get their drinks. She watched him push through the working-class crowd, out of place in his white dress shirt and the trousers from his tux. When he came back, he carried a tray with two small glasses of whiskey and two beers to wash them down. "I didn't trust them with anything other than liquor served straight up," he said lifting a glass and clinking it with hers. "To us. Let's get stumbling drunk."

She nodded and took a sip. The whiskey slipped down her throat with an anesthetizing sting, and she drank it down quickly with the cold, pale beer, but the alcohol didn't mute anything and she couldn't stop thinking about Arthur. He'd kissed her. What had that meant?

"I need to find additional work," Charles was saying. "But auditions are hard to come by."

"There must be lots of opportunities in New York."

"Not so many." He finished most of his beer with a few swallows. "Did you hear that Patrick is getting married?"

"No," she said. "That's a surprise. Had he been planning on it?"

"No, it's a sudden decision, based on the fact that there's a position he wants at Curtis, and marriage will make him a more attractive candidate."

"He told you that?"

"No, but I can guess his motives. I can put two and two together."

"Who is the girl?"

"Someone his mother introduced him to, the daughter of a family friend. I've just been introduced briefly."

"What is she like?"

"Blond hair, very neatly done-up. Average height and weight. She laughs a lot. I met her after a rehearsal, and I asked her what she thought of the music. 'Lovely,' was all she could muster. She kept laughing as if the music was a joke she'd just told me. Patrick turns very silly around her. He becomes someone else."

He said more about the girl and Patrick and their plans for a wedding, then he went back to the bar. When he returned with more drinks, he said he'd ordered french fries. "I hope they're dripping with grease."

Reenie drank the second round more slowly, and gradually, the alcohol began to soften everything—the boisterous voices at the bar and the other tables, along with her thoughts. She couldn't have said anything to Arthur. It wouldn't have come off right. There was no way. Ghostly neon lights glowed in the windows and smoke hung over the room. Nearby, someone pounded a tabletop and everyone laughed. Charles had asked her to come to the concert, but Arthur had seemed surprised. *I can't go with you. Have other plans.* What had he whispered before he left?

Someone brought over the plate of fries with a bottle of ketchup, and she dumped too much on them and began to eat, suddenly ravenous. Charles was still talking about Patrick. "He hardly knows the girl. She was simply convenient, and his mother told him she'd recently been jilted, practically at the altar."

"Poor thing," Reenie said.

"Yes, well I'm the one who's left, pulling the petals off daisies."

"Maybe you should find someone else," she said vaguely. She couldn't see his situation any more clearly than she could see her own.

"I confronted him and we had a big row. He'd come over to my apartment for one last time together, only I didn't realize it was the last time, I was still in the dark, then later that night he told me he couldn't keep coming over or seeing me. He expected me to understand. It was an inevitable moment, he said, as if it couldn't be helped, and when I got upset, he kept saying to keep my voice down. It was very late at night, and the people who live above me started banging on their floor because of the noise."

"Oh God," she said.

"He actually thinks getting married will solve everything. His beastly habits will be forgotten because of her beauty."

"Is she beautiful?"

"I don't know. I hardly looked. Not in a Marlene Dietrich way. More like a less attractive Katharine Hepburn, boyish but with none of Hepburn's intelligence or humor. I was hoping she would come tonight and that all of us would go out together afterward. I wanted your opinion. But maybe Patrick is keeping her away intentionally, while he sings her praises. 'She's so practical and down to earth, just what I need. She had on a blue dress that showed off her eyes. How long should I wait to ask her? Several months is customary, but we're both older and we're ready to begin our lives together. We know what we want.'" Charles raised his voice in imitation and waved his arms as he spoke, even though Patrick was always so contained.

"We need another round," Reenie said cutting off the rest of his story. While Charles took their glasses back to the bar, she went to the bathroom—a tiny room with a tiny, dirty looking toilet and a lock that didn't work so that she had to lean forward while seated to keep anyone from coming in. When she came back out, Charles was there with fresh drinks.

"Good thing we're not far from the train station," she said.

"Why? It's not even eleven yet."

"At this rate, I will just barely be able to stumble down the street to the station. I'd never manage a cab ride."

"If we weren't here and we'd gone to the bar near my apartment, we could stay out until morning."

She upended the ketchup bottle and tapped the bottom, pouring more out over the fries. Normally she hated soggy fries, but these tasted better, the more they were drenched. "Is Arthur seeing someone new also?"

Charles shrugged. "He's not like Patrick who keeps talking about his new interest, torturing me. He talks as if they'll be married in a month or less, but he has yet to ask her. At least, I haven't seen a ring."

"Weddings take months to plan," Reenie said vaguely.

"She's the type who will want a wedding. She wouldn't be satisfied with just a license." He ate the fries at the edge of the plate and pondered. "I think you're right when you suggest I should find someone else. I have to get over him. I've tried, really, but because of the quartet I'm forced to see him and endure his comments about Angie this and Angie that."

"If you had other work, something that kept you busier."

"That is absolutely what I need."

They clinked their glasses together in a toast to other work, and Reenie went back to the bar for more beer. The place was still crowded, and the men at the bar stood close together jostling one another, but were careful not to bump her. She smelled tobacco and sweat and smoke. "Going home?" someone asked.

"Not until I finish this round."

180

She waited for the bartender, and when he came around, she ordered more beer. "Why are you sitting over by the wall, honey?" one of the men asked her. "We can get a stool for you here. Sam, give her your stool."

"I don't need one," she told them. "I've got my friend at the table."

"Your pansy," someone else said. "I'll buy your drinks, then you'll be obliged. Hey, Derrick. Put the lady's beers on my tab."

"No, let me pay," she told the bartender, and she left her dollar bills on the bar even though he waved them away.

She carried the beers back to their table. "We should get going after this," she told Charles. "My train comes in less than an hour, and I'm ready to get out of this place."

"There's plenty of time still before your train, and I haven't finished telling you my story," he said. "It's the saddest story there is. I could tell it over and over." His voice rose. "I've been jilted by my lover, who's left me for a woman he doesn't even want. Where is the justice in that? Where is the humanity?" He lifted his beer glass and drank.

"Quiet down," a man at the next table told him.

Charles lowered his glass. "I'm not any louder than anyone else in here, and I won't be silenced."

"No one wants to hear about your lover. You're corrupting the young lady."

Charles laughed. "Do you feel corrupted, Reenie?"

"No, of course not," she said. "But let's go." She stood abruptly, leaving her beer untouched.

"Well you're corrupting me then, and my girlfriend," the man said, gesturing at the woman next to him with pasty makeup and bright lipstick.

"I don't believe your girlfriend could be corrupted," Charles said. "She looks past corruption." He stood, walked in a wavy line to the bar, and called out, demanding another whiskey.

"You're cut off, Bud," the bartender told him, loud enough that Reenie heard. She also heard Charles's response that he was not drunk, no one was cutting him off, and his name was not Bud. He said he had every right to have as many drinks as he wanted.

Reenie swept together their things. She felt suddenly clear-headed and crossed the room in a few steps, walking straight up to Charles, pushing past the others. "Come on. You said you'd walk me to the train station."

"After another drink," he said.

"One more drink and we'll stuff you under that table," the man next to him threatened.

Charles straightened up and his expression went dangerously blank with what she knew was a mask of reserve. He was putting together a speech that would go on and on and challenge his challengers. The men at the bar were turning away from him, and it was the moment to slip out, but his lips pressed together and his jaw set into grim lines. She saw he would do anything to keep the altercation going.

"I'm leaving," she said, shoving his jacket at him. She turned away and hurried to the door, hardly noticing that she had to weave between the tables to get to it. She was quickly outside on the sidewalk in the cold night air, struggling with her coat when Charles came out behind her.

"They're all assholes. If they hadn't been so obnoxious, we'd be having a last drink."

She turned away and began walking. The street was poorly lit, but she saw lights up ahead at the intersection. Charles quickly caught up with her, walking close and bumping against her. "Sorry Reenie," he said.

She kept walking, head down, not looking at him, feeling furious. "I've got fifteen minutes before the train leaves. I just want to make it on time."

"You will. It's just a right turn up there and then down a block or so." He flung an arm over her shoulders and tried to draw her toward him as they walked. She shook him off and didn't slow her pace even when he stumbled, but when he suddenly stopped, she was forced to turn around.

"God," he moaned. He was bent forward, his hands on his thighs for support, his shoulders heaving as he gasped for air. "I can't stand it."

"The station's not that much farther," she said, hoping what he couldn't stand was the pace of the walk. "We can slow down a little."

He looked at her, then down at the sidewalk. His head swung back and forth. "I hate myself. I really do."

She walked back. She couldn't just leave him like that. "It's all right," she said. Maybe he'd still gather himself, so she could make the train.

He heaved once, then twice, but didn't throw up. "We must get you to the station. You'll miss your train and it will be my fault. I'm such an idiot. If Patrick had heard me go on like I did back there tonight, he wouldn't speak to me again."

"Just take a minute, and then if we hurry I'll still make it in time." Charles went on trembling, but it was less convulsive. He sobbed loudly a few times and then was quiet. "Are you okay?" she asked.

After being in the noisy bar, the dark street felt exceptionally quiet. Everything but the two of them melted away. She bent and put her arm around him, and after a minute he nodded, seeming calmer. He straightened up, and they began to walk slowly but steadily toward the lit street up ahead that would lead to the station. They got halfway down the block, then someone from behind them called out, "Wait up, Bud."

Reenie turned. Three of the men from the bar were walking toward them. For a moment she was disoriented, having not heard or noticed them coming out of the building, and while the men seemed at first to be moving at a regular pace, suddenly she realized they were walking quite fast. She didn't have time to respond, and she had just registered their presence when the men were upon them.

One of them shoved Charles off the sidewalk, into the street. "Watch out, you might get hit by a car," he said in a tone of mock concern.

Charles stumbled onto the pavement from the push, then veered back toward the sidewalk. She watched a car turn off the bigger, lit street up ahead and drive slowly toward them. For a second she thought it would stop, but it didn't. As it passed she glimpsed Charles's panicked expression in the glow from its headlights. The man who'd pushed him moved toward him and seemed to lift him up. He tossed Charles back into the street, then came after him.

"Hey, did you hear what my friend said?" one of his friends called out following them into the street. "Are you listening? You might get injured out here. I'd hate to see your white shirt get dirtied."

Reenie tried to go after them, but the third man blocked her. "Stay on the sidewalk, honey."

The other two shoved Charles again. Then all three men surrounded him, their voices playful and teasing. "Come back here. My friend is talking to you. Don't you have something to say? You had plenty to say back there at the bar."

They stood close together and passed Charles from one to the next so that he fell into each of their arms like an object in a game.

"What's the matter? Can't you keep your balance?"

"The pansy can't hold his liquor. He's so drunk, he can't even talk anymore."

"Leave him alone," Reenie yelled. She told herself to walk into the street, but her legs didn't move, and she stayed watching from the sidewalk, stuck in place.

"Stop!" she yelled louder. "You'll hurt him!" One of them glanced back at her, but they kept tossing Charles around their circle, laughing until one of their shoves landed Charles on the pavement. Then they all stepped toward him, and Charles disappeared. All Reenie could see were the three men.

"You've got nothing to say now, do you? Back there, you had plenty to say. I was just trying to drink a few beers and unwind, but instead I had to listen to your complaints about your lost lover boy crawling through my brain."

A booted foot drew back, and Reenie heard the thud as it made contact. Charles groaned.

"Come again? Did I hear you moan? Are you enjoying this? A bunch of men surrounding you, and you the object of their attention?"

He stepped back and swung again. Reenie glimpsed Charles lying on his side. The kick landed as he was pulling his knees up to his chest. His glasses skidded across the pavement.

"Get off him!" she yelled, as what had been fear erupted into something else, raw and powerful. She ran into the street, grabbed one of their arms and yanked on it. "Stop! Get off him!"

The man pushed her aside, and she stayed there a minute, panting. Charles groaned as the other man kicked him again and again. Then the door to the bar opened, and someone came out onto the sidewalk. "Help!" she screamed. "Get the police!"

The person who'd left the bar called back inside the opened door for help. Suddenly, all at once, the assailants backed away, walking quickly down the street. They had just turned the corner when a police car came from the opposite direction. Reenie flagged the car to a stop. She knelt down next to Charles. "Help him," she yelled when an officer got out of the car. "Those men were beating him up."

The bartender came out onto the sidewalk and told the officer that there'd been some trouble but it was over now. "I'm the owner of that bar, just a few doors down." He pointed. "This street is so poorly lit. I keep asking the city to put up more lights. It makes muggings easy."

"This wasn't a mugging. Those men were in the bar with us," Reenie insisted. "I saw them. My friend and I were just trying to walk to the train station, and they left the bar just after we did and came after us for no reason except to beat up my friend."

"You sure you didn't recognize them?" the officer asked the owner.

"Yeah, I'm sure. I was bartending all night, and I'd have noticed if they were in there."

"You weren't close enough to get a good look at them," Reenie said. "I was, and I recognized them. One of them was sitting at the table next to us."

"I could see just fine. Those men weren't in my bar, but you and your friend were sitting in there for a few hours. I had to cut your friend off when he got so drunk he was disturbing everyone else. It wouldn't surprise me if he started this fight himself when he came out here. He sounded pretty angry about something."

The other officer had got out of the patrol car and was asking Charles if he could stand.

"Yes," Charles groaned, but he didn't move.

"He needs a doctor," Reenie said.

"I'm okay," Charles kept moaning.

"I don't like this kind of thing going on in front of my bar," the bar owner said. "It's bad for business."

"Can you take us to a hospital?" Reenie asked.

"He said he's okay," the officer told her.

"The men who beat him up just went around the corner. They attacked us for no reason. We'd been in the bar having a drink, and they followed us out. We were walking toward the train station, I was supposed to catch a train at 11:30, and they came after us and pushed him into the street and started kicking him."

The bar owner threw up his hands. "People will say anything, just so they come off being victims."

"It's what happened," she said.

"All right, all right," the officer told her. "We'll drive down the street in a minute and see if you can spot the assailants. But

186

first we need to get your friend into the patrol car. We'll get you two off the street and drive you where you need to go, that is if you're cooperative. If not, we can cart you down to the station on a drunk and disorderly."

"Trouble makers," the bartender said. "Let them spend the night in jail."

"We were not drunk and disorderly," she yelled. "This is absurd. What about those men who beat up my friend for no reason?"

"No reason," scoffed the bartender.

"I told you, we'll look for them," the officer said. "But you'd best quiet down. Did you miss your train?"

"Yes," she said, glancing at her watch. "It's probably just now leaving the station." She listened for the sound of a train, but didn't hear one. Maybe it had already left, and she hadn't noticed.

The officer's partner crouched beside Charles asking if he could stand. "I'll be fine," Charles kept saying. "Just give me a minute."

"Where do you live?" the officer asked.

Reenie heard Charles say his address. She picked his glasses up off the pavement. "They're broken," she said, holding them up to the officer as proof. "The lenses are shattered. They were knocked off when those men pushed him down in the street. And we weren't doing anything except trying to walk to the train station." She looked down at Charles, still on the pavement. "He needs an ambulance, not a police car."

"An ambulance," the bar owner laughed. "Good luck with that in this neighborhood at this time of night. What he needs is to dry up."

Charles pushed himself up partway. He made a terrible choking sound.

"You all right?" the officer with him asked.

"Just a minute," Charles gasped. He knelt, his head lowered to the pavement, and heaved, throwing up.

"I had to cut him off in there," the bartender told them. "He was stumbling drunk."

The two officers got on either side of Charles and hauled him to his feet. "We can take you and your friend in and book you both, or we can drive you home, courtesy of New York City taxpayers. Which will it be?"

"Book us?" Reenie yelled. "What are you talking about?"

The officer waved a warning at her. "You said you missed your train. I'm trying to decide where you'll spend the night in our fair city."

Charles was standing now, walking with help toward the patrol car. "Take me home," he moaned. "Just get me a cab. I'll be fine."

"Get him out of here," the bar owner said. He turned and began walking back to the bar as Charles got into the patrol car.

"We'll drive him home," the officer told Reenie. "You coming?"

"All right, but I want to see if the men who beat him up are still there."

He nodded. "Get in."

She went around to the other side of the car and climbed in the back next to Charles. He was curled up on his side, lying on the seat, and she squeezed in beside him, lifting his head and placing it on her lap. He groaned again. "Just take me home. I'll be fine."

"You won't be fine," she said as the officers got into the front. The patrol radio buzzed with static as the engine started. "You need a doctor."

"Take me home," he repeated. "I'll be fine."

"You should take him to a hospital, not to his apartment," Reenie said.

The officer shrugged. "Can't take him where he refuses to go."

They drove slowly down the dark street toward the lit one. Behind them, the bar owner had gone back inside, and the street

188

was quiet and empty. Inside the car, the patrol radio buzzed, and Charles's head was heavy and warm in her lap. She touched it gingerly, feeling for injuries. The car turned onto an avenue, lit with overhead street lamps and neon lights above storefronts. Ahead, Reenie saw the train station. Here and there people stood huddled on the sidewalks, but she didn't see the three assailants anywhere.

"Slow down so I can look more closely," she said, but even though the car slowed a little, she didn't spot the attackers.

"It's unlikely you'll find them," the officer on the passenger side told her. "And better that you don't. If they had a different story from yours, we'd have to haul all of you in before a judge. Bad enough that you've missed your train, I don't think you want to spend the rest of your night with New York City's finest."

Charles groaned and said something indistinguishable.

"But why can't you at least take us to a hospital so he can be treated?" Reenie asked. "Whatever it is you want to pretend happened or didn't happen back there, he's injured."

"We can't. Not unless he asks us too."

"Charles." She stroked his head. "You need a hospital. Tell them."

"Home," he said, speaking clearly.

She stared out the window and quit trying to make Charles get help or to watch for the men from the bar who had beaten him. The streets of the city streamed past in a blur of neon and darkness. Streetlights turned from green to yellow and red to green. They passed other patrol cars, the round red lights on top of their cars flashing, and they turned many times down different streets, until each new street seemed like the one before it. She saw clumps of people on sidewalks, an officer running. Dark human forms slumped against doorways. They passed an ambulance with flashing lights stopped next to a sidewalk, and she might have pointed it out, but she knew it would do no good by then and said nothing. Through the open door at the back, she glimpsed crouching figures and a stretcher with someone on it being moved. In the front seat, the officers discussed calls coming in through the static of their receiver. It was past midnight by now, and the city was alive with emergencies.

Eventually they pulled up in front of Charles's apartment building, an older, brick building that took up a quarter of a block. A paper advertisement blew past as she stepped out onto the curb, and a couple hurried by and went into the building, not stopping to see what a patrol car was doing on their street. She got out and bent down to help Charles. As he stood up, he leaned on her heavily.

"Stay out of trouble," the officer closest to them said through the opened window.

"I told you, the attack wasn't instigated," Reenie said back. "He didn't do anything. We were just trying to walk down the sidewalk."

"Then keep away from trouble." He rolled up his window, and the patrol car moved off.

Charles led her through the building's entrance to a narrow stairwell, and they slowly climbed three floors of steps with Reenie in the rear and Charles's hand gripping the rail. When he'd unlocked the door and they'd got inside and switched on a light, she went to the bathroom where she found iodine, scissors, a few gauze pads and tape. She assembled them on the kitchen table where Charles had set a bottle of whiskey.

"I hope you're not planning to drink that," she said.

"No," he said. "You can use it to clean me up." He pushed the bottle toward her along with a handkerchief.

She opened the bottle and dampened the handkerchief with the alcohol, then touched it to a scrape on his face. He winched. "Don't tell Patrick what happened. Don't tell anyone."

"Patrick is sure to find out. You'll be bruised for a while," she said, examining his head and neck.

"We won't see each other for a couple of weeks. He'll be so busy enacting his marriage plan. He probably won't even call. If I do run into him, I'll figure out what to say. I'm good at inventing stories."

She felt his head for lumps. He had one forming on the side. "You're lucky they didn't knock you unconscious." She found a raw, bloody scrape on his forearm and cleaned it, then applied the iodine.

Charles didn't even wince when she used the alcohol, and as she cleaned more scrapes and checked for wounds, he became very still. Eventually, he laid his head on the table. "I've had worse from drunken falls."

"I doubt that," she said as she moved her hands down his back, pushing gently on his ribs. "You should have asked to go to the hospital."

"If I'd done that, it would have turned into a worse scene, with me getting blamed."

"You would have gotten help. I think you may have a broken rib."

"It'll heal. Nothing they can do for broken ribs."

"You'd better piss and see if there's any blood in it, in case they injured something internal."

"They didn't. My innards are fine." His tone was between a groan and a dismissive shrug.

She helped him out of his shirt and brought a basin of warm water to the table with a washcloth. Carefully, she washed his hands and arms and used more alcohol to clean another scrape. With the warm, wet cloth, she gently wiped his back where bruises had begun to blossom. After cleaning him up, she found aspirin in his medicine cabinet. She said she wished they'd never gone to a bar near the train station and that she shouldn't have insisted, and he argued it wasn't her fault and she should stop worrying about him and phone for a cab and go to the train station.

"It's too late now," she said. "I'll wait until morning."

One minute he agreed and told her to go in to the bedroom to get some sleep, and the next he pleaded with her to leave him. "I'll be fine," he said. "Just don't tell Patrick. You can't tell anyone. You must promise not to tell."

She did promise several times, and she gave him his broken glasses, then went into his bureau and dug through a drawer for a spare pair. It was early morning by then, just an hour or so before dawn. She said she would make him some breakfast and found eggs and bread in the kitchen, along with a block of butter, jam and a bowl of oranges. While Charles dozed at the table, she brewed coffee and made up French toast with the eggs and bread. She piled two plates with food, and Charles ate heartily, finishing the French toast and then eating three oranges, peels and all.

While they were eating, the sky in the curtainless window turned from black to gray. She glimpsed another brick building several feet away. Dawn was creeping between them, and above the buildings a narrow wedge of gray sky showed. She'd been waiting for dawn so that this night would finally end and she could leave for the train station, but now that it was here, it seemed more desolate than the night had been. It rubbed out the shadows and streetlights, and there was an awful finality to how real it made everything seem.

Charles laid his head on the table. He'd put his dirty, bloodstained white shirt back on and his eyes were closed, but his face was still tense. She knew he wasn't asleep. She felt numb and her head throbbed dully as she cleaned up from the breakfast. Standing before the sink, washing their dishes, she thought she heard Charles weep, but when she turned off the water and walked over to him, he was quiet and still.

"I'll help you get into bed," she said, and he rose, allowing her to lead him. She drew a blanket over him.

"Thank you," he murmured as she switched the lights off. "We'll see each other again soon. I know we will."

She used his phone to telephone for a taxi and went down to the street to wait for it. Minutes later she was riding through the city again. The streets were gray and shuttered now, populated with only a few street cleaners and a person here or there hurrying somewhere. The bodies huddled against doorways the night before had vanished.

When she reached the station, she paid the driver and went inside. She bought her ticket and feeling jittery and wide-awake, went up to the platform even though the train wasn't due for a while. She walked past other passengers to the far end where the tracks disappeared into a black tunnel and stood there, shivering with the early morning cold. Eventually the train she was waiting for rushed toward her, and when it stopped, she got into the last car, which was nearly empty.

"Going to Boston?" she asked, checking with the conductor.

He nodded. "Eventually. Take a seat and get out your ticket."

She sat alone, and even when the car began to fill, no one sat next to her. The gray overcast morning sped past in the windows, but she didn't watch it or notice the stations where they stopped. She adjusted her seat back and shut her eyes, thinking she would sleep, but she couldn't slow her heart rate, and her thoughts raced behind her closed lids. She was leaving New York for good and returning to her life in Boston where she would continue teaching at the academy and marry Benjamin. She would never tell Arthur about the pregnancy. In fact, she didn't want any of them to know about it. She would try not to even think about any of them ever again.

About half way between New York City and Boston, her abdomen began to cramp. It started higher up, as a stomach pain, where the breakfast she'd eaten with Charles had congealed. She clamped down around the pain, bending forward. Her mouth watered with nausea, but she was determined not to throw up. Then gradually the nausea subsided, but the cramping spread and worsened until she doubled over then curled on the seat, lying on her side in a tight protected coil the same way Charles had lain on the street the night before.

She was miscarrying, she told herself, wondering vaguely if she was getting blood on the seat and what would happen if someone noticed. She'd phone for a cab when she reached Boston, she told herself. No one needed to find out. She'd tell Benjamin and her mother that she'd gotten sick on the train. She could make something up. She tried to reassure herself of this as the pain became more regular, as if she were being squeezed hard by a hand deep inside her.

Station houses appeared suddenly, flushed out of trees or brush, followed by factory buildings or track housing. A businessman across the aisle asked if she was okay and did she want a section of his paper. She accepted the comics and sat up for a while, trying to distract herself with Blondie and Li'l Abner, but the cramping did not abate. It seemed to be the only thing her body was capable of.

Finally, she steeled herself and walked the length of the car to the lavatory. There was a wait when she reached it, and she had to hold a seat back as the train rounded a curve in the track that ran along the Rhode Island coastline.

When it was her turn, she squeezed into the narrow space and fumbled with her slip and girdle. Underneath them, her abdomen was firm and round, and she felt immediate relief after pulling the girdle down. She rubbed her underwear with her thumb and felt the slick, dry nylon. There was not a hint of blood anywhere, not on the paper when she wiped herself, nor on her fingertips after she'd gently probed her opening. Her heart was pounding—danger averted, danger encountered, she didn't know which. Or would the cramping come first, the bleeding later?

The toilet sloshed below her as the train rounded another curve. She heard the brakes squeal and was pulling her girdle back up when the train lurched to stop and she bumped up hard against the sink. She got her skirt down, not bothering that the slip was folded up around her waist, and squeezed back out of the lavatory and down the aisle as more passengers boarded.

She found her seat and sat down hard as the train began to move again, then settled against the seat back and shut her eyes.

As she slipped into a light sleep, she felt the cramping lessoning. It turned into a dull ache that she associated with the childhood dread she'd felt when she'd started school or when she'd ruined her clothes or skinned her knees up riding too fast on her bike. She hadn't wanted to ride the school bus, and her brother had teased her about it until she'd hit him and been punished for it. Was that Samuel, who'd been killed on the ship in the ocean? Or Robert who missed World War II, and then somehow missed Korea, slipped right through the wheels of the administration, as her father told it. Robert was safe, but they'd buried an empty coffin for Samuel because his body was at sea. Her father's full coffin was in the ground next to the empty one. I'm having a miscarriage, she told them. Just don't tell anyone.

When the train stopped at a small-town station, she woke suddenly. A woman who'd sat down next to her was saying, "You were having such a nice nap, I tried not to wake you. You'll have the seat to yourself now. This is my stop."

She thanked the woman who was busy gathering her bags, and after the woman got off, she stretched out as best she could. The cramping had stopped altogether by now. She didn't even feel an ache. There was just pressure low down in her belly and a feeling of heaviness, the weight of something very solid. As the train sped up, the solid weight settled against her spine, and on the one hand she didn't believe it was real, but on the other hand she knew it was very real, an undeniable fact. She draped her coat over her, and the train established a steady, comforting rhythm, thrumming away underneath her. She was dimly aware of small movements under layers of fat and muscle, deep inside her abdomen. Her body felt strangely separate from her, an unknown entity. She thought of Benjamin, that she'd see him the next evening. They had a date to go out to dinner. Then she slept again, this time deeply and dreamlessly, until she reached Boston.

Later that week, she saw a new doctor, one recommended by Gloria, who separately confirmed her pregnancy after she told him she'd missed her monthly period. Then the following weekend, she told Benjamin about the missed period and positive pregnancy test while they were driving to his professor's house for a dinner he was hosting for his graduate researchers.

"I thought you couldn't get pregnant the first time, but the doctor said the test was conclusive."

"Of course it can happen the first time," Benjamin said, sounding irritated. "It's always possible, even around the time of a woman's menstruation."

"It *was* close to my period. That's how I became concerned a few weeks ago when my period didn't come. I waited a little, hoping it was just late."

"You'd only be a month or so along," he said, more to himself than to her. "That gives us time, but I suppose you'll be showing well before May."

"Yes, I think some women show right away."

They stopped at an intersection and sat there a minute or so before continuing through it. "I should have withdrawn—not that that's foolproof. If we'd been married, we'd have had something on hand, or we'd have discussed it at least." He sounded annoyed still, but it was mixed with resignation.

"We'll need to get married sooner," she said.

"What will we tell everyone? We've already announced the wedding date. They'll know why we changed it when the baby's born." It had been getting dark earlier and earlier in the evening, and now, even though it was only six o'clock, the sun had nearly set. They were moving into the darkest months of the year. He turned his headlights on.

"We'll just say we decided to not wait," she told him. "Later if they guess, it won't matter. We'll already be married, and they'll be excited about a new baby."

They turned onto a side road, then entered a neighborhood where the houses were far apart and there were no streetlights.

When they stopped at an intersection, the street signs were hard to read, and she wondered if he knew which way to turn. Then, just when he seemed about to drive forward, she felt him turn to look at her. Her heart skipped a little. She waited for him to say or ask something, but after a few seconds he looked back at the road and drove on, turning left down another street.

When they reached his professor's house, they parked on the road and had to walk down a long driveway. Neither of them spoke, and when she tried to think of something to say, she couldn't. Words failed her.

After a few minutes, they reached the house, lit festively with small lanterns. Benjamin held the door as she stepped inside, then helped her with her coat. Minutes later, he introduced her to their hosts and the other research assistants as his fiancée. She watched him for any sign of hesitation, but noticed nothing. He talked about their plans to get married giving the date they'd set in May, and everyone congratulated them. After dinner when their host proposed a toast of congratulations, Benjamin seemed genuinely happy.

Later, they held hands while walking back out the long drive. It was cooler by then, and she shivered in her coat. Before they reached the car, they stood for a few minutes and looked up at the sky. The stars looked brighter than usual, like slivers of ice. Benjamin pointed at the largest, a round, glowing burst of light. "I believe that's Jupiter up there."

She wanted to lean in and kiss him, but didn't, couldn't somehow. They got in the car and turned on the heat, and he sat for a minute, warming up, rubbing his hands together. "Did the doctor give you a due date?"

"Sometime in June. I didn't have good records of my cycle."

"But we know the date of conception."

"Well, I think the length of a pregnancy can vary."

He was quiet for a few minutes, flipping on the headlights and navigating the dark streets of the neighborhood. She wondered what he was thinking, but if he was questioning the due date, he didn't say anything about it. Instead, just before they came to the main road, he said, "We should get married soon, before you begin to show, but it'll be hard to get the use of the church on short notice."

"I'll look into it," she told him. "But let's not tell anyone else yet, not until we've sorted it out."

"They'll know soon enough." He glanced at her. "It'll be all right in the long run. I suppose it happens like this all the time."

"I was nervous about telling you."

"I'm sorry. I just hadn't expected it, but of course I'm happy about it. I wish it had waited a little longer, or I guess that we had waited, but you can't plan everything, and in the end it will just mean we'll marry a little sooner."

They went on talking about where they might live and how many rooms they'd need and how they'd tell their families, and little by little her anxiety dissipated. She relaxed against the seat and said in a joking manner that a year from now they might regret it all when they had a baby crying in their midst.

He laughed. "Our baby will never cry," he predicted.

A few weeks later, they were married in front of a justice of the peace with their families present. Afterward, they honeymooned on the coast, where he tromped contentedly along the windswept shore collecting rocks while she napped in a small rented cottage. She was suddenly more tired than she'd ever been in her life, and she could nod off even while playing her cello. They lived with Irena's mother for a few months, then moved into their first apartment, a small efficiency. When the baby was born, they put the crib next to the kitchen table, but a few weeks later they moved it into the bedroom area, behind a partition, and set up their bed in the living space where a couch had gone. The baby would not sleep on any kind of schedule, and it cried day and night, so often and so loud and for such long stretches of time, that Irena couldn't think straight. For that first year, she didn't teach at the academy and went for long periods of time without even trying to play her cello. She had no more thoughts about Arthur and The Modern Strings, and she was so exhausted she didn't even think about music. Benjamin, who was finishing his final year of graduate studies, ended up writing his research dissertation in the bathroom, with the water running to block the baby's cries. They couldn't get her to go to sleep, and when they finally did, she woke again if they made the slightest noise or even if a door closed too loudly in the adjacent apartment.

This went on for weeks and months. Irena lost track of time, and she thought she would go crazy if she had to listen to a crying baby any longer. Then one afternoon, feeling especially desperate after an hour of trying to get the baby to sleep, she laid Judith in the crib, picked up her cello and played. Bach's notes beat against the baby's howls. At first the baby cried louder, as if competing, but gradually, her cries softened. It turned out the music could quiet her. After that, Irena sat for hours next to the crib playing. At first, she only played Bach, afraid of risking anything else, but she eventually learned Judith loved any and all of the music she played and would smile contentedly while drifting off to Brahms or even Rachmaninoff.

Benjamin didn't question the pregnancy or the timing of the delivery, which was a few weeks earlier than expected, and that night on the drive to his professor's house was the only time she sensed he might have wondered about how she had shown up at his doorstep in the pouring rain. Judith looked like Irena from the beginning, but as she grew older, everyone said she had Benjamin's eyes and personality. She walked like him, raised her eyebrows like he did when she emphasized a point, and showed his aptitude for the sciences. He doted on

her, and as she grew older, she seemed more and more his du-
plicate, to the point where others remarked upon it, and Irena
had to agree, the resemblance really was extraordinary.

Chapter 12

What is that?

A piece of music someone wrote for her. The composer was famous, I think, at one time.

Really? I've never heard of him.

That's what her daughter said. They're arranging for a performance.

She could not, had thought she never would. Her body had taken over, and the baby's birth had happened with such speed she had no choice but to be carried along with it. Nothing else had felt as real as that, not her music or her love for music, and not her encounters with Arthur Cohen. Someone else had come from her and made demands on her, making any thoughts of Arthur and The Modern Strings feel foolish.

She was in the memory unit remembering. The pieces slid through her, then slipped away. They vanished like flashes of light and became smaller and smaller. She became smaller, shrinking to the size of an ant. She stopped climbing and did not try to reach the pinnacle. When she looked she saw she was already there. Below her swarms of tiny ants like herself struggled up the long incline.

Her playing had been lovely and accomplished, charming and delightful, extraordinary, unexpected, astounding even. People said she was a virtuoso, an unexpected talent, and a prodigy. They said she would become a soloist. As she grew older they said amateur orchestras were lucky to have her, and what a stroke of luck for her students, other prodigies that she ended up teaching. She was fortunate they said. One day professional orchestras would accept female cellists. Gender would not matter. In the basement there were boxes of sheet music she'd once played and programs from her concerts. Some were written upon or torn, others were in pristine condition, as if newly printed. After Benjamin died when she had to sell the house, Judith carried the boxes upstairs and they sat in the living room looking at the music. Mother, Judith kept asking, what concert was this for?

Irena didn't know and later two men arrived who loaded everything into a truck. All those boxes, a labyrinth. One couldn't stop or give up. One had to devote. She had taught at the music academy for twenty years, all that time playing with the civic orchestra, along with minor chamber groups, waiting for a chance to play again with professionals. In between her work, she'd raised Judith. At one point she got pregnant again and lost the baby at four months, no known reason the doctor said. Benjamin wanted another child but after the miscarriage, she didn't conceive again. When birth control pills became available, she asked her doctor for a script and hid them in a drawer.

You had to bide your time, had to exert patience. It was the late 1960's and 1970's before major symphony orchestras began to audition women, and even then, they hired only a few—mostly violinists, flutists and harpists. The cello was more difficult, took longer. It was considered a man's instrument. When major orchestras and professional groups were told they had to audition all qualified musicians including women, the hiring committees hung curtains between themselves and the auditioning musician, meant to hide the musician's race and gender, but some of the curtains were thin enough that they could still see the musician's shape. In other cases they asked the auditioning musician questions, forcing them to speak. You had to answer or be disqualified, but as soon as you spoke they heard a female voice. Few women cellists were auditioned and fewer still were hired. They were not sought after.

She did not know anymore, could not say. The doctor

claimed her condition would worsen and confusion was to be expected. Benjamin could explain it. He understood the human body and the brain, had researched the exchange of proteins. She no longer recognized the nurse or the person who did the straightening and sometimes even Judith seemed a stranger, that woman who said *Mother* and talked of the upcoming performance of Arthur Cohen's sonata with an enthusiasm that would have pleased her if she'd understood it. Her memory was everything now. It trampled all present-day concerns about nutrition and hydration and where all this was headed. She did not think about where she was headed. She'd wiped her slate, pulled the wool away. A flash of light, a lightning bolt or wave of electricity that exposed the story it had stored, the knowledge it had known. A bullet and a barrage of bullets. She had taken them in the back of the head, in the front and on all sides. The strokes had broken synapses, strings of neurons that were so complex she could never grasp her own mind.

After Benjamin's death, when she and Judith were cleaning out the house to put it up for sale, they'd found his aquariums in the basement. The glass shone as if it were new, and he'd stored the pumps and filters so neatly in those plastic bags. It made Irena cry because he'd always been so meticulous and must have spent hours cleaning and storing everything. Judith held up a bag of polished marbles. "Mother, look at this. He saved all these."

Each thought flashed like a light sparking. She flashed and the spark stayed lit. She watched them from her window. *Beautiful* Benjamin said. He was next to her and they lay for hours quietly amazed by all the flashes of brilliance that came from her.

Let's see.
Let's have a little more.
Mother, did you hear what I said?
I hope she can go to that performance.
I think it would matter.

It all mattered, each flash of brilliance. She saw them in their entirety, a whole universe.

She didn't see any of the members of The Modern Strings for nearly fifteen years, but in 1968 when she learned Arthur Cohen had composed an opera and there was a staged premiere planned in Central Park, she wrote to him at the address for the opera company, saying she'd love to perform his music again, love to be in the orchestra. He didn't respond, but a few weeks later she got a phone call from the conductor's assistant offering her a position in the orchestra's string section.

Benjamin didn't want her to go. He said he didn't like her going to New York City alone, and they argued about it up until the last minute when he was driving her to the train station. Judith sat in the back seat and Irena remembered an awkward, brooding silence.

"Call me when you arrive," he said when he pulled up in front of the station.

She said she'd manage her bags by herself and not to bother with parking, then said a quick goodbye through the car window at the side of the busy street.

On the train, she looked over the score, and when she arrived in New York City, she went straight to the park for a dress rehearsal. Walking past the rows of folding chairs still being set up for the evening performance under the large tent, she spotted Arthur standing near the orchestra with a pad of paper, making notes. He wore a black shirt and black jeans, even though it was summer, but other than that and his dark framed glasses, he looked the same with his longish hair that was now fashionable.

They greeted one another, and he told her that Patrick was also in the orchestra. "You'll see him shortly, Reenie," he said.

"What about Lawrence and Charles?" she asked. She hadn't had any news of the quartet in years.

He said the quartet had disbanded several years ago and

204

that Lawrence had taken a teaching position in Minnesota of all places. "And Charles," he said. "Well, you may not have heard, Charles passed away."

"No," she said. She hadn't known, she hadn't seen him since she'd come to New York that last time to hear the quartet perform. They'd written once or twice, and he'd called her a couple of times during that year when she'd gotten married and had Judith, not long after her disastrous trip to New York where she'd missed her train home. "When?" she said. She couldn't remember if she'd spoken to him or not the last time he'd called.

"Three years ago now," Arthur said. "It was an accident, very sudden. We were all shocked. He was hit by a car."

"An accident," she repeated. "Where? In the city?"

He nodded. "It happened late at night. He was crossing a street on foot, and some idiot ran a red light. We were all devastated of course. Before that, I hadn't seen Charles for months, maybe even a year or more. Patrick called to tell me. The driver got away with negligence. He paid a fine is all, most likely. There was a funeral a week later, and the driver sent a lavender funeral wreath covered with lilies, so many of them, they stank. I'll never forget that smell. Patrick said it was meant as a comment on Charles's lifestyle. Someone, I forget who, threw the wreath on a pile of rubbish at the back of the cemetery."

Arthur spoke quickly, intent on telling the whole story, even though more musicians and singers were arriving, and someone was trying to get his attention. "Where is he buried?" Irena asked before he turned away.

"Out on Long Island. I'll give you the address if you want to drive out there while you're here."

She said she'd like to, even though she'd have little time while she was there, and she didn't have a car to make the drive. Then she sat in the last seat at the back of the string section suddenly unable to even picture Charles. All she could see was the awful wreath Arthur had described, and it made her feel sick. She had answered his first letter with a short note and not answered the second one. She remembered one phone conversation after she'd had Judith. She'd said nothing about having had a baby, and instead they'd talked about a violinist Charles had met when he'd played with a small orchestra in upstate New York. Charles had fallen immediately in love with the man, but they lived so far apart, which meant they'd only seen each other once since then.

"Love is such a tease," he'd said.

The area in the tent around the stage was filling up with orchestra members, singers, and sound technicians. Other musicians were introducing themselves to her, and when she said hello to Patrick, he showed her the photos he carried of his wife and two children—a boy and a girl. When she said she'd just learned about Charles, he nodded, but the orchestra had started tuning. "Sadly enough, life happens," he said as he took his seat.

The rehearsal took place in the daylight, but by evening when she arrived for the performance, the light was fading and they were given small flashlights for their music stands. The sky was cloudless, and someone said the stars would be very bright. That was the thing about an outdoor concert—seating was unlimited but bad weather could alter everything. Thank goodness for a mild summer night with no hint of rain.

Arthur sat in the first row, just twenty feet or so away from the orchestra. His face showed little expression, but his eyes were piercing and intently focused. Someone said the lead soprano, a new, unknown singer, was in love with him. The sun had just set, and past the large, open tent was a wall of dark trees. The audience filled the inside of the tent and spread out on the grass beyond it. No one had expected such a huge crowd, and everyone in the orchestra was talking about it because there was just the one performance planned and the singers, while good, were not well known. The setting was minimal, even the lighting was restricted to a few spotlights. The music was experimental, juxtaposing classical with jazz and rock, and the score was difficult because of the mixture. There was an electronic synthesizer and extra percussion.

The subject of the opera was war and like the music, the libretto was also very modern and contained pieces from current news clips about Vietnam alongside World War II headlines and references to distant mythic wars where men had fought with swords. The chorus interspersed singing with shouts of protest. They sang lamentations, marched into battle, fought with guns, explosives and swords, then shouted the protests of angry crowds, showing that war destined humans to play three roles, a turning gyre of fighting, protest, and lamentation.

The score mixed the three themes. Violins screeched out a warning, an English horn sounded a battle cry, and the tympani became a cannon. Later the strings whispered a lament. All the instruments played the protests, which roared with a chaos of sound, greater than that of the battles. It was hard to stand the music at certain points, and Irena sensed it was meant to be uncomfortable, to crawl beneath the listener's skin.

Sitting with the orchestra, focused on playing her cello, she missed some of the words and the costumes, but she felt the pounding rhythms and heard the clashing sounds. She felt the excitement of performing something new and different and difficult. The music could not be predicted. It went in one direction and then another, turning from a banging rock rhythm to a Bach inspired lament without warning. It was nothing like the music she'd been performing with the civic orchestra. The writing for the strings was lovely and sad and ghostly like the folds of lamentation. Something would have to break—protest or lament or the fight. There were bodies being attacked or kept in starvation. She glimpsed the suggestion of horrible acts. A soprano's high voice cried out, followed by the chorus's shouts: "Inside the cradle of the world, Jehovah is calling. Inside the arc where the bombs won't stop falling." The wind instruments whistled several measures of piercing notes, and then there was a single gunshot. She glanced up at the stage where a figure knelt as another human shape bent with a pistol held close to the kneeling figure's head.

"Assassination," chanted the chorus. She heard the outrage of the thundering percussion. A singer turned the attack into a protest, while behind him the chorus became soldiers carrying machine guns under the sound of whirring helicopter blades. Then the strings took over. They made a rainstorm of Napalm that fell on forest and fields and singers and children. A monk chanted in a different language at the edge of the stage as the music reached a crescendo, followed by a coda as the chorus sang another Jehovah refrain.

The notes teetered on a jagged edge, but then the music softened into the subdued sounds of a requiem. This was well after the intermission and toward the end of the opera, during the final act. The singers' faces were painted white for the finale. She glimpsed them floating above her. They were the dead. Or they were marching for the dead. The music became solemn and absolute. This was the truth at the center of the gyre—all had died. Nothing but ghosts remained.

The players and performers were squeezed into the large tent with the audience. Beyond the tent, people who had bought cheaper tickets sat on the grass. Later the newspapers would estimate that well over five hundred had gathered to hear the opera. Some were opera or music lovers, but many were young war protesters, tired of the draft and the atrocities on television and in the newspapers. With so many people flooding the gates of Central Park, there had been no way to control the open seating outside the tent after dark when the opera began. Those without tickets had skirted the ushers and ducked under ropes and around partitions.

The opera ended to a standing ovation, and the conductor let the orchestra know that they would repeat the lead soprano's lament as an encore. Afterward, echoed shouts of "Jehovah!" rang out from the audience even while they were dispersing. As the orchestra members began packing their instruments, the audience flooded toward the stage.

"Be careful leaving the area," the director advised. "Give the audience a chance to leave the park first. It's a very large crowd. Don't try to push your way through it."

The warning quickly proved useless as more people from the audience swarmed the stage and orchestra pit which was set up behind it, knocking over music stands and props. The orchestra members needed to walk out of the park to the street in order to get cabs. "Come with us," one of the violinists called out to Irena, and she quickly packed up her instrument and walked with a group toward the park's entrance.

People pressed close on all sides, and she grasped a horn player's arm, trying to keep together with the others. She couldn't see where they were headed, but everyone was moving in the same direction. They were being funneled, like fish into a net, as they walked through the sparsely lit park. With each step, she felt the crowd grow and tighten, so that pretty soon she was nearly shoulder to shoulder with those next to her. The group of musicians became separated and she had to drop the horn player's arm, but she kept close to him and one of the violinists. They walked on and on, and the way out of the park seemed much farther than when she'd arrived. All around her the crowd pushed forward. She couldn't see beyond it to where it stopped, and she couldn't understand why they hadn't yet reached the entrance. Eventually, she lost the horn player, and then the violinist. They drifted apart, submerged by the crowd, and she became surrounded by people she didn't recognize, many of them young people carrying protest signs—*War is Hell! End the war in Vietnam now! Nixon is a Pig! End the draft, we won't go!*

She walked on, hoping she'd soon reach the street and trying not to bump up against anyone, but someone grabbed hold of her arm. "This way," they shouted. She was pushed and pulled. Trees loomed darkly above the sea of people, and everything was rippling. She was part of a tide made of moving bodies.

She gripped the handle of her cello case and kept walking, had no choice. She walked and walked but couldn't reach the end. From behind her and in front of her, she heard pieces of the chant— "Jehovah! Jehovah is calling! Inside the arc where the bombs won't stop falling!"—as the crowd began singing the chorus from the opera. Someone called out a warning, *Watch out*, or *look out!* All around her, she saw strangers and above them black branches and a few stars through the leaves. The strangers pressed against her, and she was led slowly forward by them, toward something.

The ground was uneven, lumpy with grass, and when someone bumped against her, she stumbled. Then everything suddenly flew open. The crowd in front of her split apart, and she looked about frantically but could find no one familiar even though this area was better lit and the moving mass of bodies had separated. Before her lay the street. The crowd was quickly spilling into it, over the sidewalk. She heard car horns blaring and glimpsed a police officer standing with his arms outstretched yelling, "Stay on the sidewalks and move along!"

A blinding light flashed, and up ahead she saw the crowd overflowing, filling the street and shouting, "Jehovah, Jehovah!" Others were shouting, "No more war! No more killing!" but the shouts of "Jehovah!" were loudest. They were an enormous wave of bodies, flooding the lanes of traffic and calling down the wrath of the old god.

She was forced by the moving crowd onto the street. Here and there, she glimpsed someone carrying an instrument, but she couldn't get close to anyone who seemed familiar. Someone called her sister. Someone else shouted at her to watch out because the bodies were so close together now that her cello hit up against those near her. The crowd, which had opened up and spread out for a brief moment when they reached the street, now pressed tighter as more and more people poured into the street, seemingly out of the pavement itself. Someone shoved into her from behind, and she stumbled forward, pulled by the weight of her cello. She hit against another body and caught herself before she reached the ground.

Up ahead, she heard police shouting orders to disperse. She glimpsed a line of officers along the sides of the road. Walled in, the crowd had become a solid mass.

She kept looking for a known face, someone she could hold onto who might know the way out, but there was no one, and there appeared to be no way out of the mass of people which moved as if they were one. Then, suddenly, up ahead, she glimpsed Arthur. She called out to him over the sea of heads, but he didn't seem to hear her. The people surrounding him were grabbing his arms and legs, pulling him somewhere or pulling him apart. She couldn't tell which. She tried to reach him, but he was quickly swept away.

After that, she couldn't make out anything clearly. She couldn't tell what was going on or where she should turn or which direction led out of the massive crowd. She saw flashes—a dark face, a red scarf, blue denim, the pale skin of an arm. Some of them wore white paint on their faces, similar to the white makeup worn by the chorus when they sang their final lament. She was pulled one way, drawn down the street and then moved in another direction. She didn't seem to make any progress. At one point, she glimpsed the horn player she'd left the park with and tried to grasp hold of him, but she was quickly swept away by the rush of the current.

Her cello was battered this way and that, hitting up against her legs and against the bodies of others. She gripped the handle of its case as tightly as she could. It nearly twisted out of her hand, then slammed into her thigh, but she didn't release it, refused. Someone who seemed to recognize her called her Sister. Someone else with war paint on his face and a fresh Mohawk on his head veered suddenly away. Was he falling? She heard music, a theme she'd played in the opera, but couldn't tell where it was coming from. Her skirt was pulled. Her stockings were torn.

Then from the front of the crowd, she heard a new swell of the chant "Jehovah!" The name grew louder and louder. "Strike them down!" someone yelled, and the imperative became a new chant. She peered over the sea of heads, trying to see where the shouts were coming from. Not far from where she stood, they were lifting Arthur skyward. Someone had pulled off his black jacket and was waving it like a flag. She glimpsed the expression on his face, which she read as fear, and she tried to push through the crowd to reach him. Then in a flash of light from a street lamp she saw him carried, held aloft by a large group. Some of them held his arms, others held his legs. There were people directly under him supporting his trunk and head. She heard his voice cry out in answer to the shouts, and she saw his face again, more clearly this time. It was not fear in his expression, but excitement, and joy even. Those who held him moved slowly away, carrying him through the crowd for all to see. Around them the chant of *Jehovah* grew softer but more insistent. They were chanting to Arthur. Earlier she had thought they were tearing him apart, but it turned out they were worshiping him.

They carried him farther down the street. The crowd seemed to part for them, ebbing and flowing around his lifted body. For a while, she kept up. She kept him at the center of her vision. He was lifted higher and higher, until he towered over the crowd, shouting "Jehovah!" in answer to their murmuring chant. Having unleashed a tidal wave in Central Park, he was riding the very crest of it.

Along with the others, Irena was moving in the wake of those bearing Arthur. She was so absorbed by his passage that she didn't see what was behind her until she heard the crack of a stick and someone crying out. She spun around. The police were everywhere, shoving people from the street and shouting. Farther away she saw the fog of what she later learned was tear gas. The crowd behind her was screaming. A man grabbed hold of her arm.

"Are you with us?"

"No!" she yelled back. "I'm a musician."

He had shoulder length hair and a beard, and she smelled the sour sweetness of his breath just before he let her go and reeled away. Then a woman grasped hold of her arm and spun her around. She saw the woman up close—her wide eyes and the braid of her hair that was coming undone. "Go home, Mama!" the woman shouted. "People like you are the reason for the war and my brother getting killed." She swung her hand, and Irena ducked, thinking the woman meant to strike her, but instead the woman reached down and made a grab for the cello. Irena felt the woman's hand on her own, painfully turning her wrist and pulling at her fingers.

"Stop!" she yelled, gripping the handle as hard as she could. "I'm just a musician."

"That's the problem with you," the woman spat at her. "You play a piece like that with no conscience."

Within seconds, the cello was ripped away from her, and the woman disappeared in the crowd. Irena spun around, looking for the large dark case, but she didn't see it anywhere. It was lost in the sea of people. She pushed forward into them, in the same direction the woman had gone, her fingers still curled at her side as if she held the handle of the case. Single shouts merged into a roar of sound. She thought she heard a gunshot. Something slammed into her. She braced herself but was pushed down, nearly trampled except that someone lifted her back up again. She searched the crowd for the woman or for Arthur or anyone she might recognize but found no one. The crowd blocked her view, and she could only see what was up close. She couldn't tell how large the protest was. She couldn't find the end of it. The protest and its crowd might have filled all of New York City.

For several minutes she stood still, caught in the press of people. Then all at once the crowd separated, and she was in the street with many people who were running. A police officer yelled into a bullhorn that everyone had better disperse. Protesters were throwing bottles at the officers. She heard cries and shouts and the sound of exploding glass. She couldn't tell which way to go and was caught in between the protesters and the officers, engulfed in angry shouts and cries, when she saw in front of her a cloud rising above the crowd. It hovered there, then began to disperse, and she knew instinctively that she needed to get away from it, only she had no choice but to go toward it. Someone yelled that it was tear gas, and everyone turned, attempting to run away in a blind stampede. They pushed her and shoved against her. Nearby, a man was knocked over. She watched as he was trampled. The gas burned her eyes, her throat, and her lungs, and she couldn't stop coughing. Within minutes, she couldn't see anything except the smoke. She heard screams and cries, then something crashed into her, and she saw a face up close, tortured and screaming. Other bodies pushed against her own. She couldn't stand still but was pressed one way and then another, always moving closer to the center of the mayhem. The flood of people went on forever with no way out, and the cloud of gas went on forever so that she couldn't see what was going on. Then suddenly she was alone in the cloud. No one was pushing her or ramming against her or trying to get past her, and a hand reached down and took her arm. An officer wearing a black mask lifted her. He directed her toward a nearby wagon.

"On your feet," he said, because she had collapsed onto the pavement.

"I'm a musician," she stammered, coughing.

"And I'm a police officer." He yanked her up and hauled her to the wagon. "Get inside, lady!"

"You don't understand," she yelled, trying to pull away from his grip. Her eyes were still tearing and her throat burned when she spoke. "I was a musician playing for the opera earlier in Central Park, and I got caught up in all this. I'm not a protester and someone just grabbed my cello."

"You picked the wrong time and place to perform." He grasped her arm a little harder and pushed her toward the wagon where the smoke cloud had dissipated so that the scene came suddenly into view. Officers were forcing people into the back of a few paddy wagons. One of them hit a young man with a billy club when he tried to pull away, shouting, "Bastards!"

"But I'm not part of this, and I need to find my cello," she said.

"As far as I'm concerned, if you played in that opera, you're responsible for this. You stirred it all up. You can tell the judge what happened when you see him."

They reached the back of the wagon. Her blouse was streaked with dirt, and her arm was bleeding from a cut. Her nose and throat stung and her eyes were still tearing.

"I was just trying to get back to my hotel, and my instrument was taken, stolen," she said, trying once more to explain what had happened as he forced her to the wagon.

He swung the back door open and pushed her toward it, motioning for her to climb in. "Explain it to the judge," he said.

"But I'm not a protester."

"Get in, now. And you too." He grabbed hold of a young man with startled looking eyes, curly hair and soft features that made him look much younger, maybe twelve years old, and shoved the two of them against the wagon so they had no choice but to climb up into it.

As soon as they were inside, the officer closed the back of the wagon, and they sat on the floor in darkness. Around her, she heard the murmurs of voices speaking. Someone was crying. She felt behind her, and someone said, "There's room for you on the bench." She scooted toward the voice, then rose and sat again, squeezed between two young men. People were coughing still from the tear gas. Some said they'd been separated from friends, and a woman claimed she'd been hurt. A man was coughing and retching. He said he couldn't breathe. Irena coughed also. Her eyes and nose still stung. Her face burned and she felt a dull pain on the side of her head. The door to the wagon suddenly opened, and in a burst of light she saw a black-masked officer push more people into the wagon. She saw others inside the wagon already crowded together and squeezed herself into a narrow line that disappeared when she closed her burning eyes.

"We each get a phone call when we reach the station," someone said when the door closed again.

"Yeah, and they won't have enough cells for all of us, that's for certain."

"Whatever you do, don't post bail or let anyone else post it. That defeats the purpose. We need the morning papers to state that large numbers of us were locked up. I don't even plan to use my phone call."

Irena shivered despite the heat from the close contact of bodies. She had stopped coughing, but her eyes and throat and lungs still burned.

"What were you doing here?" a woman asked her.

"I was a musician playing for the opera," she said.

"Cool. What instrument?"

"The cello."

"That's the big stringed one, right?"

"Yes," Irena told her. "I lost it in the crowd. Someone grabbed it from my hand."

No one said anything for a while. There were more shouts outside, and something hit up against the wagon, rocking it. Those at the back tried to force the doors open, but couldn't.

"This is hell," someone said.

"This is freedom," someone else said. "This is what it takes."

They went on sitting in the dark. Someone was still crying, and the inside of the wagon grew hot because of bodies pressed together. Underneath the smell of the tear gas, which was everywhere on people's skin and clothes, was the stench of sweat and anger and fear. Irena sat silently. She heard a rumbling sound

216

of an engine starting and felt the wagon jerk forward, knocking her against the others. She held onto the seat under her and tried to keep her place on the bench as the wagon swayed, veering one way and then another. She was thrown against the others as the wagon turned a corner, and when it stopped suddenly she slid off the bench onto the floor. Someone grabbed her arm and helped her back up while they sat for a moment unmoving. Inside the wagon all was dark, and it was impossible to tell where they were and if they were still surrounded by a crowd or well away from it.

"They might never let us out of the back of this thing," someone said.

"They have to. It would be illegal to keep us here."

"They don't care about legal or illegal."

Eventually, they started up and bumped over uneven ground. Then they stopped again, and this time, the back of the wagon opened and they were told to get out. Irena lowered herself to the floor of the wagon, then stretched her feet down, feeling unsteady. An officer told her to get in the line that was forming, and she followed the others inside to a large holding cell where she listened to confusing rules about phone calls. She looked about her for Arthur or other musicians or singers but recognized no one. The cell was full of young protesters. Some wore white paint on their faces, and she saw a few programs from the opera trampled on the floor. She was allowed to go out in the hall and wait in a long line for the bathroom, then directed back to the cell. The cell was dirty and brightly lit. The lingering smell of tear gas mixed with the smells of cigarettes, perspiration, and urine to form a stink that she felt sticking to her skin and clothes like the film of grime that covered her.

"Will they let us go?" she asked someone, late that night as they filed down a hallway to line up before a judge.

"Hardly."

She kept watching for anyone she knew, but still saw no one. The long line of protesters went out the door and down a hallway. She was so tired when she reached the judge, that she had trouble standing, but speaking clearly, she quickly explained her story.

He sighed. "Wrong choice for an opera."

"I didn't write it," she told him. "I only performed in it. If you're a musician, you have to take work where you can find it."

"Well," he said, gazing past her at those behind her. "I think you probably had more choice than you indicate. In the future, I'd advise you to consider the music more carefully before you agree to perform it. I'm going to go ahead and release you, but don't involve yourself in anything like this again. I see here that you live in Boston. I'd advise you to return home as quickly as possible. Does your husband know where you are?"

"What about my cello?" she asked, ignoring his question about her husband. But he was already waving her ahead and focused on the next person in line.

"You'll have to come back here tomorrow if you want to fill out paperwork on the theft. You'd have a very long wait if you tried to do that tonight," he told her as an officer motioned her toward the exit.

Back in her hotel room, she took a shower and eventually slept, despite aching all over. She woke early and went back to the station first thing and insisted on filing the paperwork about the theft, even though the detective said they could do nothing to find the cello beyond putting out an alert to local music stores in case whoever stole it tried to sell it. It was worth thousands of dollars, she told him. Her father had bought it years ago for her at an auction. It had special meaning to her because of that, and she had to have the instrument for her work. Didn't all that mean anything?

The officer only shrugged and told her the department had little time to waste on random theft that had occurred in a crowd, and since she couldn't state any identifying details about the person who'd grabbed it, they'd have nothing to go on.

218

She took a cab from the station back to the hotel and phoned her mother and then Benjamin, leaving a message about the reason for her delay. Then she phoned the opera director's office to see if they could help her. The director's assistant said she would let everyone there know what had happened in case one of them had seen the theft or noticed her cello. Then, less than an hour later, Arthur himself phoned to apologize. He offered to drive round to get her if she needed to go back to the police station.

"No," she said. They'd told her to wait until the next day. They'd contact her if it was found. She was planning on staying over for a couple of days, hoping to get the instrument back.

"I'll come by to see you," he said. "I could take you for a drive while you're waiting. At least you wouldn't be sitting around. Maybe you'd like to see where Charles is buried, if that's not too depressing."

"Yes," she said. "I'd like that."

Chapter 13

An hour later Arthur drove up to the front of the hotel in a rust-orange-colored Ferrari, a new car he said, bought just months ago, with a tight interior that smelled of new upholstery. The bucket seats were close together, and his hand brushed against her when he shifted gears. He drove fast, with the assurance of a cab driver, squeezing between cars and through intersections as stop lights turned red. Tall city buildings loomed suddenly in front of them as they rounded tight corners.

Right away, he asked what she thought of the opera's score. "Your honest opinion," he said.

She talked about the excitement of the score, with its mixture of classical, jazz and rock and the unexpected, chaotic rhythms.

"But was it moving? Did it convey the emotions of war? That's what I was after."

"It caused that big protest," she said. "I think you would have to call it moving, especially the requiem with those costumes and painted faces."

"Well, the idea for the white painted faces at the end was mine, but I was barely consulted on the costumes."

"The lament played by the strings in the final act was lovely."

"Lovely?" he asked.

"Emotional," she added. "Haunting. But I don't know much about the war. I'm not political."

"You don't have to be political to notice the current feeling against the war and the government. It's everywhere. That energy and confusion were what I was after with those three conflicting themes. My first opera wasn't even recorded, and you might not have heard about it, because it was performed only once and got no reviews. I wrote it during the few years when I was teaching, and it's impossible to do anything truly creative when you're tied to a university, I'm convinced of that."

"Well you certainly did move people with this opera, an entire huge audience that went out and caused a riot in the streets. And you got reviewed this time," she said.

"Yes, and the article about the protest on the front page of *The New York Times* will help, even if it wasn't directly about the music. It did include my name, more than once." He smiled.

"I saw you just before my cello was taken. You were in the street, not far from where I was standing. The crowd lifted you in the air."

He shifted the car into higher gear. They were leaving the city quickly behind now, headed for a bridge that would take them to Long Island. "I couldn't see anything, beyond that mass of people. It was crazy, wasn't it?" He glanced at her, laughing at the memory. "I felt like I was flying when they lifted me. When they put me down, we were away from the main part of the crowd, on a side street."

"Did the police arrest you?"

"No, there was a car waiting on the side street, and I got dropped off near where I met some of the others for drinks. I don't know how they knew where to take me. It felt almost like it was planned, even though it must have been spontaneous. It was good fortune, after being carried above the crowd and seen by so many of them, I was whisked away. We meant to have a cast party at the bar, but with the protest, hardly anyone made it."

He turned and glanced at her. "You weren't one of the ones rounded up, were you?"

She said she was and described the large cell where she'd stayed and the hearing with the judge who'd let her go.

221

"I can't believe the police, arresting musicians. An article should be written about that. We should have given you combat training at the rehearsal. Were you there when they threw the tear gas?"

"Yes," she said. "It was terrifying."

"Terrifying?" he asked. "Or exciting."

"Well, both," she said trying to see it as he saw it. "If they'd handed out maps of the area showing escape routes, that would have been helpful, although there were so many people, that even with maps escape might not have been possible. How many were there, hundreds?"

"The estimates are well over a thousand, and that's just for the concert attendance, including the ones on the grass. There were at least twice as many who didn't buy tickets, and there were even more at the protest it caused afterward." He smiled at that. "And they say classical music is out of touch and can't attract an audience the way it used to or make a meaningful statement."

They left behind the tight streets, high buildings, and crowded sidewalks of the city, and after crossing a bridge, they soon got off the highway onto a smaller, two-lane road. They traveled faster, past billboards, factories, and wide expanses of trees until they came rather suddenly upon the cemetery. It spread for miles, and looking out the window as they watched for the entrance, she saw what must have been thousands of gravestones covering a hillside and beyond—white against the dark green grass. They parked and Arthur, relying on memory, led them up the long hill. They passed a tree or a bush here and there, but mostly there were just rows and rows of stones, and it was slow going because they had to walk carefully between them. The sun cast shadows of the stones over each grave. She tried to avoid stepping on the graves, but it proved impossible. She was walking next to the dead, over them, and among them.

"Is all of New York City buried here?" she asked.

"Possibly," Arthur said. "At least all of the dead."

It was very windy on top of the hill, and the grass was less cared for. Dandelions and crab grass grew between the stones. She was wearing a full skirt and one of those Mexican blouses that were becoming popular, with a loosely gathered neckline, and she had to keep hold of her clothing, alternately tugging on the skirt and wrapping her arms around her middle. Arthur couldn't remember the exact location of Charles's grave, and they read rows and rows of stones before they found it. There was nothing different about his site, nothing to set it apart from the others. The words on his stone read, Charles Breedlove, 1927-1966, Loved by Many.

This is what is left, she thought. Nothing of his humor or his passion. "Do you think that driver hit him on purpose?"

"No," Arthur said. "Besides, there's no way to know something like that."

"But you said the driver sent that awful wreath."

"That doesn't mean he ran a red light with the intention of killing someone. He wouldn't have known ahead of time that Charles would be in the crosswalk."

"Still, if it was on purpose, it makes me feel sick."

He glanced at her. "It could make you feel sick either way."

She hugged herself tighter. "Do you remember when I came down to hear the quartet perform, shortly after I substituted and just after Lawrence joined?"

Arthur nodded. "We were playing a new piece of mine. It was just a couple of months after the festival, one of the first times Lawrence performed with us."

"Afterward you and Patrick and Lawrence went out somewhere with your musician friends from New Jersey, and Charles and I went to a bar together near the train station to have a drink, because I was getting the train back later that night. When we left the bar, a group of roughnecks followed us out. They shoved Charles down on the sidewalk and kicked him. I didn't think fast enough. Finally, the owner of the bar came out, and I screamed and the police arrived and the men ran off."

"I think, unfortunately, he was used to that sort of thing. He wasn't good at watching out for himself."

"I stayed with him until morning to make sure he was all right. He was pretty badly injured. I was fairly certain he had broken a rib or something, but he refused to go to a hospital." She glanced at Arthur. "Do you know what we talked about?" she asked.

Arthur didn't speak or nod or shake his head.

"Patrick," she told him. "It started in the bar while we were drinking. He said Patrick was getting married, because he wanted a position at Curtis."

"Well, that was maybe Charles's interpretation," Arthur said warily. "Patrick certainly wouldn't have described it that way. Charles had a very strong imagination."

"But Charles and Patrick were close, very close. Lovers even. Charles told me they were."

Arthur was staring at the stone, looking troubled. "They were close friends, and there might at one point have been a few shared intimacies, but nothing more than that. Patrick admired Charles's playing. We all did. He had an immense talent, even though he abused it. That's the way it is with alcoholics." He turned away from the stone and looked at her. "And they have distorted views because of their drinking."

He didn't say anything more, but he continued to watch her for a response and his expression was guarded. "But the rejection, the fact that Patrick didn't fully reciprocate, that's what drove him to drink," she said.

"Nothing drove him. He drank too much, and it wasn't because of his lifestyle or his desires or passions or anything else. After he died, they found dozens of paper bags full of empty bottles in his apartment. He didn't know when enough was enough. It had gotten to the point before he died where he often couldn't function, and because of that he had no work. All that talent, wasted."

"But…," she began.

He cut her off. "I don't mean any insult by this, Reenie, but you knew us all for a very brief time."

She nodded, said nothing, and after a few minutes, turned away from the grave, needed suddenly to walk. He'd told her she hadn't known them and that what she thought she'd known wasn't true. She couldn't stand to hear anything more and made her way down the hill. She wanted to get back to the car quickly, but the gravestones forced her to move slowly, stepping sideways to avoid them. She slipped and stumbled, then bent and took off her shoes. The grass was cool and damp on her stocking feet. A stone punctured the nylon and stayed against the arch of her foot even after she tried to shake it loose. She tried to hurry faster, to get to the bottom of the hill, and slid on a steep, grassy spot. She landed sitting on her behind, inches from a headstone just as Arthur caught up with her.

"Lost something?" he said, sounding amused as he held out the shoe she'd dropped when she slid.

She took it, got up from the ground, and brushed off her skirt. When she looked down toward the road, she didn't see his car, but started off again anyway.

He kept up with her. "I was just trying to explain what happened," he told her. "After that festival in Newport, I saw less and less of Charles, and when I did, he'd usually been drinking. Then he came to Patrick's wedding in that condition, and I was the one who had to get him out of the reception. He threw up in the parking lot. The wedding took place out here, not far from this cemetery. I ended up driving him to a diner to get him a cup of coffee. Charles kept saying he wished he were dead. Actually, the way he put it was something like, 'I can't stand to be among the living.' I sat with him in that diner for a couple of hours and then drove him back to his apartment. I hated him for threatening to ruin Patrick's day and for forcing me to keep him from ruining it. He kept calling me, Arthur, the white knight. Arthur, the gallant, in that silly, ironic voice he sometimes used. I dropped him off without going up to his apartment, and frankly I hoped I wouldn't see him again."

She was breathing heavily, and when she looked down to the bottom of the hill she saw they must have veered too far to one side. His car was still not visible. "Was that the last time you saw him?"

"No. We saw each other for another couple of years because of the quartet, but less frequently. There were fewer and fewer performances, and eventually the group disbanded. Charles behaved professionally, mostly at least, but he was unreliable enough that we were always nervous he wouldn't show for a performance or that he'd arrive drunk. Once I remember he was very jovial, and he and Patrick were carrying on quite a bit, like in the old days. Afterward, they left to go out somewhere together, but I don't think there was anything more between them. If there was, I never knew about it."

They walked for a while again, saying nothing. The wind had died down, and she no longer held on to her skirt to keep it from blowing. They came down another level of the rise, and she spotted his orange car below them, not too far away. The last part of the descent was steep, but Arthur didn't hold out his hand or offer to help her when she stumbled. He seemed hardly aware of her. She thought it was unlikely he hadn't known there was more than friendship between Charles and Patrick, and she disliked him for denying it. She wondered if he'd felt anything at all when he learned Charles had been killed.

When they reached the road at the bottom of the hill, she stopped to put her shoes back on, and he came alongside her. They walked up the gravel road toward his car. Then, partway there, he put his hand on her arm. She stood breathing a little heavily still, trying not to look at him.

"You can't know what it was like at that funeral. Patrick fell apart. His wife hadn't come, something about the children. The two of us had driven together. Afterward, we sat in my car talking for what felt like hours. We remembered that festival you played in, after Les broke his arm. In many ways, that weekend was the quartet's pinnacle."

He paused long enough that she looked at him and saw the seriousness of his expression, saw that he meant what he'd said.

"I really thought the quartet would rise to the top after that performance—whatever the top meant," he continued. "I thought my music would have a real impact."

"Well it has," she said. "You just had an opera performed."

"By a small company. And I had to struggle for that even. It almost wasn't performed at all. I had about given up when the conductor contacted me."

He paused, then said, "Charles could have wandered out into the street that night he was hit, especially if he was drinking. There is no telling. And even if there was something between him and Patrick, it doesn't change anything. It's not an excuse for his bad decisions."

He spat the last words, and she didn't know what to say back. Up ahead of them was the orange car, gleaming in a streak of sunlight. The air felt warmer, hot even, now that the wind had stopped. Here and there, trees lined the road. For a few minutes, they walked through shade and then back into the sunlight.

When they reached the car, he unlocked it and let her in. It felt like they'd been gone a long time, years even, but the car looked just the same. The black seats were still new looking, as if no one had ever sat on them. She noticed the speakers behind the seats and the shiny finish on the console. She was full of many things to say, but didn't say anything, didn't even know where to start or even what all the things were that she needed to tell him.

He got behind the wheel. "I don't mean to sound harsh. It was all just very hard."

She nodded, forgave him some of it.

"What will you do if your cello doesn't turn up? How long will you stay on in New York?"

"I'll go back in a day or two, either way."

"Did you have it insured?"

"Yes."

"Well, that's something."

He started the car, and they sat for a moment with it idling. The sun was bright on the windshield, and she had no sunglasses with her and had to shade her eyes, squinting from the glare.

"I heard you have a husband and daughter," he said. "Patrick told me."

She nodded, didn't look at him, couldn't have seen him because of the bright sun.

"Have you any photos?"

"No," she said. "Not with me."

"How old is she, the daughter?"

"She'll start ninth grade in the fall," Reenie said, pausing, considering before she gave Judith's age. "She's fourteen."

There was a moment when neither of them spoke, and she went on holding her hand above her eyes and squinting at the windshield. "You must have married shortly after that festival in Newport," he said finally. "Had you known each other long?"

"Yes," she said. "We'd known each other most of our lives."

She felt suddenly, strangely peaceful. She'd told him how things had turned out. She'd said the most important thing she'd needed to say, and it no longer seemed to matter whether he responded or asked more questions. She read his silence. She assumed he guessed but couldn't ask. Later she wouldn't forgive him for not asking, and when she looked back many years later when Judith was older and married herself with a child, she would hate him for not ever inquiring or wanting to know. She wouldn't see his silence as proof of strong emotions. She would see it as indifference or cowardice. But now she forgave him without his asking, and she forgave him everything else, including his resentment and callousness toward Charles. Sunlight broke across the glass as they turned onto the main road and came out from under the dappled light of the trees. The glare was sudden and so bright, she shut her eyes and saw it play across her closed lids, a red undulating warmth. The car gained speed. She felt them moving faster and faster away from the graves. The warm air blew wildly through the open windows, and she had to twist her hair back behind her head as they drove over the bridge and back into the city.

Eventually, the car slowed when they entered heavier traffic. They hadn't said anything for a long time, and when they stopped for a red light, she glanced across at him, but he was staring straight ahead, watching the windshield. His fingers tapped the steering wheel, and she couldn't guess what he was thinking, if he was angry about her swift marriage or wondering about the child she'd had. Then the light changed and he sped forward, sliding easily from one lane to another and around other cars and trucks and cabs. He ran yellow lights, honked at cars that tried to cut them off and seemed intent on reaching her hotel as quickly as possible. She said nothing, and when they pulled onto the street that would take them past the hotel's entrance, she wished suddenly that Charles was there, ready to take her out and get her drunk after Arthur dropped her off.

The street in front of the hotel was crowded with traffic, and Arthur had to double-park to let her out. The car behind them honked loudly when they stopped, and a steady stream of traffic passed them in the other lane, so there was no way for the car stuck behind them to go around.

He put his hand on her arm as she reached for the door handle. "What I was trying to say earlier is that we did you a favor, not asking you to join that quartet. It fell apart several years later, and if you'd joined the quartet, you would have been involved in the mess with Charles and everything else."

He paused. The car behind them was still honking, joined by others stuck now behind it to form a growing chorus, but he ignored them and stared down at her arm and his hand there. "You would have moved to New York and hated it, and I'm not someone you'd have wanted to be involved with, not for long anyway." He took her hands and squeezed them.

She stayed very still, not wanting to glance up at his face and meet his eyes or to move away. She ignored the cars behind them, and on the one hand, she felt ridiculous not getting out, and on the other hand, she felt as if sitting there and not moving was completely necessary and the only thing she could do. He grasped her shoulder and drew her toward him, over the console. His hand slid underneath the short, gathered sleeve of her blouse. Her arm came instantly alive.

"What is happening?" she said.

Up close she saw his teeth slightly crooked and the stubble on his chin. He kissed her and pulled at the strings that gathered her blouse at the neckline. She was not aware of anything except his mouth and his hands—one gripping her bare shoulder and the other against her blouse.

"What are you doing?" she whispered, but it wasn't a question that expected an answer, and they went on kissing, ignoring the cars behind them. She was not aware of anything else, and she thought, *I will keep this.*

His hand slipped under her blouse, it grazed her skin at the edges of her bra. His hair touched her face, and he stared down at the blouse, intent on that. She felt his mouth against her collarbone. Then he drew back for a moment, and she looked into his dark eyes. They stopped her from noticing anything else. There was no going backward or forward. She saw her younger self, naïve and too afraid to understand. This was something larger than reasoning, and it forced her to do things she couldn't anticipate.

She felt his breath against her ear. He moved over her, one hand inside the blouse firm against her back and the other nudging her bra aside. His head blocked the windshield and anything she might see through it. She pulled him closer, ignoring the horns behind them. She forgot everything else, forgot her cello and the fact that it had been taken from her and that she'd determined to do anything to get it back, forgot what he'd said earlier that had made her dislike him so much, forgot Benjamin and

Judith and the music she'd learned and memorized and taught and performed, forgot even the opera she'd just played and how Arthur had been carried like a hero or a god down the street by the angry, jubilant crowd. She forgot what he'd done and how he'd acted fifteen years ago. She saw only the fact that they were in his car together, and she found that this was greater than all of everything else added together.

He murmured words, said he'd been connected to her all those years when they hadn't seen one another, because of the music. One lived another life inside of the music.

Yes, she thought. The world they made with music was real. It was the important world, the one that mattered, and she went on ignoring the shriek of horns and the angry shouts of drivers as more vehicles were trapped behind them. She pressed her mouth against Arthur's, and his tongue against hers was an undeniable fact.

The man in the car behind them stuck his head out the window and shouted, "Assholes! This isn't a make-out zone! Move your God-damn car!" He laid on his horn and didn't let up. Arthur pulled away from her and turned to look behind them. She followed his gaze. The backup stretched all the way to the traffic light. The man behind them punched his fist in the air through his open window.

Arthur waved good-naturedly at the other drivers. "I guess this isn't the best place," he said, turning back to her with a smile, and she thought he would suggest going inside to her room, but instead he told her about a dinner he had to attend. "It's not a commitment I can get out of."

She was still seeing him through a tunnel, as if nothing else existed. She was split into many pieces.

He kissed her again. "If it weren't for this damn dinner." The man behind them yelled more curses. "I'll come with you tomorrow when you go to the precinct. I have nothing all day. We could spend it together."

She nodded. "Yes. All right."

"Good, I'll phone the hotel."

"I'll see you then," she said and they leaned in and kissed again, more quickly.

"I would come around and let you out, but this is such a crazy street."

"Don't bother, I've got it," she said as he reached over her to lift the door handle. Then she slid out and stood on the sidewalk watching as he put the car into gear and the rust-orange Ferrari pulled away.

She was not shaking or trembling and instead felt steady, standing there watching his retreat. She went on standing at the curb even after the car was too far away to see anymore. The man who'd been trapped behind them pulled up to the newly vacated spot and leapt from his car, leaving his lights flashing. "Idiots in love," he shouted as he passed her.

She stayed on the curb as the other vehicles piled up again and the honking of horns commenced, more desperate and angrier now that they'd thought they were about to move but had been deceived. Then the man who'd left his lights flashing came running back and jumped into his car, and there was the sound of engines and gears being engaged as the drivers pushed forward. One of them made a vulgar, angry gesture at her as he passed, but she hardly noticed it and didn't care. None of it felt real. The cars and the street had no substance. She turned away and walked through the hotel's entrance. She passed a group of men and a porter pushing a cart of luggage but didn't look at them. When she reached the desk, she asked the clerk if she had any messages.

The clerk nodded, handing her a sheet of paper. "Your husband called a couple of hours ago and I wrote it down."

She read the message: *They have your cello at the precinct. Someone turned it in late this morning. You should pick it up immediately. I reserved a ticket for you back to Boston at six-thirty tonight. It gets in at eleven. I'll meet you at the station.*

"Your husband said to tell you he missed you. It sounded

like he felt bad about the whole cello thing."

She thanked the man, folded the message and put it in her purse, then walked quickly back out of the hotel, still moving as if she were inside a tunnel and nothing outside of that tunnel had any meaning for her.

A cab pulled over almost immediately, and she got inside it and gave the driver the address of the police precinct. He pulled back quickly into traffic. She glanced at her watch, saw it was after four-thirty, and wondered suddenly if she'd end up reaching the precinct too late to claim her instrument. She'd missed Benjamin's telephone call, and she didn't trust the police to hold onto her cello. If she hadn't gone with Arthur, she'd have it right now in her possession.

It was late afternoon on a Sunday, but vehicles were piled up all over the city. She heard the roar of an engine, the blare of a nearby horn, and the cab driver's mutters of frustration. The cab's interior smelled badly of cigarette smoke, and she unrolled her window and felt a rush of warm air. "How long will it take to reach the precinct?" she asked the driver.

"Uncertain. There's generally less traffic on a Sunday, but it's nearly five, the witching hour. You in a hurry?"

"Yes," she said. "I have to reach the police precinct to claim an item that was stolen from me, and I'm not sure what time they close."

"If it's at five, it'll be close." He braked suddenly as another cab pulled out in front of them. "Damn you," he bellowed.

They turned down another street, and she noticed everything—the lines of vehicles flashing in the sun, the red light up ahead, and the towering buildings that cut off a wide view of the sky. Everything snapped suddenly into place as if she'd had cold water thrown on her. They passed buses and trucks and sat in lines of cars for what felt like several minutes at each light. She peered out the windshield at the stoplights and watched until they turned green and she felt the cab inch forward, then speed ahead, veering into any small space created in the adjacent lanes.

When they were two blocks from the station, she handed the fare across the seat and let herself out. She walked quickly down the first block, then began running, not noticing drivers honking as she dashed across an intersection. When she reached the police precinct, she had to wait a few minutes, but then she was brought back to a desk, asked several questions, and told to wait again while they fetched her instrument. When an officer carried it out, she opened the case immediately and lifted out the cello. She ran her hands over the familiar wood, turning it, looking for dents or scratches in the finish, but it was unharmed, as if the case had never been opened. Her copy of Arthur's score was just as she'd left it, folded and tucked under the cello's neck.

"It's yours, I take it?" the officer asked her. "The one you reported missing?"

"Yes," she answered.

"Someone brought it into the station earlier today, then dis-appeared before the officer at the window could get any infor-mation from her. He checked the instrument, and since it looked unharmed, didn't see any reason to chase her down."

"Yes, the instrument seems fine," she said as she signed the paperwork he handed her. "It looks untouched." She closed the case back up, thanked him and stood to leave.

"Sorry for the inconvenience," the officer called after her.

She went back onto the street, determined now to get out of New York quickly. Standing at the curb, she searched for an-other cab. It seemed like the traffic had only worsened in the little time she'd been inside the police station. Cabs and taxis streamed past, all filled with passengers. People hurried down the sidewalk, and families swept by, moving in packs. When she finally got a cab to pull over for her, it was well past five. She had a little over an hour to retrieve her things from the hotel and get to the train station.

I cannot, she thought, seated in the back with her cello and watching the cab make small inroads toward her hotel. She glanced down and saw that her blouse was still loose and pulled the strings, retying them. "Can't you turn down a side street?" she questioned the cab driver.

"Sure, but they'll be slow as well. This is nothing. Try driving across town on a Friday at five-thirty."

She shut her eyes. She had her cello, that was the main thing, and Benjamin was planning to meet her at the train station in Boston at eleven. If she missed the train, she'd phone him and take the next one. The cab driver made a few quick turns, and they had good luck at a couple of the stoplights. Several minutes later, he pulled up into roughly the same spot where Arthur had sat earlier when he'd dropped her off. She paid and went quickly to her room, where she packed her things, not bothering with the few toiletries she'd left on a shelf in the shower. She carried everything downstairs to the lobby, then checked out, and caught another cab, determined to meet the train Benjamin had made the reservation for.

While there was less traffic on the way to Grand Central, it was still late, nearly six-fifteen, when she walked into the station. She moved on instinct, past porters and other travelers, then stood in line at the ticket window and saw that the train to Boston was on time. The elevator was just down the hall, but she didn't risk it, and instead hefted her things up the stairs. Reaching the top, she was out of breath, but she arrived at the right track just in time to hear her train thundering into the station. It screeched abruptly to a stop in front of her.

Once inside the car, her momentum kept her moving, and she didn't stop even when she spotted empty seats. Carrying her suitcase and her cello, she made her way through several cars in the moving train, until she reached the dining car where she stowed her things and sat at one of the tables. When the waiter came, she ordered a whiskey. He brought it with a bowl of pretzels, and she sat eating them one by one as she sipped the drink. She hadn't eaten all day, and as she chewed the pretzels, she felt her stomach slip into high gear. As the train sped through New York and into Connecticut, she ordered another drink and a hamburger, which came on a paper plate and was tough and rubbery. She covered it with ketchup, and then dripped the ketchup onto her blouse as she was eating it. She tried to blot the material with a damp napkin, but the stain just spread. Never mind, she thought. The blouse had been a gift, but she would throw it out when she reached home.

Closing her eyes, she could still feel Arthur's mouth on her mouth and see his face close to hers, tipped to one side. She hardly knew him, just the effect he had on her, which was stronger than the effect of anyone else she'd ever known and was like a light flashing brightly all through her. He was at least forty by now, an interesting but not notable composer approaching middle age. When she'd told him how old Judith was, he hadn't even inquired about her.

It would never make sense. She didn't know or understand, had been forced to decide. She would go back to Boston and apply for more performing opportunities. She'd keep applying, even if she was repeatedly turned down. Arthur had told her she was good and that counted for something, but she would not return to New York. He made it seem as if there was something between them, but the past fifteen years proved otherwise.

Streaks of copper colored the horizon. She had another drink while the windows of the dining car turned navy blue and then black, spotted intermittently with passing lights. She'd loved Judith as soon as she was born. She'd felt the warm head under the palm of her hand and cradled the sleeping body against her chest. Benjamin had been there with her sitting on the bed, equally in love, as they watched and felt the baby's breath rise and fall. Life streamed in, then poured out. That pink mouth and the ears with their delicate curls—she would never tell Arthur about any of this.

She heard the train's whistle—a long, soft howl in the darkness.

"Are you all right?" the waiter asked. "Is everything all right?"

236

"Yes," she said. "But can you bring me another of those drinks?"

"Dessert as well?"

"Yes, some ice cream please."

He brought the drink first, then the ice cream, a scoop of vanilla in a small silver dish. She poured some of the whiskey in it and stirred, watching the ice cream melt into a thick pool. Then she spooned the sweet cold cream into her mouth. Arthur had gripped her arm and she could still feel that. He had kissed her mouth. In the window, she saw the lights of a town, far away, remote in the darkness. Charles was dead, hit by a car three years ago, and she had not guessed. Everything had stopped for him in a second. He had stopped, and she'd never hear his voice or see him again.

The train was nearly an hour late coming into the station in Boston, and when she found Benjamin waiting on a bench inside, it was close to midnight. He'd taken Judith to Irena's mother's house to spend the night, and he'd sat the last hour or so waiting for her, reading a newspaper. She walked into the station with her fellow travelers and found him, sitting with the others who were waiting on the late train.

"There you are," he said when he saw her. He stood up to kiss her cheek, then took her suitcase, and held the door for her as they walked toward the exit to the street.

"How was the performance? I thought you would call to let me know what was going on, but you never did after you left that message that your cello was missing."

"I'm sorry," she apologized. "It was all so rushed after I lost my cello. But the performance was fine. Central Park, good weather, a large audience. The reviews were very good."

They stepped out onto the sidewalk, and the dark air swam all around her. She swam through it. Part of her was still in New York, and another part was still on the train, swaying from side to side at the table in the dining car. Only a small piece of her had gotten off the train and walked through the station, sobered somewhat by the coffee she'd drunk just before they reached Boston.

Benjamin opened the trunk and began loading her things. The few cars parked beneath the streetlights looked mysterious and large and silent. "Be careful with the cello," she told him.

He glanced up at her. "Was it damaged?"

"No. It didn't look as if it'd even been taken from the case."

"A police officer phoned the house when you weren't at the hotel earlier today. He said a woman brought it in saying she'd found it. I asked if the incident was being handled as a theft, but he said your report described it as a loss."

He was standing next to the passenger side, holding the door open for her, but she was still behind the car by the trunk. She leaned against it to steady herself before walking around to her door.

"It was taken from me, and I certainly did not state that it was lost when they took down the report. The whole thing makes no sense—why someone took it, or why it was turned in. And the police were no help."

"Whoever took it must not have known its worth," he said as she lowered herself into the car. "Later, I imagine she was afraid of getting arrested for the theft."

He pushed the door closed, and she shut her eyes as he went back around to the driver's side. She felt like she was moving even while she was sitting still.

"I read about the protest in the newspaper," he said when he was settled next to her. "It sounded more like a riot than a protest. How did you make it out of Central Park?"

"I didn't, exactly." She lowered her head and squeezed her eyes shut, trying to shake the unsteadiness. "I mean, I did, but I ended up in the back of a paddy wagon, and then in a holding cell until I could talk to a judge."

"Good Lord. I've always said New York City was more dangerous and crazier than Boston. That proves it." He started the car. "You look tired. You were stumbling on the stairs as we came up."

238

"I had a drink on the train," she confessed.

"One?" he asked as he pulled out onto the dark, nearly empty street.

"Yes, one. You don't need to monitor me," she added.

"I'm not monitoring. I just asked. Sometimes you have more than one."

"So do lots of people—half the population of Boston, likely." She rubbed her fingers between her eyebrows. "Can we not talk about this?"

He sighed. "All right." They drove without speaking through the city then toward their house in one of the outlying towns, not far from the place where Irena had grown up. The interior of the car was dark, brightened by only a few small lights on the dashboard. She stared out the windshield at the lit cones of air extending from the headlights.

"I heard while I was there that someone I knew, a violinist I played with at that festival years ago in Newport, was killed, hit by a car a few years ago."

"Really? In New York City?"

"Yes. He was walking across an intersection."

Benjamin shook his head. "There's proof of what I just said and of why I don't like you going there. You risk rioters or worse."

They entered the highway, moving faster now. Exit signs loomed suddenly in the windshield, then disappeared, left quickly behind.

"Is that why you're so morose, that violinist's death?"

"I'm not morose. I'm just tired. I had a long couple of days with the rehearsal and the performance, and I hardly slept after getting arrested and losing my instrument."

"They dropped all charges against you, right?" he asked as they pulled off the highway and drove down the smaller streets of their town.

"Yes, of course. I don't even think I was formally charged, just held with a group of protesters and taken before the judge, who said I was free to go."

He glanced across at her. "How did you end up in a group of protesters?"

"It was very crazy after the concert. The audience itself was huge, and then all those protesters arrived. The park and the street were packed. You could barely move."

"It sounds awful, like a mob scene. Those protesters will go to all sorts of ends to get what they want, which is an end to the war. They'll settle for nothing less even if their actions compromise the greater good."

"What is the greater good?" she asked.

He turned into their driveway and gave her a long look as he shut off the engine. She felt his gaze rather than saw it, as she had her head lowered. "It's whatever is the best outcome for the majority."

A moment later, he came around and helped her out, then brought her suitcase and cello into the house. She went straight upstairs with her cello, not answering his questions about whether or not she'd eaten. She took her instrument from its case and played a few notes just to hear its sound and know that indeed it was fine. Instantly, upon drawing her bow across the strings, she felt settled, and minutes later she was in bed, fully dressed and curled on her side. She was careful not to move, but the world would not stay still, and images revolved inside her head. She spun down hallways, past cellos and lines of Ferraris. She looked for Charles but couldn't find him. Arthur handed her a piece of music he'd written. He parked at the cemetery and said, "I'll be back for you in the morning." Gravestones as tall as buildings towered over her. There was no space for her to walk between them. Steady yourself, voices inside her said, but she didn't steady herself. Instead, she let go. She flew down streets of white stones and past tall buildings. She flew through intersections. It was a long ways and Arthur led her through rooms filled with music, past all those notes and up a steep incline that was necessary to reach the coda. She drew a bow

240

across her cello strings while violins played the melody. The music went on and on, and the rooms were so full, she couldn't see anything else.

The next morning, she woke suddenly when the phone beside the bed rang. It was her mother, calling at eleven a.m. Should she drop Judith off, or did Irena have teaching commitments? How had the concert gone? And what had happened with her cello? She'd heard about the protest after the concert. What a crazy story.

Irena said she'd phone back after she had breakfast, then roused herself and went to the bathroom and turned on the shower. The water falling on her was hot, and it quickly steamed the room, clouding the mirror. If Arthur phoned the hotel this morning, he'd learn she'd checked out just after he dropped her off. Then what?

She would get dressed and make herself breakfast—eggs, bacon, orange juice and two aspirin. Benjamin would call from work, Judith would come home, and at four Irena would leave to teach for two hours. She'd carry her cello with her, which was unharmed and still the same beautiful, resonant instrument it had been when her father had given it to her just after her acceptance to the conservatory—a Montagnana cello he'd spent too much money on at an auction.

"It will see you through," he'd said.

The water from the shower-head poured down on her, heavy and forceful. I'll become the first female cellist to play with a major symphony orchestra, she told herself, and knew suddenly that it was the one thing that would matter. She had a premonition it would happen, and that it was the thing she was destined for.

She stood under the hot water, then stepped from the shower and rubbed the clouded mirror with her towel.

"There you are," she said to her watery reflection. She was steady now, inside her actual life.

Chapter 14

Mother, can you hear me?
Do you think she'll wake again?
Do you think she'll open her eyes?
Let's turn her over. Let's raise the bed a little.
She was a cellist, you know.
She played in the symphony orchestra.
You should put on one of her CDs.
Put on one that she loved.
I arranged for that concert in her honor.
I hoped to take her.
I wanted her to hear it.

This was how morning sounded. It was long ago and she would get there on time. She was the one who remembered, that concert that was planned, those notes in a key she'd always known. The sound beneath all other sounds. She would bear music. She would carry the notes on the train and in a car and up the hill. She would not let them go. Music had lifted her spirit. Certain words sung, certain melodies or phrases played with precise timing. Strings strummed, the air vibrating. The sounds went on echoing. She heard them and thought she knew what God knew, those notes she'd listened to throughout her lifetime.

She'd been married to Benjamin for fifty-six years. They'd traveled to Paris, heard the orchestra perform, traveled to London and Vienna and Germany. They'd lived in a modest three-bedroom house where she taught music lessons privately after her arthritis got bad enough that she couldn't perform anymore. Even in the dark or in a long hallway, she'd followed the beat, that great sound beneath all other sounds. Mozart knew it.

Beethoven worshiped and feared it. She had loved it.

She came to a door and kept going, could not prevent it. She went on hearing sound, bearing it, a steady thrumming that pushed air through all the vents. A great whoosh of sound, the first and last, the sound beneath all sound.

When she'd finally got a seat in the symphony orchestra, she'd begun to work her way up, practicing long hours and playing better, faster. She became third then second cellist. She went out ahead and proved her worth. She didn't stop. She spun through the hallways and to the end of the finale. She reached the pinnacle and was declared first cellist, a position she held for eight years.

Benjamin said, now you can relax but she worked harder, practicing difficult passages of music late into the night. She played solos and was singled out on programs. The audience rose clapping.

She didn't know couldn't say. She heard another note, a string of notes, that eternity of sound which kept firing, kept climbing the hill.

Let's have a little water.

Let's raise the bed.

It will help her breathe easier.

The sound was louder now, rising from the basement, the sound she was in love with.

That concert, when are they performing it?

Next week, at one of the colleges. Do you think I should cancel it?

No, and you should attend. She'd want that.

Who was the composer?

Arthur Cohen. Once, years ago, he was well known.

Oh yes, you showed me the music book when it arrived.

He knew my mother.

She performed his music with him, at a music festival long ago.

The final time she saw Arthur Cohen was in 1990, when she attended a concert of his music in Boston. By then his music was little performed, and hardly any of it had been recorded. A small orchestra in Boston devoted to performing modern music had chosen to perform a pastorale of his. She'd heard about the concert from Phyllis, a violinist in the symphony orchestra who knew Irena had once performed something of his.

Not knowing what to expect and knowing that Benjamin wouldn't appreciate being dragged to another concert, especially one of modern music which he found unmusical, she decided to attend alone. She did not much like modern music herself anymore. Atonal music had never caught on with the listening public or with performers for the same reasons she'd voiced in 1953 at the festival—it was too difficult. There were too many large leaps and rapid exchanges in rhythm and pitch, making it hard for performers to play and hard for audiences to understand or follow with the ear. The modern composers in the 1950s and 60s had had many big philosophical ideas. They'd felt a mandate to compose music completely different from their predecessors. They'd tried to divorce music from time and space to make it abstract like art without recognizable images, but without melody, meter and rhythm, many argued that musical phrases were empty. It was not music anymore. Those theories about the new, atonal music, which had so excited her years ago when she first heard about them from Arthur Cohen, now seemed wrong instead of bold. Much of atonal music was empty music, experimentation for the sake of experimentation. What had once seemed necessary and exciting and new had not held up, and Arthur Cohen was viewed by the world of music as a very minor composer. Hardly anyone knew of him.

She guessed that he would attend the concert since his music was so rarely performed, and she wanted to see him again. She drove across the city after a long rehearsal session and despite bad weather in order to get there. She wanted to hear his music again and see if it lived up to her memory of it, and she wanted to let him know she was now playing with a major symphony orchestra. She had achieved what had seemed impossible, while he had not achieved what had seemed almost guaranteed.

It was midwinter and snow had begun falling earlier that evening, so the audience was sparse, embarrassingly so. She sat toward the back where she could search for him unobserved, but she did not need to search as the conductor introduced Arthur when he introduced the piece, and Arthur, seated toward the front, stood briefly turning so the audience could view him. He was still thin, wiry, and youthful looking. His hair was still dark and longish, worn in a similar cut. He looked unchanged.

The small orchestra was made up of a few string players (two violinists, a violist, and cellist), a pianist, two percussionists, a flutist, a clarinetist, an oboist, and a couple of horn players who each played two different instruments. The piece, a pastorale, began with the piano and strings playing reoccurring chords and tone intervals. As additional instruments joined, the music became denser and harder to follow. She didn't know how to interpret it and later couldn't describe it, but she went on listening, despite her reservations and her initial conviction that she would not find the music interesting or enjoyable. Increasingly, she became absorbed, and increasingly she felt that she was seeing or hearing that the surface of the music, formed by the interplay of rhythm, pitch and duration of sound by the various instruments, was just a layer through which she could feel the actuality of sound. She sensed this actuality rather than hearing it. Underneath that musical surface, and because of it, emotions were magnified. Increasingly, the music was not just heard, but felt. It pulsed with life and pushed aside the listener, just as she sensed it had pushed aside the composer.

Long notes hovered. Clear patterns mixed with random occurrences. Whereas Arthur Cohen's earlier music had been

245

more controlled and deliberate, this later piece hovered between control and chaos. It produced many layers or veils—music as narrative or as memory (the memory of other note patterns) and music as symbol—but underneath all that, the pastorale was saturated with sound. In the density of many sustained notes, the smallest changes in pitch and rhythm sounded huge. The music made her hear differently, and undeniably she heard that an intrinsic beauty and excitement filled it.

She went on listening intently, and in the second half of the concert, for a few seconds or moments—she couldn't tell for how long—reality disappeared and she heard other sound worlds. She felt that they had existed all along and would go on existing, that the music had given her a way to sense them or know them. They lay on top of the reality of the written score like pieces of colored glass. Each piece or layer was a different set of notes and some layers were in patterns she'd never heard before. All the layers were playing at once, making it impossible to identify them, but she felt them, that was the main thing. She marveled. She slid through them and associated colors with them—golden brown, a field of yellow grasses.

Later when the concert was over and she went out into the entrance hall to look for Arthur, she heard others from the audience talking about the music. Some said it was too confusing or even that it defied music, but others expressed the experience of hearing Arthur Cohen's pastorale as remarkable. Opinion was divided, and someone said that compositions like his that pushed the boundaries of what was already established about musical form would always divide responses.

It was completely dark outside by then, and the large windows around the doorway looked out on the falling snow. Many of the concert-goers were putting on their coats and hurrying to leave, as the snow was sticking. Someone said there was already an inch of snow on the ground and walkways. She saw a car drive up to the entrance, covered with snow, its wipers working furiously. Snow was falling so heavily that nothing was distinct. Cars, trees, and the lampposts with their thin, yellow light blended into the falling snow and became lost in it. The outside world was covered.

She waited in the lobby, stood watching the falling snow and heard pieces of conversations about slick roads and black ice. The transit system had canceled its trains, and it would soon be impossible to get anywhere. Still, she waited and finally when Arthur stepped out of the performance hall, he came alone and stood just past the entrance. She walked over to him, noticing that up close he looked a good deal older. He'd always been thin, but now the thinness looked hollow. His suit seemed too large. It swallowed him.

She said, "It's been years since we've seen one another, but I had to tell you how much I enjoyed hearing your music performed again."

His face lit immediately with recognition. "Reenie. Reenie Siesel," he said, and she didn't correct him. "Wonderful to see you here. Wonderful that you came."

"I heard about the concert last week from a fellow musician. I was glad she told me about it. There wasn't much publicity."

"No. These events are not wildly popular."

"How are you?"

"I'm older. And you, are you still playing the cello?"

"Yes, I'm still playing. I'm performing now with the symphony orchestra. I've been with them for nearly ten years."

"Congratulations." He reached out and warmly shook her hand. "I hadn't heard or known. I haven't kept up."

"You would have had no way of knowing. We've been out of touch for years."

"Yes, I recall a couple of phone calls which you didn't return." He smiled a little sheepishly. There had been two calls after her trip to New York to play in the orchestra for his opera. The first time, she'd answered and they'd had a brief conversation, the second time, Judith had taken the message and she

247

hadn't phoned him back. "I thought maybe you were angry with me."

"No, not angry."

"Just fed up?" He smiled again. "You wouldn't have been the first to feel that way. Or the last, I'm afraid." He gestured at the other end of the room where a small crowd had gathered around a table with drinks and cookies. "My wife, Lynn, is over there getting me something to drink."

"I'm sorry I didn't return your call," she said. "I can't remember what was going on then. I became very busy after the opera. I had so much work with the teaching and trying to perform. Several years later I got hired by the symphony orchestra and then everything clanged. I stopped teaching at the music academy."

"Playing for a symphony orchestra is a major achievement for any musician."

"Yes. I was the first female cellist hired by them."

"You were a great musician even back when you'd just graduated from the conservatory. I continued to think of you years later when I composed. I imagined you playing my notes. I think I said this once before—you inspired me."

She didn't know how to reply, said nothing. She wanted, believed, and for a second was flooded with that.

"Here comes Lynn," he said. "I'll introduce you."

She glanced across the room and saw a pretty woman some ten or so years younger than Arthur with short, neatly cut, dark hair approaching them. The woman handed him a plastic cup.

"This is Reenie," Arthur told the woman. "She's a cellist. She played in one of the first concerts where my music was performed, in that quartet I told you about, The Modern Strings."

"I thought Lawrence was the cellist," the woman said.

"She played with us as a substitute before we got Lawrence. It was at a classical music festival in one of those mansions in Newport, Rhode Island. She was the only woman performing at the festival, with a whole big group of us men. She

248

was young, just graduated from a conservatory, and she was an outstanding musician. The instrument just opened up and sung under her hands. I think we were all a little in love with her."

Lynn smiled. Irena shook her hand, said she was glad to know Arthur had married.

"Lynn came along just when I was ready," Arthur said. He was smiling, and his expression seemed relaxed and genuine. He seemed less driven and maybe less haunted than he had years ago.

"We had trouble getting here from New York," Lynn said. "The storm was moving up the coast and the train was delayed. I'm sure the audience would have been larger if the weather had cooperated."

Irena agreed and then the conductor came across the room to them. He had once guest conducted at a musical event she'd played in, but it had been long ago and she'd been just one of many musicians. He gave no sign of recognizing her. "We're taking you out to dinner soon," he told Arthur. "I'm arranging for someone to drive you. Several of us will go if you're fine with that. They want the chance to talk with you."

"Yes, that's fine," Arthur said. "Looking forward to it. You did a marvelous job with the pastorale. Can't wait to discuss it with you." He said more, that it was an honor, that he felt privileged.

Irena stepped to the side and turned to Arthur's wife. "So nice to have met you." As the conductor hurried off to make final arrangements, she told Arthur, "It's been wonderful to see you and to hear your music performed, after so many years."

"Come to dinner why don't you, if it's not too late." He glanced out the windows by the doors. "If there's not too much snow. A storm always makes things more difficult, but one has to rise above events like the weather. I'll find out where they're taking me, and you can meet us there."

"I can't," she said. "I wish I could, but I have to get home. I'd better go now while the roads are still drivable, before they're worse."

"I heard they're already worse," Lynn said. "Slippery."

Irena nodded. She told Arthur, "It was so good to see you again and hear your music performed. Are you composing a lot?"

"No," he said. "I'm mostly just playing. And you know..." She missed the rest of what he said. She wasn't concentrating. She realized she had said nothing about his pastorale and how much it had moved her. She wasn't thinking, couldn't.

"Of course he is," Lynn said. "He's always composing, but he doesn't like to talk about it. That might jinx things." She leaned in toward Irena. "He's very superstitious."

The conductor waved at Arthur from across the room. "I've got a ride arranged." There were just a handful of people left.

"You had a daughter, didn't you?" Arthur asked her suddenly.

"Yes, Judith. She's grown up now. She recently had a baby in fact. She's a teacher."

"Ah," he nodded. "Does she play an instrument?"

"No. I tried to get her to take lessons as a child, but she was always more interested in her father's passions—biology and science."

He nodded and seemed about to say something, but the conductor was coming back with the others, and she said, "I should go."

Arthur grasped her hand. "So good to have seen you. So good of you to come."

She said goodbye and backed away as he released her, then turned and walked to the doors, pushed them open, and stepped out into the cold night air where the snow was falling in thick wet flakes so dense it was hard to see anything else, hard even to keep her eyes open. She blinked away the flakes and felt them course down her cheeks. The snow came down in heavy wet swirls, and her hair and coat were immediately wet. By the time she reached the parking garage where she'd left her car, she was shivering. She got inside but didn't start the motor or turn on the heater. She sat for a few minutes, hunched over herself, teeth chattering.

He'd phoned her after she came back from New York with her recovered cello, wanting to know if she'd found it and why she'd left so suddenly without explanation. Was she upset that he'd dropped her off at the hotel and gone to his engagement?

She said all that was fine, and that she'd only left early because she'd had to. Her husband had phoned and she needed to return home quickly. She'd gone to the police station to retrieve her cello right after he'd dropped her off at the hotel.

"I should have left you a message," she said. "But I was in such a hurry to make the train."

The second time he called, Judith wrote down a message, which Irena tore into pieces and threw away. She had not called him back. He would never, and she would never. She could not even acknowledge to herself the depth of her disappointment. She'd erased what had happened, and eventually she erased everything related to what she had erased—she ended her lifelong friendship with Gloria over a small argument, and she burned the medical records mailed to her from her old doctor's practice when he retired. When Judith needed a medical procedure, they learned that both Judith and Benjamin were the same blood type, type A, and Benjamin, qualifying as a close relative with the same blood type, donated the blood for her surgery. The truth was not possible to tell, and she hadn't ever told it.

Sitting alone in her car in the emptied parking garage, she saw the layers of subterfuge, couldn't ignore them. She had never, would never say, couldn't tell anyone, and the keeping of that felt like the worst thing of her life. A sob welled up. It filled the car with a sound that frightened her so much that she wiped her face, turned the key in the ignition and spun the dial up all the way for the heater. She sat waiting for the car to warm up enough that the defroster would work. I cannot, she told herself. After all these years, I will never.

She left the parking garage and drove slowly, forced to concentrate on the slippery roads. Twice she felt the car begin to skid, but she braked with slow precision and brought it back under control. None of it had mattered in the end, not her superiority which she'd gone to the concert of Arthur Cohen's music to assert, and not even the fact that he'd composed such unusual and beautiful music. The music world had ground him up and spit him out, without giving him recognition. As it turned out being a permanent member of The Modern Strings, which had seemed poised to change and influence all classical music to come, would not have amounted to anything. Better for her that she'd returned to live in Boston. He'd said himself he wanted nothing serious, that he couldn't be pinned down, and pregnancy was weighted. It was a solid, very real event.

She saw herself in a rush of images—hopeful then dashed, a naive young woman then a mother. Events had conspired and insisted, forcing her actions. She would have married Benjamin eventually anyway, she'd have come round. That's how her brothers had put it when they'd congratulated Benjamin—Irena's come round. We knew she would. That was destiny. Judith was more Benjamin's daughter than hers, she was so like him with her passion for biology, and who was to say in the end or to judge outcomes.

It was all too complicated. If she had told Arthur years ago about the pregnancy and they had married, there was no telling what would have happened. People said anything was possible, but often the human reach did not go far enough. You had to let go of reaching and leave hindsight behind. She couldn't tell and never would. She had done what she could, including loving Benjamin. She'd only had one child, but she'd had a career as well, had played divinely, superbly. *Play me that way, Honey. Think of the sounds we could make.* She'd made beautiful sounds—Mozart, Beethoven, Debussy, Bach, Haydn, Tchaikovsky, Chopin, Schumann, Stravinsky, and more. She had lit up churches and orchestra pits and stages, had known practice would make the difference, a single-minded devotion. She'd known beyond all doubt what it would take.

The driveway when she reached it had not been shoveled, but she was able to pull in far enough to get the car off the road, then wade through several inches of snow to the house. The bright outside lights were on, and she had no trouble seeing her way. She went inside and immediately took off her damp coat. Benjamin had laid a fire in the fireplace and pulled up two chairs. There was a pot of beef stew with carrots and some rolls on a plate, all still warm. Her cloth napkin, her plate, and silverware were set up on a small folding table, waiting for her.

She sat in the chair, already feeling the warmth from the fire. Benjamin said, "Late night?" believing she'd been at an orchestra rehearsal this whole time, and for a second she felt something hard and unyielding under the comfort of being home. Anger, regret, guilt? She pushed it away.

"Yes." She groaned a little, sank into the chair, its old cushion that knew her body. She took off her wet shoes and leaned forward to place them in front of the fire. "And it's snowing."

"I saw. Were the roads bad?"

"Not too bad, but they will be. It's a very heavy, wet snow. We'll need to have the driveway plowed in the morning. You might want to go into work late."

He picked up the wine bottle by his chair. "Want some?"

She nodded and after he poured it into her glass, she drank. "I needed that." She hadn't overdone it for years now, and for a while when she'd first been hired by the symphony orchestra, had stopped drinking altogether. Now the dark red wine spread through her, warming her, and she didn't worry about drinking too much. She didn't worry about anything. She forgave herself all transgressions. Gratefully, she pulled off her wet socks and wrapped the shawl on the chair back around her.

"I went to a performance over at one of the universities after the rehearsal," she said.

"You should have told me about it. I could have met you."

253

"I didn't decide to go until the last minute. Someone at re-hearsal mentioned it—a performance of some music by Arthur Cohen. Do you remember him? I performed his music years ago at that festival in Newport."

"Of course, and you played his opera in Central Park. You lost your cello afterward in that protest. It was against the war. You almost didn't get it back, and you were arrested, or rounded up, or something crazy."

She nodded. "The composer, Arthur Cohen, had a moment of fame. He was even in all the newspapers. I assumed, I think he probably assumed as well, that he'd go on to become more famous, that we'd hear of him. He won a Pulitzer a few years later, but even so, his music was never much performed after that. He disappeared from the scene."

"A flash in the pan."

"Yes. His music is forgotten and I don't know why. The concert was a performance of a pastorale."

"Was it any good?"

"Yes, that's the thing—it was very good. Other worldly even. Maybe his music is too modern, too different. No one has known what to make of him, or how to listen to him." She stared at the fire, warming up now more deeply. Her muscles and bones relaxed with it.

"You seem sad," he said.

"Just hungry," she said. It felt good to talk freely about Ar-thur Cohen in this way, as if nothing but an interest in his music had existed between them. She got up from the chair, lifted the lid off the dish of beef, and spooned out the stew onto the plate he'd set out for her. She took the napkin and a roll.

"I thought he'd achieve more, and that by comparison I would achieve very little. Not that I'm famous or anything, but I'm still performing."

"And performing at your height."

She nodded.

"To say nothing of the fact that you were the first female

cellist that the orchestra ever hired."

She heard the pride in his voice. "Yes. No one can say how things will turn out. No one can know."

As she ate the beef and the sweet carrots and drank more of the wine, she became wonderfully sleepy and forgetful, slipping off for a while into the sleepy warmth of the room.

Benjamin said, "Should we put on some music?" But they didn't. They went on sitting in front of the fire, and all around them the house turned chilly and dark, but the space in front of the fireplace grew warmer until eventually they carried the dishes to the kitchen and went upstairs to bed where they warmed the sheets and each other, thoroughly, without hesitation, and she felt no remorse or regret. Everything was as it should be. Life had occurred as if by design.

Chapter 15

This was the last. She lay back on her bed with her eyes closed. There was a great thrumming in the bowels of the building, a sound that permeated everything and the more she listened the more she heard it, the one sound underneath all other sounds, where all other sounds came from, where music itself began. She was still capable of hearing it and it never stopped but went on even at night in the silence that surrounded it, pouring out of the vents that tunneled behind walls and under floors and above ceilings. It was a wondrous sound that made all else, notes divine and inspired, possible. It was coming for her, that sound, coming at her.

Benjamin was gone. Her parents and brothers had died before her. Arthur Cohen was gone, as was Charles and her old friend Gloria whose funeral she'd attended a few years ago even though it had been years since they'd spoken. Sound had stayed and it had lasted even though the music ended with two final dark bars in the signature. After that there were no more pages and the musicians packed up their instruments.

Let's turn you over.

Let's make you comfortable.

She lay back on the bed. It billowed around her, carried her like a boat. She had played that Étude by Chopin and won an award. She'd had the distinction of being first. The bed was wide and brightly lit, so she could barely see past it to where the audience gathered. They migrated around her. Someone was waving in the distance and her brother Samuel ran across the yard. His hands were muddy and he had a rip in the knee of his pants.

Benjamin bent over the bed, whispered in her ear.

Let me give you a little water.

Let me cool you down.

Her tongue was a sheet of paper and the roof of her mouth closed over it. All around her were the musicians with their instruments—violins, cellos, horns, trombones, and a woman with a harp. Franz Liszt stood next to Stravinsky who wasn't stern like she'd imagined but smiling. They carried her and the stage was a high platform ringed with lights. Someone was humming a tune, someone was playing the theme from Beethoven's Fifth and the stage grew very crowded with many pieces of music, piles of scores and the entire string section along with brass and percussion. A pandemonium of sound as all the notes at once were played.

Here, Arthur said, it's the sonata I wrote for you. They bore the stage up higher and the string section played the third movement all the way to the end as the conductor signaled her to take her solo.

You're so warm, Benjamin told her, *burning up*, and then Judith came over for dinner with her husband and the new baby, and they ate outside in the warm evening and had a cake afterward because it was a celebration.

Mother, I'm here. I've been sitting here all morning.

I put on a favorite piece of yours, that symphony by Ravel. Do you hear it?

She did hear it. It filled the stage, a wondrous sound.

What about this CD? Should we play it also?

Yes, she loved that recording. Music was everything to her. It was her religion.

She had donated her body to science, made the decision months ago, giving herself away to be studied, including the ear with its inner spiral, that cornucopia of sound, and the all-important nerve in the brain that carried vibrations. She had an innate sense of rhythm and acute hearing that enabled her to discern A from C, and A from other A's, other lesser A's. There was never a perfect A, the perfect note perfectly pitched. Her mind had grasped that early on, but knowing she could never reach perfection had not prevented her from delight in trying. Arthur had taught her that and she had never forgotten, had heard and played music differently because of him.

I'm going to put on this concerto by Dvorák.

Yes, she said. That would be lovely. Benjamin had his binoculars because a pink thrush had lit singing on one of the branches. A recording of Dvorák played in the background and she drifted among the notes. He stayed with her and they listened for many days, years even. The notes fell on her, rained down from the ceiling and blew through the air vents across the field. An entire world of sound and so many notes possible. Her ears were filled, her brain was bursting.

She recognized a string of notes she'd played as a child over and over to get them right when Miss Mahony had said— faster now, play them faster. The pleasure of that. She heard one note after another, heard them briefly as they slipped past while everything else converged as time and rhythm collapsed and the walls of the mind fell inward. She heard it all—the sound which the world had come out of and was reeling back toward. How could one make sense? One had to, and now it seemed a supreme effort, the making of melody and harmony, one note after another, the arrangement of sound from a vast eternity of notes. She had done that, achieved what seemed impossible. Note by note, beat by beat, a rhythm of the world's comings and goings, its measures and moments, its pleasures and struggles. Her rhythm, the rhythm underneath all rhythm. The notes were now strumming all at once. She heard the vast hum of the universe, its turning through darkness and light.

Shall I put on the Bach CD?

Yes. Do you hear it, Mother?

It's playing for you.

She heard but didn't hear. All those notes.

A cornucopia.

That concert of the music that was composed for her, it's in a few days.

Sound that went on indefinitely.
Sound that was going out.
Sound that had been everything.

The Coda

Listen.

Come here.

Let me show you.

It was October and the leaves were falling. The sky was drenched with color, and the light was sharp and clear, not the white light of summer but the bright autumn light that shown through the thick dark oak leaves and the orange and yellow maples, feathering into many colors. A concert was taking place, the premiere of Arthur Cohen's sonata, dedicated to Irena Reynolds, the great cellist who had recently passed away. The pianist was Deborah Cohen, Arthur's niece, and Judith Reynolds, Irena's daughter, sat in the front row. The two women had worked hard to plan for this.

Outside, cars and trucks rumbled past, and underneath the building the furnace had fired up. Heat poured through the tunnels. Life was endless. Sound was endless.

The university's auditorium was nearly full. It was a modern concert hall with a circular structure and a wide, well-lit stage. The pianist and cellist began to play. Their notes filled the space, and all those seated there, the music lovers and the students studying music, heard them—such passion, such depth of feeling and desire. Inside the notes was a golden field and inside that color lay a dream of summer nights. Inside the dream were two instruments playing, two strands of notes. Inside the music was a life, and inside the life were the sounds of the dream.

She had come a long ways. She had reached the top, had carried her cello up the long hill where they were playing. The sun had come up. She saw the musicians in the bright air. The hillside was flowering and the composer had written something new. A field of golden grasses shimmered.

She was at the top where the musicians were warming up and she took off her clothes. She took off her dress and her underthings and shoes. She took off one shadow after another. She removed each layer—hope, love, disappointment, regret—saw they didn't matter. Beauty was at the top. Someone said, someone knew.

The musicians were beginning to tune and she found her place, as if she'd never left but had stayed at the top where the concert was taking place. She tuned herself, strummed each string. The air was dry and airless and the hilltop was like a giant sheet. She fell into it. All around her now the music was beginning. Sound would last. Beauty would last. She unwound the last bit and saw herself briefly in a train window. The image flashed then went out. She took the music out of herself. She removed the notes and the coda.

You play like an angel her father had said.

She had not forgotten, had played most of her life.

Now she touched the bow to her strings. There was no conductor. He was not needed. The sounds came from her as if she'd played this piece all her life. She had played it. It had played her. The strings stretched all through her and she took off her skin and flesh and muscles and bones. She was the strings and they were her. She saw the mind did not matter. She poured out its contents.

I loved the third movement.

Wasn't it beautiful?

So unexpected.

This was the pinnacle. She'd climbed the long ways and was herself music. She released the bow. She released even her wooden body.

Play, someone instructed.

She played beauty and beauty played her.

Their vibrations filled the air.

Acknowledgments

For centuries women were denied the pleasure of performing and composing music. Their efforts were thwarted, and their accomplishments were unacknowledged or trivialized. Countless female musicians and composers have been lost to history. For those wanting to read more about this and the extraordinary women who prevailed in this field, I found *Unsung: A History of Women in American Music* by Christine Ammer a comprehensive accounting of this struggle in American history.

There are many great books about modern music and the changes that occurred in classical music composing after World War II. *The Rest is Noise: Listening to the Twentieth Century* by Alex Ross was a comprehensive and clear guide. I also found *Give My Regards to Eighth Street, Collected Writings of Morton Feldman* (Edited and with an introduction by B.H. Friedman and an Afterword by Frank O'Hara) a fascinating account of the mind and experiences of a composer writing music during a time period when suddenly, as for all of the creative arts, music and what constituted music was undefined. There are also many great books about jazz in the 1950s, but I found the first-hand accounts of listening to jazz in the clubs of New York City by Julian Olf and Baron Wormser the most helpful.

I have enormous gratitude for Linda Shockley and all her work on the behalf of my books, and for all those early readers who read parts or all of this novel, including Janet Osborn whose encouragement, as always, inspired me, Shannon Jenkins, my devoted reader, and fellow writers Alison Bass, Roger King, the late Julian Olf, a playwright and generous editor and friend who is enormously missed, and for the wonderful Carrie Brown who always spoke the perfect words to me at just the right time. Thank you also to Joe Taylor and Livingston Press for all their work, and to the writing community at Enders Island for listening to and reading parts of this in progress. Your inspiration and support are invaluable. Finally, I owe a huge debt of gratitude to the pianist Linda Osborn, whose creative spirit and knowledge of music and preforming informed every page.

Karen Osborn is the author of four novels: *Patchwork,* which won a Notable Book Award from *The New York Times*; *Between Earth and Sky; The River Road; and Centerville*, which won the IPPY Gold Award in Fiction. In reviews, she's been compared to Ian McEwan, Jodi Picoult, and Russell Banks. *The New York Times* has called her work, "psychologically sophisticated" and *The Washington Post* has said her writing is "an extraordinary effort to engage the American condition as we find it now." In addition to being an author, Ms. Osborn teaches fiction writing in Fairfield University's M.F.A. program.